RED DIRT

RED DIRT
Growing Up Okie

———————◆———————

ROXANNE DUNBAR-ORTIZ

Foreword by
MIKE DAVIS

University of Oklahoma Press
Norman

Library of Congress Cataloging-in-Publication Data

Dunbar-Ortiz, Roxanne.
  Red dirt : growing up Okie / Roxanne Dunbar-Ortiz.
    p. cm.
  Originally published: London : Verso, 1997.
  ISBN 978-0-8061-3775-9
  1. Dunbar-Ortiz, Roxanne. 2. Rural poor—Oklahoma. 3. Whites—
Oklahoma—Social conditions. 4. Oklahoma—Social life and customs.
5. Oklahoma—Biography. 6. College teachers—California—Biography.
I. Title.
  CT275.0718A3 2006
  976.6'053092—dc22
                                                    2005055453

The paper in this book meets the guidelines for permanence and durability
of the Committee on Production Guidelines for Book Longevity of the
Council on Library Resources, Inc. ∞

3 4 5 6 7 8 9 10

In memory of my mother,
Louise Edna Curry Dunbar, 1909–1968;
and for Michelle, and the generations to come,
so that they will remember

Contents

Foreword to the Oklahoma Edition

I am one of several million baby-boom-era Californians who grew up with a bittersweet relationship to the ancestral land that our parents had fled during hard times. We were the children of internal migrants, and we inherited ethnic ties less to Western Europe than to the Great Plains and other hardscrabble parts of the American heartland.

The "old country" in my case was Ohio, but most of my childhood friends in the blue-collar El Cajon Valley east of San Diego had parents who spoke with the pleasant cadence that others derided as an "Okie drawl." In reality, there were as many sons and daughters of West Texas, Nebraska, and Louisiana in my elementary school as true Oklahomans, but "Okie" was the generic insult hurled across the class divide of Main Street in 1950s El Cajon.

Later, in the caste system of my high school, "Okies" occupied an ambiguous position below the "Good Mexican" kids but slightly above the "SAs" (Bad Mexicans) and Native Americans. (No African Americans lived in our segregated western town). Although as a Roman Catholic I was used to a certain quotient of episodic local bigotry (usually after a revival passed through town), I was perplexed that some of my friends, mostly fervent Baptists, should be patronized as if they were Little Abner characters or, even, not quite white.

Then one evening, while hunting for hot-rod novels on the shelves of the local library, I found a book that mesmerized me for life. I had no idea who Woody Guthrie was, but *Bound for Glory* was exactly the mixture of blowing-down-the-road adventure and rebellion that I craved at age fifteen. It introduced me to depression-era America and experiences that still haunted my parents but of which they rarely spoke. It also explained that "Okie" was just a proud synonym for the Rooseveltian common people – people with names like Woody and Roxie.

Bound for Glory, in other words, was my private burning bush. It was a key to understanding my immediate social world and bolstered my affection for the gritty, sly, and often hilarious kids that I grew up with. With Woody Guthrie, as well as Buddy Holly, the Freedom Riders, and the Beatniks as inspirations, my friends and I even instigated a small rebellion or two.

Years later, when I was working with Verso Books, Roxanne ("Roxie") Dunbar-Ortiz showed me her extraordinary memoir. Like *Bound for Glory, Red Dirt* simply blew my socks off. This tough-minded, wonderfully evocative autobiography from the other end of Route 66 is nothing less than the secret history of poor white people in America. She recounts a family history that runs backwards in relation to national myth: a fall from middle-class grace to ramshackle and embittered poverty.

Downward mobility, of course, has always been one of the most taboo subjects in our national culture. When Orson Welles, for example, tried to portray the decline and fall of a midwestern dynasty in *The Magnificent Andersons* (his most brilliant and subversive film), the studio forcibly substituted a more optimistic conclusion and Welles was ostracized. Both New Deal liberals and anti–New Deal reactionaries insisted that American history must result in a happy ending.

The original sin of radicals always has been their dissent from this deceit of happy endings and forward, continuous progress. Indeed, in the case of Dunbar-Ortiz's family history, downward mobility was made all the more poignant because it was punishment for her visionary grandfather's stubborn belief in One Big Union and the Cooperative Commonwealth.

When she evokes the great socialist tent revivals on the banks of the Canadian River or folk resistance to Woodrow Wilson's war (the Green Corn Rebellion), Dunbar-Ortiz is of course opening up Oklahoma's collective closet. How many other descendants of the "sharecroppers and tenants and cotton pickers and wheat thrashers" don't have a Debsian great-grandmother or Wobbly grandfather in their genealogy?

In Dunbar-Ortiz's childhood, the family's radical heirlooms – a framed IWW Constitution and a red membership card hanging on a string – were still proudly displayed next to her grandfather's veterinarian diploma and a framed picture of Jesus. Indeed, Grandpa – long dead, mysterious, and utterly charismatic – ultimately became the lodestone that helped Dunbar-Ortiz shape her own defiant, radical path.

The tragedy of modern Oklahoma, in contrast, is that too many preachers, politicians, and vengeful reactionaries have been allowed to turn a rich history of plebeian revolt into scorched earth and to expunge rebel ancestors like Grandpa Dunbar and Woody Guthrie. Even the state's enduring icon, Will Rogers – whose New Deal politics would be an anathema today – stands uneasily and probably sadly upon his pedestal.

Historical amnesia, of course, is not an Okie franchise: it is the ontological disease of most Americans of poor white ancestry. Most Okies at least know – and many even boast – about the sharecropper's shack or sod cabin or teepee in their ancestry. Dunbar-Ortiz urges her readers to return to that point of origin: to root around in the red dirt and debris of memory.

In her case, it was one of Grandpa's old horseshoes that became the starting point of her reconciliation with her father as well as her daughter's initiation into the meaning of being "Okie." Dunbar-Ortiz then discovered an almost identical experience in a poem by Wilma Elizabeth McDaniel (a California dust-bowl daughter), which, in turn, sparked their extraordinary friendship.

These epiphanies recall a literary counterpart. In *Grapes of Wrath,* there is a famous scene along Route 66: some Okie men are squatting on their haunches, doodling in the dirt with sticks, and talking about the disasters driving them west. The comparison of their individual but common experiences precipitates a sudden recognition that in Steinbeck's time would have been called "class consciousness."

Dunbar-Ortiz knows how difficult such conversations have become, but her memoir is full of examples of spontaneous solidarity even on the part of the two rabidly anti-hippie LAPD cops whose rage becomes kindness when they hear a down-home drawl. *Red Dirt* illuminates the complex battleground of poor white identity and, indeed, even points the way to its transcendence, as Indian grandmothers join with IWW grandfathers in a chorus of difference and dissent.

Dunbar-Ortiz does not romanticize her Okie background or white working-class culture. There were too many crazy demons of racism and sexism in her childhood and too much cultural and moral suffocation in her little town. Oklahoma, she argues, has become America's most "protofascist" state.

Yet the bedrock of *Red Dirt* remains the conviction, ratified by "growing up Okie," that the past still has the power to speak to the present and that the lived experience of class still produces radical self-knowledge. I can't think of another book that so eloquently confounds the prevalent, reified view of "red versus blue" states or challenges the persistent stereotype of the Okie "other."

It was an honor to publish the original edition of *Red Dirt* in Verso's Haymarket Series, which I co-edited with the late (and much missed) Michael Sprinker. It is exciting that this unforgettable memoir is now back home, where it will endure as a classic, at the University of Oklahoma Press.

MIKE DAVIS

Acknowledgments

Thanks to Matt Bokovoy, acquisitions editor at University of Oklahoma Press, for bringing the book back home to Oklahoma, and to Mike Davis and John Womack, Jr., for supporting that effort.

Verso Books originally published *Red Dirt* in 1997. I again want to thank all those involved, especially Mike Davis, Colin Robinson, Steve Hiatt, Kevin McMahon, Lee Smith, and thanks as well to Rachel Guidera and Amy Scholder in the New York Verso office for consistent support.

Special thanks go to poet Wilma Elizabeth McDaniel – the "Okie Poet Laureate" of the California Central Valley – who read this book at all its stages of writing. Permissions to use her poems are generously granted by Chiron Review Press, Hanging Loose Press, Mother Road Publications, and *Prenumbra Literary Journal*, and by the poet herself in contributing previously unpublished poems.

Except for my mother and father, both deceased, I have chosen to use pseudonyms for most of the people in this book to protect their privacy. My brother Fred Dunbar – Hank in the book – has been a great source of support in publicizing the book. My daughter, Michelle Callarman, inspires me with her unconditional love, generosity, and encouragement.

Red Dirt

Prologue

The Great Good Luck
of the Found Horseshoe

O grandfather tell me
is it true you worked the land,
and the tools that you used
you made with your own hands?

PETER ROWEN,
'Before the Streets Were Paved'

A cold, still December day in 1992, the sky a bright blue, so bright it almost blinded, the red earth spread west to the horizon miles and miles away, not a soul or a house or an animal or a vehicle in sight.

The three of us – my brother Hank, my daughter, Michelle, and I – stood silently in front of a long-abandoned sharecropper's shack, where my family had lived when I was a toddler.

Michelle and I had driven from San Francisco to Oklahoma for Christmas. It was a singular occasion: we had never 'gone back' – as California Okies tend to term it – together, and she had never met my father. She knew my two brothers and my sister and their children and she had visited Oklahoma dozens of times, but always with her father and his second family, and always his clan. She had never seen where I grew up, my childhood haunts, the shacks I had called home, the cemetery where my mother and so many other relations are buried. Nor had she ever expressed any interest in doing so. She knew from her father telling her throughout her childhood that there was something dark and shameful about that side of her heritage, something that added up to 'white trash.' And I suppose she assumed

1

from my silence on the subject that it must be so.

At the time we made that trip, I had begun writing what I called 'life history,' about growing up rural and poor in Oklahoma, a kind of historical study that would tell the story of a people and a place through one life, mine, and about our people who went to California, and about the Los Angeles Police Department and Thomas Jefferson and Andrew Jackson and everything else.

I knew I needed to address the role of Scots-Irish frontier settlers, like Jackson, and their descendants, like my father's family, like the family of Will Rogers, Jr., and, especially, Okie migrants to California, who have either resisted or carried out the will of the Anglo-settler elite. And I decided to do so in April 1992, when a nearly all-white jury in southern California found four Los Angeles police officers innocent in the videotaped beating of Rodney King, an African-American man. My first thought on hearing the verdict was the same one as when I had read about the change of venue for the trial from Los Angeles to Simi Valley: What do you expect, Simi Valley is an Okie town where cops come to retire; why do you think Ronald Reagan built his presidential library there? A large number of Simi Valley homeowners are second- and third-generation Dust Bowl and Defense Okies, the ones who 'made it.' Yet I noticed that none of the plethora of news reports mentioned that fact – they would point out that Simi Valley was virtually all white and was a suburb favored by Los Angeles policemen, but they did not mention that many of those cops had grown up there, or nearby in other Ventura County and Central Valley towns.

Although trained as a professional historian, I felt I needed to ask my father questions. I had been estranged from him off and on since I'd left home at sixteen. I had sworn to myself when my daughter was born that I would never allow him to meet his granddaughter, a trump card I could always use against him, something I knew that he as the patriarch of the family cared fiercely about: his progeny, even the females.

But now I needed to hear my father's stories, his language, the cadence of his speech, and, yes, even his maddening provincialism, his bigotry. I needed to figure it out, to understand. I vowed I would go simply as the professional historian specializing in oral history that I was trained to be; I vowed to treat the old man like any other source. I also determined to grow up and put away hate and revenge, and to let my daughter meet him. Since he was then eighty-six and would soon be gone, I reasoned, she deserved to know her grandfather even if I thought he didn't deserve to meet her.

Every time I return home, my brother Hank, who has never left Oklahoma, takes me on a pilgrimage to the places we grew up, sometimes with Daddy in tow to tell us his stories. We always begin at Matthewson Cemetery to visit my mother's grave, then go on to each old home-place or the empty space where one had been.

Hank drove us to that old sharecropper cabin that he remembered well, that one and the other half-dozen ones in Canadian County, Oklahoma where my family had sharecropped and rented for a decade before I was born and for the first six years of my life, until we moved to town and Daddy exchanged farming for a paycheck. After we were grown and gone, he moved to The City – Oklahoma City. Each time we take that pilgrimage through our childhoods, my brother rummages around those old home-places, looking for something, some item from that desolate past. That December day with my daughter and me restlessly waiting to get out of the freezing wind, he struck gold. 'Well I'll be, look here, a horseshoe. I believe I remember Daddy making this horseshoe. Boy, this will make a good Christmas present for him.' He handled the rusty, crude old U-turn piece of iron as if it might break or turn to ashes like bone. With his bare fingers he brushed the cold red dirt off the horseshoe. His dark eyes glowed, and he suddenly appeared to me as the little boy he used to be rather than a fifty-six-year-old man.

Michelle seemed a bit perplexed by her uncle's enthusiasm, but she joined in the spirit of celebration, carefully cradling the old hunk of iron the thirty-five miles back to Daddy's place in southwest Oklahoma City, where she presented it to him.

That was the first encounter between my daughter and my father. I detected a watery softness in the old man's white eyes, but he kept his cool. He took the horseshoe into his gnarled hands and touched every inch of it, as if he had just pounded it out fresh, and he told the story of the place, of the time (1939), of the horse the shoe was made for, of the meanness of the landlord, of the disastrous New Deal agricultural policy, of the coldness that winter living in the drafty shack, of the baby (me) who nearly died of asthma, and of the three-year-old boy, my brother who had found the horseshoe, who tailed him everywhere he went and who had watched him make it.

Michelle listened intently – the stories took about an hour before they started repeating themselves – and you would have thought this grandfather and granddaughter had always been the best of buddies.

'He won,' I said to myself, 'damn him, he won, won my daughter's heart – and mine, too.' No turning back now. 'Damn, damn, damn,' I repeated to myself, 'now I'm going to miss him when he dies, and miss all the years lost to revenge.'

After that trip I returned to California knowing if I were to write my life history, I had to start over. I came close to giving up – and then I met Wilma Elizabeth McDaniel. I had come across Wilma's poetry in various collections on the California Central Valley compiled by the writer and scholar Gerald Haslam, but had not paid much attention to it; after all, those of us who did not leave Oklahoma during the Dust Bowl thought ourselves somewhat more righteous and superior than those who fled during the thirties. What caught my attention was an advertisement for a new book of poetry by Wilma called *Prince Albert Wind*. Included in the publicity materials was the poem 'Buried Treasure,' which so duplicated my experience that Christmas with my daughter and brother that it was eerie:

> Elbie Hayes ruined his
> expensive shoes
> squashing around the autumn
> desolation
> of a sharecropper farm
> in Caddo County

> Okie boy
> turned fifty
> searching for anything that
> had belonged
> to his father
> when he was fighting the
> Great Depression

> Kicked at a lump
> behind the caved-in cellar

and uncovered a rusty
Prince Albert tobacco can

Stowed it away
as he would a saint's bones
in his Lincoln Continental
and headed back to Bakersfield

I searched in bookstores and libraries for everything Wilma Elizabeth
McDaniel had ever published and found *A Primer for Buford*, in which
Wilma calls on Okies to recover and pass on our memories, cap-
sulized in the title poem, 'A Primer for Buford':

Uncle Claudie Windham's life
has weathered to the color of
wisdom
only a few things bother him
now
mainly his grandson Buford Windham, Jr.

He laments
That boy ain't growing up right
in Berkeley where his mother teaches
I mean he don't know nothing
his daddy done
when he was a boy in Oklahoma

Why he don't even know our language
if you told him there was a roller
coming
he'd think you meant a steam roller

Uncle Claudie shakes his head
I reckon Buford need a primer
like we had in the first grade
start from scratch
and learn where he come from

Pretty soon
there won't be anyone left that
can tell him.

Then I met Wilma herself, and she and her work have inspired and informed me ever since.

I suppose that all of us who become self-conscious about being Okie have also read John Steinbeck's 1939 novel, *The Grapes of Wrath*. That novel, together with the 1940 epic movie based on it, etched an indelible picture of the Okies in the minds of a whole generation, so that for them and their children the book represents not fiction, but truth. Steinbeck was already a celebrity author due to his 1935 best-selling novel, *Tortilla Flat,* when he met Tom Collins, an organizer for the Communist Party's Cannery and Agricultural Workers Industrial Union; Steinbeck published *In Dubious Battle,* which, although sympathetic to the Okie farm workers, also characterized communist organizers as cold manipulators. Despite this portrayal, the Party sang Steinbeck's praises as a Popular Front novelist, and Steinbeck began research, guided by Collins, for what would become *The Grapes of Wrath* in the Federal Resettlement Administration's facility for migrants in Arvin, California, the Weed Patch Camp.

Steinbeck's great novel was fueled by myth, but the writer did not create the myth; he merely reported and dramatized it. He told our story, our mythology. In a 1936 essay published before the novel, 'Their Blood Is Strong,' Steinbeck focused on the racial superiority of the Okie migrants, portraying us as preindustrial and deeply democratic:

> Having been brought up in the prairies where industrialization never penetrated, they have jumped with no transition from the old agrarian, self-containing farm, where nearly everything used was raised or manufactured, to a system of agriculture so industrialized that the man who plants a crop does not often see, let alone harvest, the fruit of his planting, where the migrant has no contact with the growing cycle … They have come from the little farm districts where democracy was not only possible but inevitable, where popular government, whether practiced in the Grange, in church organization or in local government, was the responsibility of every man.

Steinbeck imagined a life in Oklahoma that had never existed. Oklahoma settlers, as Dan Morgan observes in his 1992 history *Rising in the West: The True Story of an 'Okie' Family from the Great Depression Through the Reagan Years*, were not innocent of industrialization: the whole area had long been one vast oil field and refinery, and coal mines were worked alongside fields of cotton and wheat cash crops. Even more romantic is Steinbeck's portrayal of town-hall democracy, when what my forebears experienced was powerlessness under the boots of 'elected' gangster rings who robbed the public coffers. Morgan convincingly portrays rural Oklahoma settlers, mostly dispossessed of their small holdings, as tramping between mines, smelters and refineries, and as tenant farmers raising cash crops.

That's the true story of my family and of the Okies, although we dream of a paradise that we wish had existed and might be recovered. But there was the land, and the love of the land.

One

Red Diaper Baby?

The working class and the employing class have nothing in common. There can be no peace so long as hunger and want are found among millions of working people and the few who make up the employing class have all the good things of life. Between these two classes a struggle must go on, until all the toilers come together on the political as well as on the industrial field, and take and hold that which they produce by their labor.

From the Constitution of the
Industrial Workers of the World, 1905

I was born Roxie Amanda Dunbar. 'Dust Bowl baby' they called me and my nickname was 'Baby.' I was a surely unwanted last child with two brothers – Laurence, eleven, and Hank, two – and a sister, Vera, nine. I would ask Daddy if they had wanted me when he told me about those hard times, and he would say, 'Sure, else I wouldn't have paid a doctor ten dollars to come and birth you.' Once I understood how really destitute they had been I realized he meant what he said. Yet on my birth certificate Daddy listed his occupation as 'proprietor of feed store' and Mama's as 'housewife,' sounding so secure.

My life began on a hot late summer Saturday, September 10, 1938, in San Antonio, Texas. I was born in the one-room shack where the five of them lived behind my uncle's house. For the first three days my name was Marvel, named after Mama's best friend, a failed opera singer who sang in honky-tonks. But Mama had a fight with Marvel and decided not to name me after her. Daddy came up with the name Roxie. He always told me he saw that name on a marquee in New Orleans' French Quarter when he went there with some other cow-boys as a teenager. He said that the Roxie club was named after a beautiful stripper. Mama always said he was making all that up.

My mother never talked about that time in San Antonio when she was pregnant with me. But I can imagine how she suffered. I know the facts because Vera has told me many times. She was nine and remembers it well. In June of that year my grandmother sold the feed store Daddy was running and they were evicted from the house they rented. During those last three months before I was born they were homeless, and it was a scorcher of a summer as always in south Texas – humid, unbearable. They took refuge with Daddy's oldest brother, a veterinarian in San Antonio. My uncle was bankrupt himself but let my family live in a one-room storage space behind his house, windowless, an oven. All that summer Mama and Daddy and the three children were stuffed in that hot, windowless room.

Some ailment struck my mother with a vengeance. They said it was poison ivy, but who knows? It was chronic, afflicting her for years before and after I was born. On every inch of Mama's body, Vera says, even inside her nose, ears, mouth, vagina, anus, were swollen welts bloody from scratching. How relieved she must have been when her body was freed at least of me. Mama couldn't nurse me because of the sores. So it was Vera who wound up caring for me, holding me and feeding me from a bottle. I long blamed my mother for my debilitating, disabling bronchial asthma that began soon after I was born, and I'm certain she blamed herself.

My father's name is Moyer Haywood Pettibone Scarberry Dunbar. When I was growing up he would read to me from the framed 1905 IWW Constitution, and tell me: 'I was born two years after the IWW, and Papa named me after the founders: William Moyer, Big Bill Haywood, and George Pettibone. They were on trial, framed up for murder in Boise, Idaho, during that summer of 1907 when I was born, same year Oklahoma got statehood. Clarence Darrow got them off. One Big Union, that's what your grandfather fought for.' Then Daddy would rail against the current trade unions.

Hanging on the bedroom wall beside the IWW Constitution was a framed photograph from 1912 of my father's entire family, my grandfather and grandmother sitting on the wide front porch of their spacious two-story house. All ten children were dressed in their Sunday best. Daddy was five years old in that picture. My grandfather, Emmett Victor Dunbar, was nearly forty, but youthful with thick dark hair, muscular, handsome. I would stand on the bed and trace my grandfather's features with my finger, and stare into his eyes. I talked to him. He began to look like Jesus to me; my mother's framed picture of Jesus in the front room never brought out a sense of devotion compared to that of my grandfather's picture.

Next to the photograph was Grandpa Dunbar's diploma in veterinarian medicine from St. Joseph, Missouri, dated 1910. He had moved his family from Missouri to Piedmont, Oklahoma in 1907, just after Daddy was born, and returned alone to Kansas and then Missouri for three years to study medicine. During those years, Grandma was practically a single mother caring for five little children in Piedmont, where her entire extended family had settled. Grandpa had joined the Socialist Party when it was founded in 1901 – eastern Kansas and western Missouri formed the southwest center of the Socialist Party – but was attracted to the more radical IWW once it was founded. Already a committed Wobbly when Daddy was born, Grandpa continued his involvement while in medical school and returned to Piedmont an organizer as well as a highly respected professional. Daddy said Grandpa rotated three teams of horses to make his doctoring calls around a fifty-mile area – cattle and horses were his specialty.

Beside the veterinarian diploma and the picture, a worn, thin red book – my grandfather's IWW union book – hung from a string, 'Emmett Victor Dunbar' scrawled inside.

'Why did Grandpa take you all to Texas?' I'd ask.

'Danged Klan ran us off, some of them same folks you see in church on Sunday. They're pretty brave when they got sheets over their heads. Nothing but cowards. Papa had to sell out lock, stock and barrel.'

Daddy was fourteen when the family moved to the border town of McAllen in the Texas Rio Grande Valley. Grandfather Emmett died in 1934, kicked by a horse he was doctoring. But my father held the KKK responsible because a dozen years before they had beat my grandfather half to death and left him with brain damage.

Daddy told me over and over about those years before the First World War when the Wobblies controlled the town and county where I grew up, and practically all of the mines and fields and woods of western North America: the glory days. My father liked to tell stories about them while he cleaned his hunting rifle; the smell of gun oil went with the story.

'Your Grandpa organized all the sharecroppers and tenants and cotton pickers and wheat thrashers, all them migrants from here to yon. Papa got himself elected to the school board, that same school you go to. One time a bunch of landlords tried to take the school with guns. Papa and all us brothers held up there five days shooting it out with them, and we whupped them good.'

'How old were you then, Daddy?'

'About your age, ten, eleven, but I was a good shot. Papa always chose me to ride shotgun on his wagon when he made his rounds doctoring.'

'What did the Wobblies want?' I asked. No matter how many times he told me, I loved to hear his agenda of Wobbly dreams: abolition of interest and profits, public ownership of everything, no military draft, no military, no police, the equality of women and all races. 'The O-B-U, One Big Union,' he would say and smile to himself, lost in memory.

The Wobblies were mostly anarchists and suspicious of the electoral system, but many of them like my grandfather voted for Eugene Debs and the Socialist Party all five times he ran. Daddy explained: 'It was different here in Oklahoma than some places. Why by nineteen and fourteen Oklahoma had more dues-paying members of the Socialist Party than any other state in the Union – twelve thousand. That year they elected over a hundred Socialists to office.'

'So what happened that the Klan drove you all out?' I asked.

'That son-of-a-gun Woodrow Wilson, him and that gangster Palmer and his goon J. Edgar Hoover wiped out the IWW, put them all in jail or kicked them out of the country. The dadgummed rich wheat farmers bankrolled the Klan. They swelled up like a tick – night riding, killing stock, burning barns and crops, lynching, burning crosses. Good Christians they were.'

Daddy, like his father, was a free-thinker. I would lower my head whenever he talked about Christians because I was a devout Baptist. Mama was a hard-shell Baptist convert, and I never missed a church service once we moved to town: Sunday morning and night,

Wednesday night prayer meeting, and summer Bible School, camp and tent revivals. My parents tried not to fight about it, and Daddy would even give me a dime to put in the collection plate. But he would break out singing 'Pie in the sky bye and bye,' from Wobbly troubadour Joe Hill's 'Preacher and the Slave,' to the tune of the hymn 'The Sweet Bye and Bye,' and Mama would steam.

Next to the Klan and Christian hypocrites Daddy scorned any kind of law enforcement authorities. The Wobbly Constitution said that any worker who joined the army, a militia or even a police force would be denied membership forever.

Despite my grandfather's former affluence, when my parents married in 1927 they returned to Piedmont as sharecroppers. 'Why are we so poor if Grandpa was rich?' I asked.

My father would shift his eyes away from the IWW Constitution and stare at his gnarled hands. He didn't like being reminded that we were poor. Down the street lived two of his mother's sisters, among the wealthiest families in town, meaning they had two-story houses with running water and bathrooms. The big family house where my father grew up still stood, one of the seven big houses in town, but it no longer belonged to our family.

'I did all right until the Dust Bowl and the danged Depression. Why even rich bankers were jumping out of windows back then. Danged Roosevelt dumped our crops in the ocean and got the bankers back on their feet, then tried to drive us all off the land. I wasn't about to be run off to no California.'

Oscar Ameringer became the Socialist Party organizer in Oklahoma in 1907. He was doubtful about organizing farmers. In his 1940 autobiography, *If You Don't Weaken,* Ameringer wrote that he had once regarded farmers as capitalists, not exploited wage laborers, as the owners of the means of production with a great deal to lose from socialism. But after a meeting in Harrah, the town where my mother grew up, he was astonished to discover an America he did not know existed, starving farmers poorer than the white and black workers he had been organizing in New Orleans.

Between 1906 and 1917, the Wobblies and the Socialist Party won converts on a mass scale in Oklahoma. My grandfather was one of the first. They adopted the religious evangelists' technique of holding huge week-long encampments with charismatic speakers, male and female, usually near small towns (indeed, many evangelists were themselves converts to socialism). Socialists were elected as local officials and the lampposts of many towns were hung with red flags. In 1915 alone 205 mass encampments were held. The Socialists never won a statewide race in Oklahoma, but their percentage of the vote increased from 6 percent in 1907 to 16 percent in 1916 voting for Socialist Party candidate Eugene Debs. In 1914 the Socialist candidate for governor won 21 percent of the vote and they won six seats in the Oklahoma legislature, along with a majority of local offices in many counties. But it was not a peaceful process.

'There was a lot of shooting?' I asked Daddy.

'You can say that again and not just shooting. Wobblies cut telephone wires and dynamited pipelines, water mains and sewers. It was all around here but mainly over in the eastern part of the state. Them Seminole Indians in it, Negroes too. Down in San Antone and the Valley them Magon brothers from Old Mexico. Boy, the Wobblies sure put up a fight.'

In speaking of blacks and poor whites and Seminole Indians rising up together in eastern Oklahoma, I know now that Daddy was referring to a spontaneous event, separate from IWW or Socialist Party organizing, the 'Green Corn Rebellion' during the summer of 1917.

In December 1994, when I was poking around in southeastern Oklahoma trying to understand that rebellion, I met an elderly Seminole Muskogee Indian woman who said that she had been only nine years old at the time, but she remembered it, and that her uncle, who she said had been a leader of the rebellion and was imprisoned afterwards, had told the heroic story over and over.

'The full moon of late July, early August it was, the Moon of the Green Corn. It was not easy to persuade our poor white and black brothers and sisters to rise up. We told them that rising up, standing up, whatever the consequences, would inspire future generations. Our courage, our bravery would be remembered and copied. That has been the Indian way for centuries, since the invasions. Fight and tell the story so that those who come after or their descendants will rise up once again. It may take a thousand years but that is how we continue and eventually prevail.'

I asked her to explain the significance of the Green Corn ceremony to the Muskogees: 'That is our most sacred ceremony, and you could call it our new year, the time of new beginnings. It occurs whenever the green corn comes, sometimes as early as late June, or as late as early August. During that year, 1917, the green corn came late, during the last week of July and early August. It was on August 3, 1917, at the end of our four-day Green Corn ceremony that we rose up.'

My father portrayed the Green Corn Rebellion as a great moment of heroism, a moment of unity, betrayed by the 'electric-light city' Socialists, who scorned it. Of course nothing about Wobblies and Socialists appeared in my US or Oklahoma history textbooks (and very little appears in Oklahoma textbooks even now), so I began to doubt my father's stories, especially about the Green Corn Rebellion.

When I moved to California and was swept up in the sixties as a student, I gained a new pride in my Wobbly/Socialist heritage, but nearly forgot the Green Corn Rebellion until it reappeared in my field of vision in the mid-1970s while I was working on the book *The Great Sioux Nation,* which grew out of the 1973 Lakota uprising at Wounded Knee. A Muskogee medicine man from Oklahoma, the late Philip Deere, told me a story in 1974 that sounded familiar. At first he did not name the event but described his memory of it and what he was told growing up. He would have been about the same age as my father in 1917, ten or eleven years old. Philip recalled the rebellion as Indian-conceived and led.

I searched for published information, trying to verify Philip's version, but found very little indeed that even mentioned the Green Corn Rebellion. Finally, I found the typescript of a 1959 undergraduate Harvard University history thesis by John Womack, Jr., himself from Oklahoma, the biographer of Mexican revolutionary leader Emiliano Zapata, and now a senior professor of history at Harvard.

By 1890, before the Native American republics of Indian Territory were dissolved by the 1898 Curtis Act that violated treaties with the Native nations and forced their communal holdings into individual allotments, white tenants had already come to outnumber the Indians two to one in Indian Territory. Breaking the law, violence and corruption were thus the rule, not the exception, in that region, setting the stage for an agrarian rebellion.

And times were hard. Over 60 percent of mortgaged farms were lost to foreclosure during the two years before the Green Corn Rebellion. More than half the farms were worked by tenants. The rates were even higher in the Southeastern counties where the rebellion took place (Pottawatomi, Seminole, Hughes and Pontotoc counties). Only a fifth of the farms in that region were worked by their owners, and half of those were under heavy mortgages that carried usurious interest rates of 20 to 200 percent.

Farming in Oklahoma was commercial, with tenants as wage laborers and cotton the king; cotton production doubled between 1909 and 1919, making Oklahoma the fourth-largest cotton producer among the states and firmly establishing a cash-and-credit economy. The other major industries were oil production and coal mining, which spawned boom towns and attracted large populations of transient workers.

When the government began to draft soldiers for the First World War, the white, black and red farmers in southeastern Oklahoma decided to resist conscription. Their strategy was to come together and seal off an area from outside interference, persuade their neighbors to join, and then march all the way to Washington, D.C., picking up recruits along the way. There they would overthrow President Wilson, stop the war, and reform the domestic economy to 'restore to the working classes the full product of their labor.' In preparation for the great march they burned bridges across the Canadian River to keep their liberated area isolated. They cut telephone and telegraph wires so the besieged could not call for help. They planned to confiscate property in the towns and on the surrounding farms. Anyone who opposed them was to be conscripted in the same way that the federal government conscripted its troops. They agreed that any local authorities who tried to stop them would be met with gunfire, and poisoned food and well water. They believed they would be joined by the working people's armies of other states and that the IWW and the four Railroad Brotherhoods would support them for a victorious march on Washington, where they would then take control (since most of the US military would already be in Europe or fighting Pancho Villa in Mexico).

I learned from Professor Womack's account that a group of African-Americans did indeed set off the rebellion. In early August 1917, a sheriff and his deputy were fired on by some thirty black rebels. Hundreds of poor whites and Muskogee Indians were involved. The rebels were well organized. They divided themselves into details, some to recruit all who had not yet joined the rebellion, others to burn barns, another to blow up the Texaco pipeline, several groups to destroy railroad bridges and cut telephone and telegraph wires, and others to tear down fences and free farm animals to trample cotton fields. After a long summer day of destruction the 500 or so rebels congregated in their new liberated zone to feast, celebrate and rest.

However, the reaction of local townspeople against the rebels was fierce. They organized huge posses to hunt them down. When faced with angry, armed citizens, the rebels dispersed, guerrilla-style. During the following days, more wires were cut and bridges hit, while more and more rebels were captured. Pitched battles took place, and hundreds were arrested.

US entrance into the European war in 1917 produced a wave of patriotism and a brutal backlash against the antiwar Wobblies and Socialists in Oklahoma. The Socialists blamed the repression in Oklahoma on the Green Corn rebels. Fiery crosses burned all over the state, and the ranks and resources of the Ku Klux Klan burgeoned. The Klan seized political power in Texas and Arkansas and came close in Oklahoma. My grandfather was one of their victims.

When a core group of native white Americans, the very foot soldiers of empire, began turning socialist and anti-imperialist, even inching away from white supremacy, the government and other centers of power acted swiftly, viciously and relentlessly to crush the movement. A wave of propaganda accompanied the repression. The D.W. Griffith film extolling the KKK, *The Birth of a Nation,* had already appeared in 1915. After the victories of the Russian and Mexican revolutions, Red Scare propaganda flooded newspapers and magazines, and formed the main text of sermons. The landless agrarians of Oklahoma were left with a recollection of hard times and hatred for big government and for the rich and powerful, but also with the memory of a failed movement.

And repression: Oklahoma was kept under careful surveillance long before the McCarthy era. As reported by George Milburn in 1946:

It is a criminal offense, for example, in Oklahoma, to have a copy of Karl Marx's

Das Kapital in one's library, and anyone suspected of possessing seditious literature is liable to search, seizure, and arrest. Indeed, certain scholarly citizens have
been prosecuted criminally and faced with penitentiary sentences, because sober
political treatises, regarded as classics elsewhere, in Oklahoma are even more
illicit than a bottle of bootleg booze.

So talk about my grandfather and the Wobblies and Green Corn
rebels thinned as the new Red Scare escalated: A Red in the family
tree was no longer something to be proud of. The rage about our
poverty was covered over with pride for just being white and 'real'
Americans.

I myself grew fiercely patriotic. Tears brimmed in my eyes when I
heard the 'Star Spangled Banner' or pledged allegiance to the flag. I
won first prize in a county speech contest for my original oration,
'America Is Great Because America Is Good.' I spent the summer of
1954 avidly watching the Army-McCarthy hearings on television,
rooting for McCarthy, adoring the young Roy Cohn. I doubted my
father's stories. And my father no longer told the stories.

During the Korean War I sold Veterans of Foreign Wars crepe
paper roses. Several young men in town were drafted and came home
wounded. One of the boys who returned sat with my brother and me
and our cousins and told us about Korea: 'Why, we're rich here in
Oklahoma by comparison. They're lucky to eat a spoonful of rice
once a day. We went through this one little village and seen an old
man, looked to be a hundred, all dried up and wrinkled, just died in
front of us. I stopped to pay my respects and as I was looking at him
wondering what his life had been like, out comes this giant white
thing from his mouth, a damned tapeworm five foot long.' And we
felt lucky to be free Americans fighting communism, proud of our
country for helping others.

Today my father says he believes his father regretted having been a
Wobbly and a Socialist, and that he had been hoodwinked by communists. I don't believe it for a minute; rather, I think he wants to
forget his father's, and my, idealism, which could get me into trouble.

Yet when I was a student during the sixties in California, Daddy's
stories of my Wobbly grandfather were my guiding light and for that
I am forever grateful. What remains mysterious to me is why my
father told me those stories. My older brothers and sister claim never

to have heard them as children, and until my brother Hank got Daddy to tell his story for an oral history of Piedmont, he had never heard them from Daddy and I think he hadn't believed me before.

Daddy shocked me recently when he told me about how brutally his father had beat him as a teenager. I had never before heard him utter a single negative word about his father. 'Boy, it hurt and sometimes put me in bed. He used a horsewhip. After I was about twelve seems like he had it in for me, and that's why I run off when I turned sixteen. I couldn't take it no more,' he said, tears filling his fading blue eyes.

That would have been 1919 to 1923, when the Wobbly and Socialist movements were being crushed and the Klan was on the rise, and my grandfather and his family were targets of KKK violence. Grandpa Dunbar had taken out his frustration on his most devoted disciple.

Two

Dust Bowl Baby

But Bessie defends him
Jess puts fresh meat
    on my table
squirrels rabbits prairie chickens
ducks and geese
We hardly ever have to eat
salt pork
if he has shells for his guns

WILMA ELIZABETH McDANIEL,
from 'We Hardly Ever Have to Eat Salt Pork'

Starved out of sharecropping in western Oklahoma, my parents had been living in San Antonio for two years before I was born, working for Daddy's mother, running a feed store she had bought after my grandfather died. But the business failed, and three months after I was born the family was back in Oklahoma. We stayed with Mama's sister in Oklahoma City and Daddy worked in a nursery but was laid off, then reluctantly signed up with the WPA, 'digging holes and filling them up,' he said, 'no more than welfare. What I wanted was a real job of work.' Then he found a farm to sharecrop near Piedmont, a town his family had been among the first to settle and where he had grown up. Daddy was tied to the land, red soil in his blood.

In a photograph of my parents taken in 1927, on their wedding day, they stand in front of a palm tree in his parents' yard in McAllen, Texas. Mama wears a fashionable twenties flapper dress. She's slim and stylish, her dark straight hair cut in a bob. Her head reaches just above Daddy's shoulder, he nearly six feet and she a half-foot shorter. Daddy's black hair is slicked back and he resembles Clyde Barrow, his contemporary of Bonnie and Clyde fame. He wears a long-sleeved

white shirt and light slacks and a horizontally striped tie and holds a
billed cap. They are a good-looking couple, glowing, healthy teenagers. In another picture, taken two years later, in 1929, they are skinny
and haggard, standing in the middle of a dried-up Oklahoma cotton
field, a bleak backdrop. Daddy holds Laurence, their firstborn. By the
time I was born they had lived through nearly a decade of the Depression and dust storms.

I always thought Daddy regretted being tied down to a wife and
baby. He dreamed of a mythical past of cattle drives and cowboys,
which he'd had a taste of during its last days. He insisted on living off
the land when it was no longer possible without a lot of money. He
continued to hunt. He refused to go to California: 'Only them with
money and a truck or car could even afford to go,' he still says.

Daddy dreamed of the rodeo as others might Hollywood or Harvard. He wanted to make it big with prize money. He dropped out of
school and ran away to become a cowboy, but ended up grubbing for
paltry wages doing miserable, unmythical work on west Texas and
Oklahoma ranches, driving postholes for fences, stringing barbed
wire, fencing the freedom he dreamed of. A few years before, maybe
even a few after, Daddy might have realized his dream Will Rogers–style, or later as a Gene Autry. Maybe he would have been less
devastated by hard times had he not had such improbable dreams. I
can well understand my mother's attraction to this handsome, talented cowboy, so her romantic dreams were equally busted by the
1930s reality of rural poverty.

Yet, until the Depression, Daddy probably had confidence that he
could do or be anything he wished, and that there was all the time in
the world. But as a nineteen-year-old father he had to find work and
no one was hiring. They lived in a tent by the river and then in a mud
dugout that Mama called a cave. They picked cotton.

During the first two years of my life my family sharecropped on
two farms near the tiny farming community of Piedmont where
Daddy had grown up and his family had once owned land. Before
they went to San Antonio that year before I was born they had
sharecropped on a half-dozen farms in that area. The only crop the
landlords allowed was cotton, a cash crop to sell. Daddy hated cotton. He wanted to raise food and stock. He wanted his own farm.
'This ain't farming, no different from factory work,' he'd say. But he

sharecropped to stay on the land. And he raised cotton, and they picked and chopped cotton.

We owned no farm equipment, not even a team of mules or a plow. A landless farmer could drive a better bargain if he had the cash to rent a farm and use it as he wished; or if he could furnish his own equipment and mules he would get three-fourths of what he produced. But a 'cropper like Daddy got only half the share.

Every time they moved it seemed like it had something to do with Daddy quarreling with the landlord, like the time he took a horse-whip to one landlord who was beating a mule with a stick to get him to move. He hated working for the landlords who drove shiny new pickup trucks and lived in nice houses in town and joined the Masons, and whose wives passed their time playing bridge.

'Moyer,' Mama said many times, 'we could move them kids into town instead of being stuck out here in the sticks if you weren't too proud to take a wage job.'

'Ain't no jobs to be had, Louise, you know that,' he'd say.

I was nearly three, and we had almost finished more than a year on the farm a few miles south of Piedmont, in a nice area down by the creek with cottonwoods, when one day in January Daddy came home and announced we were going to move ten miles northwest, out on the flat plain, and caretake a horse ranch. In the deal we would be allowed to have a vegetable garden, corn field and some stock and chickens. My brothers and sister and mother were relieved about not having to chop cotton anymore, and I was happy I wouldn't have to when I was older. Laurence was excited because he would have a horse to ride.

Everything we owned fit in that pickup – two mattresses and metal bed frames and slats, a canvas army cot, the Singer sewing machine, a saddle and bridle, blankets and clothes, pots, pans and dishes, the kitchen table and six unmatched chairs, the piano, a shotgun and a .22 rifle.

The day we moved to the Barnes Ranch was Groundhog Day, a day that felt like springtime. The air was soft and warm, the sky the color of the bluing Mama used in the wash and without a cloud. For a week rain had fallen and melted the ice and snow. The roads were no longer muddy but still ruby red from the rain. The wheat fields on the plains had turned pale green overnight. For me a hard winter of asthma would soon end and a new life begin. Asthma varies with the victim, but mine was always related to catching the common cold or dust and pollutants, not to allergies. An ordinary bad cold would become a life-threatening asthma attack.

We stopped in front of a peeling white frame house, somewhat better than the sharecropper cabin we left. The outhouse had two holes. Of course there was no electricity or running water, but there was a windmill and a huge water tank for the horses and a pump right outside the back door of the house. Laurence, who was four-teen, was happy to have a horse, but he didn't like being so far from school, nor did Vera, and Mama wanted to move to town to be near the Baptist Church.

Despite the others grumbling, Hank and I were excited about the new place. We spotted dry creek beds all around, good for hiding, and new places to explore. An oil pipeline passed nearby and there was a tall white board fence around the horse corral, both good for tightrope-style walking. And there was a huge hay barn with a loft to play in. Then there were the horses, two dozen of them, all colors, all a little walleyed as if they hadn't been around people or ridden much.

I figured Daddy was proud of what he'd done by getting the place, but he complained anyway and pointed out the drawbacks. 'House is gonna be drafty and hard to keep warm in the winter. No cellar for twisters. But it'll just have to do for now, Louise.'

'No need interfering with God's will,' Mama said. Daddy was afraid of tornadoes – unlike Mama, who believed that God would decide the day and time you died.

The whole family set to work fixing up the new place. The boys would have one bedroom and my parents the other. Vera would sleep in the living room. My bed as usual was the canvas army cot; in the new place they put it near the kerosene stove in the living room to keep me warmer.

I followed Daddy around the next day after the others caught the school bus. He showed me where he would plant the vegetable gar-den and corn field at the next full moon and where he would hang the tire and rope swing and where he would build a rabbit cage for me. He had promised we could have pet rabbits at the new place.

Then we went to the horses. Daddy talked to each one. 'Baby, fetch the currycomb and we'll shine them up good,' he said to me. I was honored to carry out any task Daddy suggested. I brought the steel-wired brush to him and he gently combed the horses head to toe, the horses whinnying in pleasure. Daddy's job was to keep the horses in good shape and ride each one daily so that on Sunday afternoons the landlord could bring his friends to go riding. He said that Mr. Barnes was a very rich man who owned many oil wells. But he was going to pay Daddy only twenty-five dollars a month in addition to free rent.

'A city slicker,' he said as he showed me the strange little saddles in the barn.

'What are those?' I asked.

'English saddles they use,' he said. He had his own worn Western saddle and bridle from his cowboy days, but he hadn't owned his own horse since the bad times began. One of the ways he made extra money was to break horses and train them. During rodeo season cowboys let him use their horses to enter roping events and split his winnings. He was well known in the county for his way with horses, and his father had been the local veterinarian and someone all the old-timers remembered well even when they disdained my grandfather's socialist leanings.

The horses took to Daddy as horses and even wild animals always did. I had heard him say many times that there was no kind of man he despised more than a man who mistreated animals.

The big day, that first Sunday, came bright and clear. I woke to Daddy pulling on his boots in front of the stove near the cot where I slept. It was still dark outside. He tried unsuccessfully to rouse Laurence for them to prepare the horses for riding. He clomped into the kitchen and ranted at Mama: 'Will you try to get that lazy boy up? I swear he could sleep all day.' He stomped out into the dark alone.

Laurence stumbled out grumbling and pulling up his bib overalls. He went out barefoot. Then Mama woke Hank. 'Henry, get out there and help your daddy.'

When the horses were all curried and saddled and their reins tethered to the corral fence, we all sat down in the kitchen to eat biscuits and gravy and thick bacon and cane syrup. It was Sunday but we never went to church except on special occasions like Easter and Christmas or for funerals. Mama wanted to move to town to go to church regularly, and she and Daddy argued constantly about it, especially at Sunday morning breakfast because Mama would try to get him to let her take us to church. Every few weeks she would win and we would drive the ten miles on the rough, or muddy, red roads to Piedmont and the Baptist church. Daddy, like his father, was not a believer and thought the Christians were hypocrites. I listened to their arguments but didn't know what to think about God and churches, except that church services bored me and I usually slept, my head in Mama's lap.

The city people arrived in two huge shiny black cars – one a Cadillac, the other a Chrysler, Laurence immediately informed the rest of us kids. Hank and I straddled the fence and waited restlessly for the party to ride away so we could inspect the cars more closely. I had never been around such fancy people. There were ten altogether, three of them women. They were all dressed almost exactly the same in heavy riding clothes, brown with black velvet collars, and they wore strange narrow red hats. Their brown leather boots came to the knees but they weren't cowboy boots, rather more like rubber boots. Their pants stuck out on the side above their knees. Each carried thin sticks. I worried about what Daddy might do if any of them were to hit one of the horses. If he got mad we would have to move to another sharecropper cabin, I thought.

I could tell which one was the landlord because he gave Daddy orders about adjusting the stirrups and bridles. He didn't even look as old as Daddy, who was thirty-four. He was blonde and tanned and had twinkling blue eyes. To me he looked like a movie star – they all did. One woman seemed to be the landlord's wife because he called her 'honey' and 'sweetheart.' She was blonde and blue-eyed and tanned too. I wondered how all those blonde people got so brown in the winter, or for that matter why they wanted to be brown when they weren't. I knew no one would want to be naturally brown as I was. I longed for fair hair and skin, for blue eyes, like my sister had.

I watched Daddy make all the adjustments the landlord de-manded, and the party rode off down the red dirt road, laughing and chattering, taking sips from a small flat silver object that Daddy said contained whiskey. Daddy stood watching the horses leave, a worried look on his face.

'What's the matter, Daddy?' I asked and tugged on the pliers hook on the side of his bib overalls.

'People like that have no business with horses,' he said. Clearly his concern was for the horses' safety and not the people's.

The riding party returned two hours later. The horses panted and were slick with sweat. 'Take a look at that hoof on the bay mare,' the landlord commanded, 'I think she picked up a stone.' Daddy did not reply but took the horses inside the barn to feed and comfort them. The city people took baskets of food and an oilcloth out of the trunk of the Cadillac. They spread the oilcloth over the table in the yard and sat on the two long benches. I watched them from the barn door as they ate fried chicken and drank out of silver flasks.

Around four in the evening when the western sky began to cloud over and turn crimson the city people prepared to leave. Laurence, Hank, Vera and I were just returning from walking the pipeline. Laurence carried Daddy's .22 and the two rabbits he'd shot for supper. We were walking back along the road when the two cars pulled out. The cars slowed and almost stopped. The landlord threw something out the window that landed at our feet. Then the two big cars dug out and speeded away, leaving us in a cloud of red dirt. We all looked down at the objects on the ground. There were four shiny pennies almost the same color as the red dirt. I crouched to pick up the pennies but jolted upright when Laurence snarled, 'Leave them. Never take handouts, Roxie.'

I loved the Barnes Ranch, everything about it, even the Sunday visits by the landlord and his friends. I liked watching the ladies. They seemed like princesses from a storybook. But they drank whiskey and smoked cigarettes, too. Mama smoked cigarettes, but always in secret in the outhouse. Daddy smoked a pipe and I had heard him tell Mama that she should smoke in the house if she wanted, but she was saved and the Baptists forbade women smoking.

The one thing Daddy said he liked about the Barnes Ranch was taking care of the horses. He curried and lathered them, doctored and shod them, rode them, and trained them for roping. But he hated the place; I'd never realized how miserable he was at the Barnes Ranch until a few years ago when he showed me the only photograph of us there, on which he had written 'The Barnes Prison' at the top.

After my brothers and sister left for school each day I followed Daddy around as he cared for the horses, and he took me riding across the plains, the wind whistling in my ears. Once we rode all the way to Coyote Hill, where Daddy said there had been a Ghost Dance among the Cheyenne Indians just after the land was opened to white settlers. He said the Indians danced to make the white man disappear, to make the buffalo and fallen warriors reappear, and to resurrect the old way of life. He said that further down south the Washita River was where Colonel Custer had killed a whole camp of unarmed Cheyenne, and that was why they did the Ghost Dance. He said that many of the white settlers had thought the Ghost Dance was a war dance and were scared, and that was why the army killed hundreds of Sioux up north in 1890 who were doing it, and that made the Cheyenne stop dancing.

'Did the dead warriors come back to life?' I asked.

'Well now, some say so. I rode the line up in the Panhandle with an ole boy that was a Cheyenne and he said so. Says they come back and settle in some living person, not just Indians. Said he thought one had settled in me, the way horses liked me and all. I never had no problem with the Indians.' As always I wanted to ask him if Mama's mother had been an Indian but I knew – I don't know how – that was a question I should never ask. And I was aware of the gaps in Daddy's supposed respect for Indians because I had heard him call my mother 'blanket ass' and 'squaw' when he was mad at her, or trying to make her mad.

Sometimes on our rides we passed through Indian communities, which were clusters of shacks with a little store or gas pump, and we passed Indians on the road. I was afraid even though Daddy said there was no reason. 'They're done conquered and won't never go on the warpath again,' he said.

'But their spirits are still alive,' I said.

'Weren't nobody better hunters or loved horses more than the Cheyenne,' he said.

The landlord had promised to provide two milk cows, two hogs to breed, and two dozen chickens, and he did. Laurence and Hank milked every morning, and Mama and Vera made butter and buttermilk. The women fed the chickens and collected the eggs and slopped the hogs. Soon we had a litter of pigs and slaughtered the hogs for bacon and loins to sell in town, keeping only fatback for ourselves. As the chickens multiplied we had fried chicken for Sunday dinner. And Mama had plenty of eggs to sell. But mostly we ate the squirrels and rabbits and possums and coons that Laurence and

Daddy shot. Mama and I did not like the wild meat. I disliked biting into the shot. So I was content with beans, fried potatoes, raw onions and cornbread, like my mother. Soon the garden gave us radishes and green onions, tomatoes and lettuce, snap beans and peas. Mama canned what we couldn't eat or sell.

I now understand why my father hated the Barnes Ranch. We were isolated, subjected to the whims of the landlord. Relatives didn't even visit on Sundays any more. Sundays were for the landlord. Always, before and after, there had been anywhere from four to ten relatives out for Sunday dinner at noon, cousins to play with. Sometimes they came out on Saturday and stayed all night, spreading pallets all over the floor to sleep on. Some of them lived in town and some in the city, but the older relatives had all grown up in the country and liked to visit. They would arrive with angel food cakes, Spam and Vienna sausages, Saltines, canned sardines, Wonder bread, and sliced bologna, and leave with Mama's home-canned green beans and tomatoes, and her butter and home-baked light bread.

The summer of 1941, just before I turned three, came in hot and dry on the Barnes Ranch. By the Fourth of July the land was parched. For a month the temperature had rarely dropped below a hundred degrees even at night. The horses suffered. Daddy, reading the natural signs, scared us: 'There's gonna come a bad wildfire.'

The city people came earlier, at daybreak on Sundays, to ride. Daddy tried to persuade the landlord not to run the horses but they did anyway. One horse died, Daddy said of dehydration. The red earth cracked and when the wind blew it was dark in the middle of the day, the air filled with red dirt. Mama's worn straw broom was useless against the thick film of dust that covered the floors. I choked on the dust and had to use a damp cheesecloth smeared with Vicks to breathe through. Another month passed without rain.

'Just like '36, sure am glad I ain't working no cotton,' Daddy said. The cotton and wheat crops in the county had withered and been plowed under, making even more dust to blow.

And then it happened just as Daddy had predicted. One night I woke to a strange sound, a sound I had never heard before, a kind of roar and crackle almost like sharp thunder but I did not smell rain, only more dust, which was no longer a smell but a presence. Yet I hoped that the racket foreshadowed a downpour. I lay listening as the sound grew louder and felt the room grow hotter. Suddenly the room lit up, almost as though the sun were rising close by, or closer than usual.

'Roxie, run!' a voice boomed from the dark. At first I thought it was God's voice but it was Daddy's.

'It's the end of the world,' Mama yelled.

'Ain't no end of the world. Worse than that, a wildfire,' Daddy said. Suddenly we were all outside. The horses screamed. Mama yelled out a verse from the Book of Revelation: 'And the devil that deceived them was cast into the lake of fire and brimstone, where the beast and the false prophet are, and shall be tormented day and night for ever and ever.'

'Why I be doggoned,' Daddy said. The wall of fire turned and headed south. 'The road stopped her but she could come back.' He told Mama to pump water and fill the tin bathtub and buckets. Daddy and Laurence ran to the barn to get the horses out. I followed them. They took all the quilts and a big tarp and soaked them in the horse tank. They put them on the roof of the barn but there weren't enough to cover it or the house.

'Let's get that hay out of the barn,' Daddy said.

I went back to the house to find Mama stuffing the picture albums, letters and her Bible into a gunnysack. She took me by the hand and led me to the fence around the horse corral and said to stay there and hold the gunnysack, then went to take the chickens out of the chicken house and the cows out of the barn.

I sat on the fence watching the wall of fire recede south. I had heard about prairie fires but never seen one. Balls of fire shot off from the main one and ignited a new area. Oil wells exploded on the horizon, sending rockets of flames into the red and black sky. Soon a wall of fire loomed on the horizon in every direction. The heat and smoke were nearly unbearable. I pressed the wet rag Mama had given me over my face. I watched Daddy and Laurence blindfold and hobble the horses, tying rope around their front legs. Daddy said the horses would panic and run into the cauldron if the fire returned.

But the fire did not return. At nine in the morning we all sat, exhausted, around the table in the yard, gazing over the charred fields. Smoke hung acrid in the air. The horses pawed the ground and nuzzled each other.

We were too jittery to go back to bed and by the time the fire left, the sunrise appeared only palely. Then the landlord's sleek black Cadillac emerged like a hearse from the smoke. Mr. Barnes did not get out but honked his horn. Daddy walked slowly over to the car. After a few minutes the landlord drove away. Daddy stood in the same spot and watched the car disappear. Then he walked back and sat down at the table in the yard.

'Reneged. That ole boy says he's gonna get rid of the horses, says there's oil beneath this land.'

'He can't do that, can he, Moyer?' Mama pleaded.

'Sure the hell can, do whatever he damn pleases – he owns the land,' Daddy said.

And so we went back to being tenant farmers. This time we moved to the Eades farm five miles east of Piedmont, where we lived in a yellow two-story frame house. There was a spring-fed creek, two big barns and cattle and a horse, a huge concrete horse tank covered with a shingled roof like a giant umbrella containing foot-long goldfish the landlord had raised, and a lot of cotton to pick. By then Pearl Harbor had happened.

The Barnes Ranch experience must have been the fatal blow that turned my mother and father into mortal enemies rather than allied survivors. Even my older brother and sister do not recall unrelenting animosity between our parents until that time. They were in their early thirties, crushed by poverty, their youthful hopes and dreams extinguished. They moved on with determination, separately, and eventually with my mother, sadly.

'Shut your mouth or I'll kill you, I mean it,' Daddy said, his voice controlled, low, cold. He held a big hunk of firewood above his head ready to strike. Mama faced him, defiant, screaming.

'Go ahead, kill me, go right ahead, better than going on like this,' she hollered at the top of her voice.

They were in the kitchen. I was maybe four or five. I stood in the doorway, cringing, wheezing. Vera, who was thirteen, tried to get between them, crying, screaming, 'Stop, don't kill her, Daddy, stop.' What I remember of that time about the fights is all of a piece, an unending war, the war reported on our old battery radio a counterpoint to their war. The arguments were mostly over Laurence, by then a volatile teenager whom Daddy considered 'too wild.' Increasingly, the arguments were over me and my asthma. Mama's argument for wanting to move to town was that I wouldn't be able to walk the mile to the school bus to go to Piedmont. Their arguments always brought on an asthma attack, and the attack always ended the argument, or suspended it for a time.

My mother and father wanted to conform, tried desperately to conform, to the traditional family pattern, but they were definitely different, neither of them ever quite fitting in, even within their own families, I realized later. My father had not followed in his father's and brothers' and sisters' footsteps in becoming comfortable landowners, and he had 'married down' to a poor, homeless half-breed. But they did aspire to normalcy. Men where I grew up were expected to put meat on the table, any meat, acquired by any means except stealing: hunting, working for a paycheck, raising stock, fishing. Daddy's answer to any complaint about being poor from Mama or us kids was, 'Ain't I always put meat on the table?' That challenge left us mute.

The rest was a woman's wish list. That the man in the family, usually the husband but sometimes an older son when there was no daddy, be sober. Or if he drank, not to run around or gamble or get killed or maimed in a wreck while drunk. That he be churchgoing, which was connected with the not drinking. That he stay out of jail, that he not beat his wife or the kids too hard or too much, that he save enough money to buy a new pickup, that he take the family to the picture shows now and then. On the other hand, if he drank and ran around and even thieved and still found a way to put meat on the table, he was considered to have done his part of the bargain. The work ethic was not necessarily a part of the equation if the man could provide by other means. But most of those men who kept meat on the table worked hard and long. They had to in order to reach that minimum standard.

Complaining was forbidden. Anything that suggested weakness was forbidden. We took pride in not being gripers and whiners, 'bellyachers.' And that was our image writ large, as in *The Grapes of Wrath*, the stoical, silent-suffering, dignified people of the soil. That's what the country and western songs were about, too, all that pride and dignity. I thought a lot about the accusation of whining because, even at my sickest as an asthmatic, I was not supposed to complain. 'What happens, happens, that's just the way it is,' was Mama's watchword.

Two people couldn't have been more different than my mother and father: Mama wanted everything, all the modern appliances. She had an icebox that required blocks of ice in summer, while in winter food was stored outside. She cooked on a kerosene stove that took a long time to heat up and smelled terrible. She pumped and carried buckets of water. She wanted a nice house with an indoor bathroom and closets, new furniture and rugs, drapes. She pored over the pictures in hand-me-down *Good Housekeeping* magazines, dreaming. She wanted an electric sewing machine instead of the pedal Singer. She wanted a washing machine instead of scrubbing clothes on a washboard. Later she wanted a television.

Daddy was the opposite. He hated gadgets or anything unnecessary. For him a knife was perfectly sufficient to open cans and for a number of other useful purposes, such as gutting and dressing the rabbits and squirrels he shot for our supper. He could keep any vehicle running and saw no need for a new car or pickup. As long as he had a knife, a rifle, a needle and thread – for mending clothes or sewing up severed flesh on man or animal – and an iron skillet, everything else was superfluous. Our houses looked like camps (as does his house today).

'Don't need no stove to cook. Nothing tastes better than what's cooked on an open fire,' Daddy said.

'But you can't make biscuits and cornbread and light bread and pies that way,' I said. Those were my favorite things to eat.

'Sure can, with a dutch oven. Iron skillet's all you need,' he said.

'You can't fry light bread,' I said. Often we had fried fruit pies and skillet cornbread we called corn pone, and boiled dumplings, but I preferred baked cornbread and pies, biscuits and especially homemade light bread.

Daddy laughed. 'You don't have to fry in a dutch oven, it bakes. You make it by digging a hole in the ground. You put your hot coals in there and cover it up with a sheet of tin or a wet tarpaulin and heat it up. Then you put your iron skillet with the pie or biscuits or bread dough in there. Bakes as good as any ole oven you can buy.'

'Where'd you learn to do that, Daddy?' I asked.

'Over there on the Osage reservation in northeastern Oklahoma when I was working on a ranch. Them Osage squaws showed me how,' he said.

I was excited by that revelation and looked at Mama, who had been listening to us talk while she got the kerosene cooking stove going to fix supper. She had been griping about wanting propane and a gas stove and Daddy started telling me the story.

'I ain't no squaw and this ain't Osage country and you ain't a cowboy no more,' she said.

'I never knew you worked over there, Daddy,' I said.

'Yup, weren't for long, when I was sixteen, worked for an ole boy who stole a big hunk of Osage land. Well, he leased it from them but they didn't have no choice and never will get it back. That ole boy ran two thousand prime Hereford on the spread. Didn't provide bunks or food or nothing for us cowhands, so we had to camp out and make do, hunting and eating beans. I sure missed my mama's good ole biscuits and cornbread and light bread. Then, like I say, them Osage squaws showed me how. A big family of them Osage invited us cowhands over for supper one night. Guess they felt sorry for us, we was so poor. The squaws served up roasted rabbits and about the best biscuits I ever had and a wild-berry pie. I seen them using a contraption they told me was a dutch oven, so they showed me how to do it. After that, us cowhands ate pretty good.'

'What are the Osage Indians like?' I asked. The very name 'Osage' felt good on my tongue, and I imagined tall, bronze people dressed in fringed buckskin, like in the picture shows.

'Oh, just about like any country folk, excepting one thing. They'd give you the shirt off their back. You just mention you like something they have and they give it to you. If they have any money they give you that, too. That's the way all the Indians was.'

Daddy says that was his idea of a good life, but that's the way Mama really was. She was the one who would give a stranger the shirt off her back. Money to her was something to be got rid of as quickly as possible, not Daddy. To his face and behind his back, Mama and all us kids called him 'Scotch,' stingy. He followed the commodities market closely and always knew the exact market prices of corn, cotton, sorghum, wheat, beef and land – and he still does today. He kept track of every penny.

How we divided fried chicken tells the real story about the pecking order in our family. My brothers preferred the drumsticks. Vera had a penchant for the neck. Me, I adored the wings. Mama claimed to love the gizzard and the back, that sparsely meated portion that she ate in the kitchen in between serving us. The liver, breast and thighs were for Daddy. When Laurence and Vera were gone, Hank had no trouble consuming both drumsticks and Mama added the neck to her choice. I still got the wings. There was never any question what belonged to Daddy.

Bathing was another indicator of status. Until I was about twelve we had a small, round zinc tub. Then we graduated to an oval tin tub that was about five feet long. Baths were once-a-week, Saturday night affairs. The water had to be heated in buckets on the kerosene cooking stove. Mama did that, of course. Daddy bathed first in the clean water, and then came my two brothers, then Vera, then me. Mama bathed after all of us had finished, all of us in the same water. Even though this was the procedure in many homes and was never questioned in ours, I despised bathing in the tepid filthy water left after four other people had been in it. Once Laurence and Vera were gone, I was advanced to third, with Mama still last.

Because I was sickly and the baby, my mother staked out complete control over me. We were alone together more than any other two people in the family. Every event was an occasion for her to instruct me in the lessons of life as she knew them.

One particular occasion stands out in my memory because it previewed my eventual obsession with justice, particularly the cruelty of the death penalty. I was five; Mama and I were home alone on the last farm we sharecropped, on the shortest day of the year, the radio said. I sat on the step outside the front door, facing east. Mama had tried to keep me inside but finally gave up. I was keeping watch.

The ground was bare and frozen, dense red ice. The world was dead and silent except for the howl of the wind – a Norther – and the cry of a lone freezing coyote. The sky was a sheet of zinc. From where I sat cars that passed on the red dirt road were visible from both north and south. During the time I'd been there none had passed. They rarely did. I stared at a point on the horizon to the north.

I was watching for teenaged outlaws on the run, a boy and a girl. In my hand was a newspaper with their pictures on the front page. The girl looked like me, especially the eyes – big dark eyes. The dark boy could have been my big brother Laurence. The radio said that morning that the two were headed south from Kansas, that they might be in Oklahoma trying to make it to Mexico, that the Oklahoma National Guard was on alert. The radio said the kids had killed a farmer and then some others when they robbed a bank. They had a sawed-off shotgun. The radio said they were staying on back roads and that people on isolated farms should keep an eye out for them, that they were another Bonnie and Clyde. I listened every night to Laurence's stories about Bonnie and Clyde, and about Billy the Kid, Jesse James, Belle Starr, the Younger Brothers, the Dalton Brothers, Geronimo. And Pretty Boy Floyd: Laurence had been six years old when the FBI ambushed and murdered Pretty Boy, the Oklahoma bandit who robbed from the rich and gave to the poor, and he remembered crying to go to the funeral, the largest funeral ever held in Oklahoma.

When the news that the outlaws might be in Oklahoma came over the radio, Daddy had said, 'Just derned no-goods,' and went off on the horse to mend barbed-wire fences. Mama pumped some water, then washed the breakfast dishes and sat down at her pedal Singer. She was not afraid.

Nor was I afraid. I waited for the outlaws to drive up because I wanted to meet them. I thought maybe they might take me with them. I knew some hiding places.

The door opened and Mama said, 'You better get on indoors or you'll catch your death.'

'Just a little longer, please.' I dragged 'please' out in a whine that I knew Mama hated.

'They caught them kids,' she said and shut the door.

I went inside and sat down by the radio. The announcer said, 'A Texas Ranger stopped to check a car on the side of the highway. The hoodlums got out with their hands up. They're sure to get the chair.'

I cried and Mama said, 'It's over now, nothing to be afraid of no more, just no-goods.'

'What's the chair?' I asked.

'You'll understand when you're older,' Mama said.

Three

Prairie Red Wing

There once lived an Indian maid
A shy little prairie maid
On the Plains ...
The moon shines tonight
On Prairie Red Wing
The breezes sighing
The night birds crying
While Red Wing's weeping her heart away.

'Prairie Red Wing,'
traditional

Saturday was my favorite day during that time on our last farm, during the war before I started school and we moved to town, that time when we lived in the big yellow house east of Piedmont. Saturday was when the whole family drove into town, the boys in the back of the pickup and me on Mama's lap, my sister squeezed in by the door. The distance was only five miles but took a half hour because of the rutted and sometimes muddy road, and Daddy drove very slowly even on pavement, switching off the engine and coasting on the slightest incline to save gasoline. After a time we couldn't drive anymore because there were no tires or gasoline due to wartime rationing, so we used the horse and a buckboard to go into town. But I liked the drive, however slow. Daddy always told the same stories on the ride.

'Who lives there, Daddy?' I would always ask.

'The Fedders. Old man Fedder homesteaded that place back in the Run and raised his brood there. Came straight over here from the Rhineland in the old country. Now his oldest son and wife live there alone – raised their brood, too. Never did put in a floor. They say they like the dirt and the animals like it, always a hog or chickens in there sleeping with them.'

At another spot Daddy pointed out an abandoned shack nearly grown over with blackjack trees. 'That there's where we sharecropped in '36 when Hank was born. The landlord, old man Jackson, died and his widder sold the farm when the drouth came. I sure wish I coulda bought that place but couldn't afford it. The new owners run us off. That's when we moved to ole San Antone.'

Just before reaching Piedmont there was a hill and from there the red earth spread as far as the eye could see. That moment always thrilled me. In my head I heard trumpets like in the Bible. It seemed like the door to heaven.

But Piedmont was no heaven, even I knew that. I had been to the three other towns around and Piedmont didn't compare. But I liked going there because I knew just about everyone. There were two general stores, one owned by a German family, and one by an Irish Catholic family. We traded at Meyer's instead of Shannon's because Howard Meyer was married to Daddy's first cousin Josie. Mama with Vera and Daddy with Laurence went their separate ways to do their business buying and selling and bartering at the meat locker, the feed store, the creamery, the post office. Hank and I joined a cluster of other children at the front of Meyer's store to read comic books that we couldn't afford to buy. Then Lee Ann and Linda, our second cousins, Josie's girls, came and took us back into the huge, dark warehouse that was filled with sacks of animal feed, flour, sugar and big cans of lard, syrup and molasses. We played hide and seek, squealing when rats scrambled at our feet, until Mama or Vera came looking for us to go home. That's when we got ice cream cones at the creamery.

On a globe the town of Piedmont did not rate the tiniest visible speck, not even on the map of the United States. Only on the Oklahoma map did Piedmont show up because it had a post office. The only other geographical points that anchored reality for me were the three nearest towns, less than fifteen miles away, each with railroad tracks running through them, Yukon to the south, Edmond to the east, El Reno – the county seat – southwest, and the City – Oklahoma City – only thirty miles southeast but another universe. Other than those parameters there was heaven above and hell below.

The county was named for the Canadian River, which flowed through it, when there was water. The riverbed cut through red shale seven miles south of Piedmont. The closest larger town was Yukon, across that river, with a large Czech population notable for its giant flour mills and a movie house. Yukon's main street was Route 66. Only red clay roads led into Piedmont except for the paved nine miles to Yukon. About eight miles east of Piedmont on the way to Edmond sat the SOHIO oil refinery and company housing. When I was growing up in Oklahoma a hundred thousand wells pumped three billion barrels a year valued at four billion dollars, the highest production of any state in the United States; Oklahoma was the Saudi Arabia of North America. I learned that in school, where my teachers took great pride in oil, it being the only thing Oklahoma was first in and known for except for the Dust Bowl and a Broadway musical. No one in Piedmont had piped-in natural gas, although a few, families we considered rich, had propane tanks.

In 1890 what would become the first families of Piedmont had homesteaded nearby on the Chisholm Trail. Five families settled there and called the township Matthewson, with one family opening a store. They soon won a post office and had established a school and a cemetery by 1898. In 1904 the settlers of Matthewson moved two miles east and one and a half miles south to form Piedmont, leaving to the old site only the cemetery, still called Matthewson today, where my mother and most of the relatives on my father's side are buried. The settlers named the town Piedmont after their frontier settler ancestors' region of Virginia and because they built Piedmont on a rise and said that 'piedmont' meant foothill in French, the language of their French Huguenot ancestors.

When Daddy was a child in Piedmont, the railroad ran through and there was a depot, three grain elevators, a flour mill, two cotton gins, a post office, three general mercantile stores, three churches, two hotels, two lumber yards, three barber shops, a meat market, three doctors, two livery stables, a state bank, two blacksmith shops, a firehouse, two confectioneries, a telephone office, Masonic Hall, a Ford Motor agency, three gas stations, two creameries, and a city hall and jail.

By the time we moved to town in 1944, the train and nearly all the businesses had gone. All that was left were two small zinc grain elevators, one filling station, two general stores, a barber shop, beer joint, post office, local telephone switchboard, and the Masonic Lodge. There were two churches in town, one Methodist, one Southern Baptist. There were no police, no mayor, no city hall or jail, no chamber of commerce, no street names, no doctors.

The core of Piedmont was crisscrossed with three east–west and five north–south red dirt roads. Thirty houses lined those dusty unnamed streets, with empty lots between most. The tiny four-room house we moved to when I started school was right in the middle, across the road from the Methodist Church, four blocks from the main street. To the east of the center was a cluster of ten or twelve houses. Twenty or so family farmers within a five-mile radius claimed Piedmont as their town of identity and sent their children to school there. Including the farming families outside town, the population hovered around a hundred, many of them interrelated, and a lot of them from Daddy's mother's family, the Jenningses.

When we moved into Piedmont, finally my mother realized her dream of owning a home in town and being a housewife rather than a farm laborer. 'I never had a childhood,' Mama would say and tell me again her stories so I would remember how lucky I was to have a mother and a house to live in and enough food to eat. She told me about how she and her brother lived on the streets when their father would disappear to drink. They smoked thrown-away cigarette butts and stole candy and bread from stores. That part of Mama's childhood sounded fun to me. But when she got to the part about being put in a foster home, I didn't like it.

'They were mean and had five kids for me to take care of and clean and cook. I ate cold leftovers like a dog and slept by the kitchen stove like Cinderella,' she said.

It took me a long time to appreciate that Mama was not like the other mothers in town. She spoiled me and my sister and brothers, especially Laurence, her firstborn. We were never spanked or even punished. Once we moved into Piedmont, every day after school Mama had homemade fudge and hot popcorn waiting for us – other kids could have treats only after eating their supper. On Saturdays she cooked dozens of hamburgers on real hamburger buns, nearly as authentic as the ones in the burger places in surrounding towns, which we could not afford. We brought home neighbor children to share the feast; they were always welcome in our house. We jumped on the beds and ran in the house, no-no's in every other mother's domain. 'I never had a childhood so I want you kids to enjoy yours,' she would say. When 'Pistol-Packin' Mama' was a top hit, Mama learned the words and tune and sang it to me even though it was a song glorifying sin and the Baptist preacher condemned it as 'worldly.'

Mama did not distinguish between what boys and girls could do and say and be. When I said I wanted to grow up to be a doctor or a fireman, she encouraged me, only reminding me that I could be president of the United States if I preferred.

Mama taught me what she called 'storying,' and no one could outdo her. 'You just make up whatever you want to be. If you don't like someone, pretend they are someone else. You can turn a dry, hot corn field into a cool, blue lake or a molehill into a mountain,' she said. Mama told many lies, stories about gremlins and goblins, her Irish father's stories. I made up stories, too, and she didn't mind as long as I never would 'bear false witness against thy neighbor,' which was one of the Ten Commandments of God. I think Mama understood in her love for Jesus that his magic resided in his storytelling, not his miracles.

My mother appeared all-powerful to me, muscular, someone who could do anything. Daddy could fix anything and breed or train any dog or horse, and of course he was physically stronger than Mama. But I perceived Mama as Atlas, so strong she could have lifted a truck or a house had there been a need to do so. The first time I heard of Paul Bunyan I thought of Mama. She was only an inch taller than me or my sister and not a powerhouse by any standard, except her arms and back, which were as strong as any man's.

In the sixties in San Francisco, I remember coming upon a group of students with placards calling for volunteers for freedom rides to the South to protest segregation. There was a folk singer strumming a guitar and singing. I stopped to listen. He was singing 'Prairie Red Wing.' The hundred or so rallying students were singing along so I joined in. I knew every word. Then I noticed I was singing different words. I was singing *there once lived an Indian maid* and *the stars shine tonight on Prairie Red Wing.* But then I noticed that their words were different. They were singing *there once was a union maid* and *I'm working for the union*. I was confused. I asked the student next to me where that song came from, and she said, 'Woody Guthrie. You never heard it?'

'Not that way. I thought it was another song,' I said.

Of course, I soon learned about Woody Guthrie and that he had grown up not far from where my mother had. My mother used to play and sing that old traditional song, 'Prairie Red Wing,' every day, pounding out the tune on our old out-of-tune upright piano with chipped keys: 'There once lived an Indian maid ...' Mama played by ear and perfected many folk songs and hymns but 'Prairie Red Wing' was my favorite. Sometimes Mama cried when she sang that song and told me it was about her mother, and at dusk on summer evenings she'd point to the evening star and say that was her mother, who died when she was five. She remembered her mother's funeral, the six white horses pulling the shiny black hearse to the cemetery.

'One day I'll be rich and I'll buy you a big house with a bathroom and give you a funeral just like that,' I would assure her.

I think Mama, as I would later, reconstructed a memory of her mother and the funeral from songs, especially 'Can the Circle Be Unbroken,' about a child's loss of a mother:

> I was standing by the window
> On a cold and cloudy day,
> When I saw the hearse come rolling
> For to carry my mother away ...
>
> Yes I followed close behind her,
> Tried to cheer up and be brave,
> But my sorrows, I could not hide them
> When they laid her in the grave.
>
> Went back home, Lord, cold and lonesome,
> Since my mother she was gone,
> All my brothers and sisters crying,
> What a home, so sad and lone.

And somehow I always knew Mama was telling me her life story when she sang about the poor little Indian maid, Prairie Red Wing.

Four

Patrimony

Which side are you on, brother,
Which side are you on?

FLORENCE REESE

By 1950, four million people or nearly a quarter of all the people born in Oklahoma, Texas, Arkansas or Missouri lived outside that region. A third of them settled in California, while most of the others moved to Arizona, New Mexico, Oregon and Washington. The best-known part of this trek westward is the period of the Dust Bowl, the thirties, when the majority of the migrants first camped, and then settled mainly in the agricultural valleys of California, but Oklahoma settlers had already been moving west ever since they began home-steading in Oklahoma in the 1890s. During World War II many of the Central Valley Dust Bowl migrants moved nearer the defense plants, particularly around Los Angeles, while a half-million more Southwestern migrants, dubbed 'defense Okies,' arrived to take war-time jobs. The great majority of them maintained ties back home.

The core group of those designated as 'Okies' are descendants of Ulster-Scot – 'Scotch-Irish' – colonial frontier settlers. Usually the descendants of Ulster-Scots say that their ancestors came to America from Ireland, but their trek was more complicated than that. The Ulster-Scots were a people born and bred of empire. They were

Protestant Scottish settlers in the English colony in northern Ireland where the indigenous Irish inhabitants were Catholic.

During the early 1600s, the English crown conquered northern Ireland, and declared a half-million acres of land open to settlement under English protection; the settlers who contracted with the devil of early colonialism came mostly from western Scotland. Scotland itself along with Wales had preceded Ireland as colonial notches in the belt of English expansion. The English policy of exterminating Indians in North America was foreshadowed by the English colonization of northern Ireland. The Celtic social system was systematically attacked, traditional songs and music forbidden, whole clans exterminated while the entire population was brutalized. A 'wild Irish' reservation was even attempted.

By 1630, the new settlers in Ulster – 21,000 English and 150,000 Lowland Scots – were more numerous than English settlers in all North America. In 1641, the indigenous Irish rebelled and killed 10,000 settlers. Yet the Scottish settlers continued to pour in, with the largest number arriving between 1690 and 1697 after King William's victory at the Battle of the Boyne. They formed a majority of the population in some areas from which the indigenous Irish had been removed.

So the Ulster-Scots were already seasoned colonialists before they began to fill the ranks of settlers to the English colonies in North America in the early eighteenth century. Before ever meeting Native Americans the Ulster-Scots had perfected scalping for bounty on the indigenous Irish. The Ulster-Scots were the foot soldiers of empire, and they and their descendants formed the shock troops of the 'westward movement,' that is, of the expanding United States continental empire.

Ulster-Scot immigration to North America represented a mass movement between 1720 and the War of Independence. Most of them headed for the western borders of the colonies and built communities on the frontier, where they predominated. During the French and Indian War of 1754–63 the English armies and colonial militias were largely made up of Ulster-Scots. By the time of US independence, Scots, mainly Ulster-Scots, made up around one-sixth of the population of the thirteen colonies, and, in some states like Pennsylvania, a third. During the Revolution most Scottish settlers –

Lowlander and Highlander, older settlers and newcomers – remained loyal to the English Crown. The Ulster-Scots, however, were in the forefront of the struggle for independence and formed the backbone of Washington's fighting forces. Most of the names at Valley Forge were Scots-Irish, my ancestors. They saw themselves, and their descendants see themselves, as the true and authentic patriots, the ones who spilled blood for independence and spilled rivers of blood to acquire Indian land, who won the land by 'blood-right,' leaving bloody footprints across the continent. The books written about the frontier settlers fill libraries, but none fulfill the dream of Oscar Ameringer, immigrant from Bavaria and US Socialist Party leader during my grandfather's Wobbly days:

> I wish someone would look up the names on the roster of Washington's army at Valley Forge and trace the bloody footprints of their descendants across the North American continent until they were washed up and washed out on the shore of the Pacific. What an all-American Odyssey it would make! What a great history of the Rise and Fall of American Civilization.

During the last two decades of the eighteenth century, first- and second-generation Ulster-Scots continued to move westward into the Ohio Valley, West Virginia, Kentucky and Tennessee. They were the predominant element in the westward population movement, maintaining many of the Scots ways, with non-Scots settlers tending to be absorbed (like Daniel Boone, whose heritage was English and Welsh). Ulster-Scots were overwhelmingly frontier settlers rather than scouts, explorers or fur traders. They cleared forests, built log cabins, and killed Indians, forming a wall of protection for the new US and during times of war employing their fighting skills effectively. They restlessly moved three or four times before settling at least semi-permanently.

The majority of Ulster-Scot settlers were cash-poor and had to indenture themselves to pay for their passage to North America . But once settled they came to predominate, not only as soldier-settlers, but also as contributors in the fields of medicine, religion and education. Perhaps most important, by the end of the eighteenth century, the Scottish Presbyterian church was the largest, strongest and most influential church next to New England's Congregationalist Church.

Ulster-Scot membership in the Presbyterian Church waned on the frontier, but the new evangelical sects retained some Calvinist doctrines, particularly the notion of the people of the covenant, commanded by God to go into the wilderness to build the new Israel.

Many descendants of the frontier trekkers moved on from Kentucky and Tennessee to Missouri and Arkansas (including Daniel Boone himself in his old age) and then moved on to Oklahoma during the late nineteenth and early twentieth centuries. This was the trek of my ancestors. Breaking every treaty with the Indians, the federal government allowed the settlers to overrun Oklahoma and Indian territories. Millions of landless farmers made the Run to stake their claims, but only a fraction acquired land, or held on to it. In 1898, the Oklahoma settlers showed their appreciation – a third of Teddy Roosevelt's 'Rough Riders' who invaded Cuba were recruited from Oklahoma Territory.

But Oklahoma was where the American dream had come to a halt. For nearly three hundred years, the English Crown and then the United States had offered free or cheap land to British and Ulster-Scot settlers, then to Germans and Scandinavians, then to Polish and Czech peasants. If a farming family fell on hard times or wanted greater opportunity, they picked up and moved on, homesteading newly 'opened' territory. By 1880 all the arable land of the continent was owned – much of it by large operators – and millions were landless. While many of those pushed off the land poured into the cities to work, most stayed in rural areas as tenants, sharecroppers, migrant farm workers, cowpunchers and miners, and later as roughnecks and roustabouts in the oil fields.

Okies and other descendants of the trekker culture do not think of ourselves as foot soldiers of empire, nor is that the image of us that dominates the popular imagination. We consider ourselves to be the true native-born Americans, the personification of what America is supposed to be, and we know that means being Scots-Irish original settlers, those who fought for and won the continent.

Okies are thus the latter-day carriers of America's national origin myth, a matrix of stories that attempts to justify conquest and settlement, transforming the white frontier settler into an 'indigenous people,' believing that they are the true natives of the continent, much as the South African Boers regard themselves as the 'true' children of

Israel, established by a God-given Covenant.

But it is not that simple: Potent memories inform my broad theories and conclusions. I cannot forget my grandfather and his time, the Wobblies and the Green Corn Rebellion. Therein lies a truly valiant history, a history little known to its millions of descendants, a history usable only if celebrated in the context of acknowledging the lie of the origin myth, and only if class is central to our future identity as the Okie subculture. Country music, evangelism, romanticism, patriotism and white supremacy have been able to coalesce my people – the descendants of the original settlers – as a people united despite class differences or social roles, mirroring Black, Latino, Asian and Native American nationalisms, which exhibit similar contradictions and limitations.

So who was I then, who were we and what were we anyway? Poor whites? Half-breeds? Hicks? Hillbillies? Rednecks? White trash? I don't remember identifying with those terms that were used to refer to people like us; on the contrary.

White Trash: I believe the first time I heard that term was when I saw *Gone with the Wind*, referring to some pretty creepy people, dirt poor, sneaking, conniving, violent tenant farmers, or perhaps migrant cotton pickers. At the time I saw the movie my father was alternately a tenant farmer, migrant cotton picker and ranch hand, but I did not for one minute identify with those whom the planters and the enslaved Africans called 'white trash.'

I identified with Scarlett, with the O'Hara family, the original Scots-Irish settlers. The fact that my father's ancestors were original Scots-Irish old settlers was what made me feel superior. And those characterized as 'white trash' in *Gone with the Wind* were surely also descendants of Scots-Irish old settlers. Their sons would die fighting to defend the very slave-owning ruling class that kept them poor. Their greatest heroes had been Confederate irregulars during the war and afterwards mythologized outlaws like Jesse James.

Often I asked my mother why my father's family name, Dunbar, was shared by a black person. In English class we read the poems of African-American poet Paul Laurence Dunbar. I hoped my mother would say he was a relative of ours because I loved his poetry. But she said that my Dunbar ancestors were 'Scotch-Irish' and had once owned huge plantations and many slaves and that slaves took the names of the masters.

'How do we know we're related to the masters and not the slaves?' I would ask.

'Because you are white.'

We Okies are those tough, land-poor losers whose last great hope in the American dream was born and died with the 'opening' of Oklahoma and Indian territories. Our great shame, like all 'white trash' and colonial dregs, is poverty, that is, 'failure' within a system that purports to favor us. The dregs of colonialism, those who did not and do not 'make it,' being the majority in some places, like most of the United States, are evidence of the lie of the American Dream.

Five

Once Master of the House

By this time [the early twenties] the Klan had so completely
captured the Masonic organization in Prairie [Oklahoma] that
the lodge became the disseminator of its doctrines ...The Klansmen in fact were decent citizens ...The Klan by this time had
captured the Baptist church ... It was difficult to go to church
without making ambiguous commitments. A speaker was likely
at any time to ask 100 per cent Americans to stand; if they rose
they were Klansmen, if they remained seated they were somewhat less than Americans.

ANGIE DEBO,
Prairie City

In rural Oklahoma we thought we knew everything. In that tiny total
universe we divided the world into opposites: male and female; animal and human; sky and earth; night and day; winter and summer;
good and bad; country and city; poor and rich; patriot and traitor;
the devil and God. The weather was extreme – miserable, cold, frozen winters of ice storms, sleeted ground and howling Northers, that
hard Arctic wind that I regarded as a force with a mind. I believed the
Norther must be God since the devil was associated with heat and
fire, red not white. Winter was neither preceded by autumn colors
nor followed by spring flowers and gentle rain; winter simply turned
into chaos along about April in the form of tornadoes and hailstorms
and hot, howling wind that carried clouds of red dirt and spread
raging prairie fires. Some years locusts blackened the sky and descended to devour all the crops.

Our world view was Manichaean not Buddhist, no yin and yang.
There was no balance, just absolutes.

For us, city people were rich, country people were poor. And in
the country, the wheat farmers and families who owned businesses

were rich and the rest of us were poor. What distinguished the rich from the poor was a flush toilet in the house and a new car or pickup outside. We were nearly the poorest of the poor, but my family's poverty was gilded with the memory of my grandfather's status as a landowner and a veterinarian and we were not the poorest of the poor, not as poor as our cousins next door who went on welfare after their father died, not as poor as the backwoodsman and his two sons down on the creek, not as poor as the few itinerant families who settled for a time, then left, not as poor as my mother had once been.

Daddy gave up farming for good the summer before I turned six. My mother argued that I could not walk the mile to the school bus in the winter because of my asthma. No other argument had budged him in his determination to farm, but that one did. It was only an excuse to rationalize the inevitable. The cotton fields were being turned over to wheat and there was no sharecropping wheat because you needed expensive machinery to harvest it. A poor, landless family couldn't make a living farming any more. Daddy bought a tiny shack on a small lot in Piedmont and fixed it up with white paint, and a new shingled roof he painted green, and he trimmed the two front windows with wood shutters he made and painted red. At first he worked as the school janitor and bus driver, then took the job he would keep for the rest of my years at home, driving a Mobil gas truck delivering fuel to farmers all over the county.

Living in town, and especially going to school, seemed magical at the time. On the north edge of Piedmont, a half-mile from our house, sat the brick school building with its eight classrooms, library and gym/auditorium. Indoor bathrooms were added when I was in the fifth grade. The school included grades one through twelve with around a hundred students in all.

'Write your story so that a spaceman from Mars could understand it. Don't take anything for granted. Explain everything. If you want to tell about the cakewalk held here in the school gym last week, don't just say there was a cakewalk but explain what a cakewalk is, every detail, how the women bake the cakes and instead of selling them to raise money for the church or some event, everyone in town comes and pays for tickets to walk in a circle marked with numbers, round and round until the music stops, then whoever is standing in the winning spot gets the cake. If you want to tell about the charivari of your older brothers or sisters when they got married, don't assume that the man from Mars will know what a charivari is or even that he would know what is a Norther or a tornado or red dirt like we have here.'

I wrote down what my teacher said, excited to begin writing. But the teacher wasn't finished.

'First, I want you to make lists of things. Write down a description of your surroundings, naming all the animals and trees and how the houses look, the sky, the crops, all that.'

I poised my sharpened yellow pencil above the Big Chief writing tablet on my desk and wrote about all I could think of that surrounded me:

Red dirt. Cottonwood and willow trees, scrub oak and sagebrush, sunflowers, morning glories, hollyhocks.

Farmers, cowboys, Indians, preachers, widows, schoolteachers.

Prairie dogs, coyotes, possums, gray and brown squirrels, raccoons, grasshoppers and locusts, prairie chickens and rattlesnakes, centipedes, scorpions, tarantulas, and along the creek beds horned toads and water moccasins. Mockingbirds, meadow larks, woodpeckers, hummingbirds, sparrows, crows and hawks.

Cows, sheep, horses, pigs, chickens, turkeys.

Windmills, oil derricks and foot-diameter pipelines, and towering, white grain mills. Barbed wire.

Red shale, red dust and ripe golden wheat fields, corn, and cotton.

Angry wind. A black cloud on the eastern horizon threatening to form a tornado, streaks of lightning followed instantly by sharp cracks of thunder, the sky raining pellets of marble-sized hail, the sky turned that green that means a tornado won't roar out of the storm clouds.

Route 66 crosses the old Chisholm cattle trail on its way to California. Between trucks and station wagons with California tags, slow-moving pickup trucks with rifles and shotguns on gun racks. Roadside billboards with 'Jesus Saves,' another for Ralston Purina.

The teacher broke the spell of my writing. 'Okay, now I want you to write down a description of each of the seasons, what happens during the summer, fall, winter and spring, what the weather is like, you know, the Norther, tornadoes, dust storms, lightning, sleet, crops.' Summer, I thought, summer had to come first.

Summer is wheat harvest crews coming though, staying for three or four days.
Summer is a tent revival somewhere nearby.
Summer is Rolando's one-ring circus under the big top.
Summer is Tom Mix and the Royal Canadian Mountie picture shows projected on
a sheet on the side of Meyer's store in town.
Summer is when other kids go to camp or with their families to Yellowstone Park,
or Carlsbad Caverns or the Grand Canyon.

Fall is school and new books, sometimes new shoes and new clothes out of the
Montgomery Ward catalog, but not always, sometimes just homemade feed sack
dresses and last year's shoes.
Fall is a Saturday afternoon when Daddy and my brother clean their guns. They
carry them around all week during the fall, shooting jackrabbits and squirrels for
supper. My brother Laurence shoots at targets, tin cans and bottles, too, practicing to be as good as Billy the Kid. Daddy disapproves of wasting ammunition so
he never shoots at any target that's not eatable and he shoots to kill, one bullet.
Fall is the odor of gun oil.
Fall is Thanksgiving dinner when we are the only ones to eat venison instead of
turkey. No matter what every November Daddy takes a week to go to south Texas
to hunt deer.

Winter is when the hunting dog and the sheep dog sleep inside by the stove and
sometimes a weak lamb, and when I wheeze and choke with asthma.

Springtime brings twisters. They always seem to come at night. Night after night
the roar like a train sends us to our neighbor's cellar that the old lady calls a 'cave.'

'Now I want you to write about your greatest hero or heroine, living
or dead, but not a relative. You can choose a real person or someone
from a story, like Little Red Riding Hood,' the teacher said.
    I wrote down three names: Nancy Drew, Joan of Arc and Belle
Starr. It was a hard choice but I settled on Belle Starr. I drew lines
through the first two. I wished I had my book on Belle Starr to look
at the pictures, but I nearly had it memorized. Laurence taught me
how to read with that book when I was five, and then gave it to me
on my sixth birthday. It was called *Bella Starr; or, The Bandit Queen; or,
the Female Jesse James*. I thought about one thing that book said: 'Bella
was not only well educated, but gifted with uncommon musical and
literary talents, which were almost thrown away through the bias of
her nomadic and lawless disposition, which early isolated her from

civilized life.' I wrote about Belle Starr:

> Belle Starr lived the same time as Billy the Kid but I don't think they knew each other because Billy the Kid lived in New Mexico and Belle in Oklahoma like me. But she knew Jesse James and the Younger brothers. They all robbed trains and banks and gave the money to poor starving farmers and Indians. They could go anywhere without being caught because the poor people hid them out.

The next day the teacher called me up to her desk and told me that I should know that Belle Starr, and the James Gang, were Confederate guerrillas who continued to fight against the federal government after the end of the Civil War, that they wanted to restore slavery and the Confederate nation, and that I should think twice about admiring such people.

Even though her warning did not faze my admiration for Belle Starr and Jesse James, that teacher made me think about many things. She told us that the world was millions of years old, that Oklahoma used to be thick with miniature horses that time erased.

'Sixty-five million years ago during the Late Pleistocene period Oklahoma was overrun by tiny horses about the size of a coyote. There were also large and small camels, rhinoceroses, mastodons, mammoths, musk oxen, saber-toothed tigers and herds of elephants. Until they were destroyed only less than a century ago there were millions of buffalo,' she said.

I was amazed by what the teacher said. Now the only wild animal left bigger than a rabbit was the coyote and he was killed for bounty.

The most startling part of her story was that human beings had been around for hundreds of thousands of years. The following Sunday, the Sunday school teacher was telling about the creation and said the world was born five thousand years ago.

'No it wasn't, it's millions and millions of years old,' I said. All the other children glared at me. The teacher was the preacher's wife and her face turned red.

'Who told you that?' the preacher's wife asked. I was uncomfortable and wished I hadn't opened my big mouth.

'Nobody, I just know.'

'Teacher said it at school, I heard her,' a boy piped up. The other children nodded.

The Baptist preacher that very Sunday in his sermon preached about godless science and told the congregation their children's minds were being poisoned by a certain teacher who everyone knew did not belong to any church and had godless ideas.

That teacher did not return the next year.

For all my love of school, Laurence remained my most important teacher until he left for California when I was seven. I was in awe of him and desperately tried to please him.

'What's a buck, Roxie?' Laurence asked. He was teaching me new words while he cleaned his rifle.

'A boy deer,' I said.

'What else?'

'A dollar.'

I wasn't sure if Laurence was tricking me into a puzzle or if it was a real word lesson. He knew everything about words and spent study hour at school every day poring over the foot-thick dictionary. He taught me how to remember words.

'Look at this word,' he'd said earlier and written down 'annihilate.' 'What does it mean?'

'I don't remember,' I said, thinking it was a word he'd already taught me and I'd forgotten.

'It's a new word. Look, right in the middle is 'nihil.' Nihil means nothing. So annihilate means to make nothing, to destroy. Savvy, Roxie?' He always asked me if I savvied something, from the Spanish verb 'saber,' to know.

And my mind had lit up with the knowledge of a new word I would never forget. But 'buck' was too easy and I suspected a trick.

'How did a dollar become a buck?' he asked. I pondered the question. A dollar and a deer didn't seem related in the same way as 'movies' and 'motion pictures,' or 'desert' and 'deserted,' as Laurence had taught me.

'I don't know. How?'

'Okay, so this is a little history lesson not just a word lesson. Back in Daniel Boone's time in the wilderness when they had to buy things to live, like an axe or a team of mules, a wagon wheel, a knife or a new rifle and ammunition, and they had no cash, they hunted deer and traded the hides for what they needed. One skin of a buck deer was worth a dollar and would buy an axe, five buckskins a wagon wheel. So instead of dollars they had bucks.'

My skin tingled with the new knowledge that I would tell my friends at school and impress them. I was sure no one else would know that, not even the teachers.

'How do you know, Laurence?' I asked.

'I found it in a book. Everything has an explanation, Roxie. You have to ask the question and then find the answer in a book.'

Daddy and his older brothers and sisters had gone to Piedmont school, too, but in a different building on the other side of town. Grandpa Dunbar and his Wobbly comrades had controlled the school board for several years until the Ku Klux Klan took over and ran them out.

Though the Klan had disbanded as such long before I was born, they were still a ghostly presence. Daddy would point to men in town and say they had been Klan, 'good Masons and good Christians all of them.' The ones Daddy fingered were mainly the better-off wheat farmers and Baptists. Daddy loved to tell about the time that his father, followed by the whole family, stomped out of a town meeting when the Klan took it over: 'Every danged one of them was Masons,' he would claim.

Perhaps that was why the Masonic Hall was so spooky to me. It was on the second floor of the oldest, and only two-story, commercial building in Piedmont. The building, which still stands and houses the Piedmont museum, is dark red brick like the other five buildings on the main street, but much grander. The entrance to the Masonic Hall was at the side of the building. The wide staircase leading up to the hall was hand-crafted of polished oak and lined with thick brass railings.

The Masons rented out their hall for other affairs such as baby and wedding showers. The hall was huge with tall ceilings and tall windows on two sides, the floor carpeted wall to wall, the only carpeted floor I had ever seen. At each end of the long room and on each side were tall wooden chairs, throne-like. When Mama dragged me to doings there, I would study that room where secret ceremonies occurred, vows, rituals involving lambskin aprons and even, some people said, lamb's blood. I would think about that time long ago when men would come to that hall and don white robes for night riding. I thought they had most likely planned the attack on my grandfather in that very room.

I wanted to know what the rituals were really like. Daddy said they were 'mumbo-jumbo. Just grown, rich men with nothing better to do than play childish games.' Though he hated the Masons he did not object when Vera joined the Rainbow Girls, the young women's auxiliary to the Masons. Later I would join, too.

As much as I worshiped Laurence I also lived in fear of his anger, which could explode for no obvious reason.

Cold winter nights, the wind howling outside the thin walls, the flimsy house shuddering, Daddy added more kerosene to the tank on the stove in the middle of the front room. The doors to the kitchen and bedroom were shut, the windowsills stuffed – we called it 'chinking' – with newspapers and gunnysacks.

I lay on the divan reading *Black Beauty*. Mama and Laurence snapped cards and barked at each other across the folding card table, playing pitch. I breathed shallowly, waiting for the fight. A pitch game always ended in chaos. The Baptists forbade gambling and discouraged playing cards but Mama was a card shark. Smoking and pitch were two things Mama would not surrender for her faith although she didn't do either publicly.

Pitch was so simple even I knew how to play, but it was fast and I couldn't keep up. Five cards were dealt to each player. Scoring was by the highest and lowest, two jacks, and game – aces counting four, kings three, queens two, jacks one, and ten-spots a whole ten points toward winning game. Bidding – here's where the gambling came in – was from one to five points. The winning bidder declared trump, and a trump-suit card, however low, could take any card in another suit, which counted toward game. If the bidder failed to make the points bid, he 'went set' or had that many points subtracted from his running score.

Hank sat cross-legged on the floor in front of the stove drawing letters of the alphabet between lines of an exercise book, trying to improve his penmanship, his only poor grade. Daddy occupied the one stuffed easy chair, next to the long narrow table against the wall, his ear to the radio, laughing at *Amos 'n Andy,* his favorite program along with Gabriel Heatter, and the *Grand Ole Opry* on Saturday nights. All the while he listened to the radio his eyes were glued on *The Last Trail,* a Zane Grey Western paperback.

'I'll be a son-of-a-bitch gone to hell, Judas Priest,' Laurence suddenly hollered and slammed his cards on the table. Laurence was a sore loser. Mama laughed at him.

'You watch your mouth, boy,' Daddy said. Daddy never swore in the house and didn't allow anyone else to. Laurence always ended up swearing when he played cards or any time he got mad, which was often.

Suddenly Daddy and Laurence were on their feet, both six feet tall and skinny, yelling at each other, fists cocked. Mama screamed and tried to wedge between them, keeping her eyes on the gun rack. Hank slipped out of the room to bed. I wheezed.

'Stop it else the baby'll have an attack,' Vera yelled.

That stopped it. It always did. But never for long. Laurence was wild and insolent and uncontrollable, and Mama would not allow Daddy to discipline him. Mama adored Laurence, and I suppose Daddy was jealous of the good times they had together, though Daddy, too, prized his first son. Those two years before Laurence left home, he and my father vied to be the master of the house.

I dreaded those evenings from dinner to bedtime, so books and learning became the center of my life. Laurence often had his head in a book and Daddy accused him of being lazy; even when Laurence worked for pay he never saved his money. Money was the main focus of the fights.

'I ain't got no spare cash for no ring, so just don't ask again,' Daddy said.

'But everyone gets a school ring, I gotta have one,' Laurence said. It was the end of his junior year in high school.

'You shoulda saved your harvest money for that instead of buying the Winchester,' Daddy countered.

My head twisted back and forth like watching a Ping-Pong game. Daddy sat at one end of the table, Laurence at the other. Hank sat beside me concentrating on eating as quickly as possible so he could escape before the fight got worse. The fights at suppertime always got worse. Vera sat across from me, picking at her food, nervous, quiet. Mama never sat down with us to eat. She ate bits while cooking and cleaning up but served us during the meal, flitting here and there like a hummingbird.

It was springtime and all my favorite dishes were on the table –
fresh-killed fried chicken and giblet gravy, new potatoes and string
beans, okra and summer squash fried in corn meal, breaded tomatoes, garden lettuce doused with hot bacon grease. And there was
fresh rhubarb pie for dessert. But the food on my plate was getting
cold. A lump in my throat wouldn't let me swallow a bite. I knew that
any minute Laurence would jump up and grab his Winchester and
Daddy would reach for his Remington and Mama would screech,
'Not the guns, oh Lord, not the guns, oh Lord, don't let them kill each
other.' Next I would cry or wheeze or both, and Mama would say,
'The baby's sick, stop, the baby's sick.' Laurence would stomp out
with his .22 to go fire out his anger on tin cans. Daddy would
methodically finish his food and take seconds, the only one to eat a
full meal, as one by one my sister, brother and I slipped away to our
own secret places. Later we would eat cold leftovers in the kitchen
while Mama washed the dishes.

Suppertime was always the worst time because of Daddy stopping
off at the beer joint before coming home. Laurence was also a regular
at the beer joint, but Daddy never caught him there. Laurence taught
me how to play shuffleboard there, so by the time Laurence left
home, I was the only female in town to have mastered the game.

The beer joint in Piedmont was one of five centers of social life –
the others were the Masonic Hall and the Baptist and Methodist
churches, which hosted showers, weddings, funerals and potlucks,
and the school with plays, basketball, baseball, cakewalks and spell-
ing bees. No dancing, except square dancing, was allowed anywhere,
thanks to the Baptists. Minor social life, mainly gossip, was carried on
in the two general stores, the post office and the barber shop.

But that men's club, the beer joint, was the most exciting because
it was the most forbidden place in town, the only place not centered
on family life. The regulars sprouted bellies the size of watermelons.
It took a lot of drinking to achieve a buzz on 3.2 beer, the only booze
legal in Oklahoma until 1961.

'You can get as much charge out of a chaw of Red Man chewing
tobacco,' Laurence said.

Johnny and Jake, two bachelor brothers, owned the Piedmont
Cafe, as they called the beer joint. Jake was fat, Johnny skinny. Jake

was loud and cussed a blue streak, while Johnny was quiet and polite. Jake had lost a leg to diabetes and hobbled on crutches. Johnny did the cooking and cleaning. They lived together in a room below the Masonic Hall.

Women didn't go into the beer joint, but girls and boys did to buy candy or peanuts, Pop Cola or Grapette. I went in as often as I could find an excuse. On Saturdays and evenings the three big round tables were filled with men, my brother always the youngest among them, drinking, smoking, swearing and playing pitch for money. And Laurence would perform his ambidextrous skills for money, especially when any stranger dropped in. Laurence was naturally left-handed but had been forced by teachers to write with his right hand. He could write with both hands at the same time with perfect penmanship.

For Mama (and for me) Laurence could do no wrong, not even when he shot Vera in the knee with his .22 and not even when he ran over his best friend and not even when he punched the English teacher, a tiny, middle-aged woman. Mama always had an excuse for Laurence – Vera was in the wrong place at the wrong time when Laurence was cleaning his gun and it accidentally went off; the boy he ran over wasn't badly hurt and it was an accident; the English teacher had slapped Laurence first.

Laurence was always in trouble at school because he knew more than the teachers and had a big mouth and thin skin. He also had a short fuse and won every fist fight. But he established a tradition for me and Hank, who were expected to make straight As like Laurence, and we did, with Laurence's help – teaching us to read and write before we went to school, teaching us geography and math tables, the names of clouds, how to spell words and diagram sentences.

Laurence was famous and infamous, respected throughout the countryside as a star ballplayer, hunter and fighter, and as a genius. He had a photographic memory. He was ambidextrous and a card shark and a marksman. He drew and painted – mostly guns, uniformed soldiers, and battle scenes. He did not believe in God and refused to go to church. He learned to read, write and speak German from local farmers he worked for. He read voraciously and remembered every word. Everyone said he looked like a movie star – tall, dark and handsome. He was the star in every school play. The stories about him as an infant and toddler were legend and Mama never tired of telling them – walking and talking at nine months, teaching himself to read at three, to write at four. One year Laurence spent his harvest money on an ancient hand-cranked Victrola he bought from an old German woman, along with dozens of thick, scratchy records – all Mozart, Beethoven, Schubert, Brahms. Daddy's cowboy music on the radio competed with Laurence's symphonies.

Sometimes it seemed to me that Laurence was Mama's only child, Hank, Vera and I pale in comparison. Mama and Laurence were buddies more than mother and son. She never asked him to help with anything and defended him when he refused to help Daddy. On weekends he slept nearly all day. Every day Mama and Daddy argued over Laurence which led to quarrels about money, mainly, and about the beer joint.

Six days a week Daddy drove into Piedmont in the red Mobil gas truck at exactly five o'clock after twelve hours of deliveries. We would be at home waiting for him, the table set for supper, Mama fussing that the food was getting cold. At about five minutes past five she found she needed something from the store.

'Go on down to Meyer's and fetch me a can of Pet Milk for the gravy,' she told Hank.

If I wasn't sick I'd tag along. To reach the store we had to pass the beer joint. And there sat Daddy's big red truck with the winged horse painted on it. Hank and I walked on to the store to buy the can of evaporated milk, or whatever item Mama had thought she needed, and walked back home.

'Did you see him in there?' Mama asked when we entered the door.

'Yeah, he's at Jake's,' Hank said.

A few minutes later a cloud of red dust blowing in the open front door announced his arrival.

'Add up all that beer you drink and I could have an electric ice-box,' Mama greeted him. He did not reply but sat down to eat.

'Nothing but bums and sinners in that beer joint,' she said. Still he did not reply.

'You don't spend no time with me and the kids, your drinking buddies are more important.'

'One beer don't hurt nobody. Anyhow, your sweet boy spends more time in there than me and you don't never say nothing to him,'

Daddy said.

'Well, Laurence is only a boy, not a man with a family to support.'

The debate escalated and deviated during supper.

'Daddy, I gotta have new basketball shoes,' Hank said.

'I ain't got no money for no new shoes till fall,' Daddy said.

'You got money for rodeoing and for going deer hunting and buying more sheep, and for beer,' Mama said.

'Yeah, and I bring prize money in, and that deer meat goes a long ways in the winter, and you know we couldn't do without that wool money,' he said.

'I never seen a penny of that wool money. You stashed it away to buy you a horse and now you use it for rodeoing. You're just selfish,' Mama said.

Daddy stomped out to feed the sheep. I wheezed. Hank said, 'Forget it, Mama, shoes can wait.'

'No siree, I'll get them shoes for you if it's the last thing I do.'

Daddy's horse was a sore point. Mama wanted nothing to do with horses and didn't want Daddy entering races and rodeos. One day Daddy had come home with a beautiful silvery dappled blue roan, a quarter horse, a rodeo and race horse. He let me name her and I chose 'Nancy,' after Nancy Drew. Daddy entered Nancy in quarter-horse races and rodeos all over the region and brought home prize money. Soon he bred the mare and she had a shiny black colt which became Hank's pony and which he named Sambo. Daddy wanted me to grow up and be a rodeo queen, and I wanted to, but Mama would not hear of me having my own horse.

Our little house was crowded and without privacy, yet I felt the others didn't see or notice me because I was so quiet, because I was no trouble. Of course during a 'fit,' as Mama called my asthma attacks, everyone noticed me and rushed to help. They would take turns staying up all night nursing me, all the time their faces filled with worry and grief. My mother would rock me and tell me stories for hours, often all night long.

During those hanging-on times when I couldn't breathe I had the sense of being an eye and an ear hidden in the wall, watching their every movement, listening to their speech and sounds. I felt as if I came from somewhere else, the tail of a comet that got sucked in by earth's gravity. It made me free and powerful, like Superman, or Black Beauty, Joan of Arc or God. I felt myself to be God's eye, watching, listening, wishing I could help them when they were sad or mad or quarreling with each other.

But it broke my heart when my big brother Laurence left home, and I think my mother never recovered from it. I remember well that night before he left.

'Listen to that wind howl,' Laurence said.

'It's a Norther on the way,' Hank said.

My thin shoulders shuddered. 'Where does the Norther come from?'

'Where the polar bears and Eskimos live,' Laurence said. He was driving our flimsy '38 Ford pickup. The red dirt road was freshly graded and nearly as smooth as blacktop. The shiny harvest moon and the headlights made the road look like a red ribbon strung out far as the eye could see.

Squeezed between my brothers I felt safe, and happy and sad at the same time. I stared at the red road and listened to the howling wind. I trembled a little in anticipation of the biting cold that the wind would usher in within a few weeks, and the asthma. I halfway expected the Highwayman to appear in the headlights. We had just seen that movie about a dashing, red-caped English outlaw who robbed from the rich to give to the poor, based on the Alfred Noyes poem *The Highwayman*, which we'd read in school. I wasn't afraid that the Highwayman would rob us because he would know that we were poor. The words of the poem kept running through my mind:

> And still of a winter's night, they say,
> when the wind is in the trees,
> When the moon is a ghostly galleon tossed
> upon the cloudy sea,
> When the road is a ribbon of moonlight
> over the purple moor,
> A highwayman comes riding – riding – riding –

I reflected on the fact that *The Highwayman* would be the last picture show I'd see for a long time. With Laurence gone no one else would take Hank and me the nine miles to the picture shows in Yukon. Tomorrow he would stand at the intersection of that red shale road and Highway 66, on the north side, to flag down the Greyhound and ride it to the edge of the earth, to California, like most other boys after they graduated from high school, or even before. I could not imagine life without Laurence – no more nighttime stories about Billy the Kid and Geronimo, about Belle Starr, no more word lessons.

The day before I'd heard Mama say to Daddy, 'Don't let Laurence go. The army will get him and send him off to some war and he'll get killed.'

'The army will get him here as good as out there. He's grown and I can't stop him from going,' Daddy answered. 'Anyway, ole Truman says he won't start no war anywhere. That's why he dropped them atom bombs on Japan.'

Everyone had thought Laurence would be discovered by a college basketball scout at the state playoffs the spring before. He was a whiz southpaw shooter and fast. But he'd been thrown out of the game in the third quarter on a technical when he slugged the referee.

'What will you do out there in California?' Hank asked. I twisted my head to look up into Laurence's face for the answer. His hard black eyes glowed like burning coals. I thought he looked like Henry Fonda, with his straight black hair and chiseled face.

'Get a job, anything but prune-picking, save money, go to college.'

Laurence dreamed of becoming a doctor, the best surgeon in the world. He could name all the bones and muscles, parts of the heart and eye and brain, and he drew pictures of them with colored pencils. And he spoke and read German. He said the best books on medicine were in German.

'Will you come back here to be a doctor?' I asked. The nearest doctor was nine miles from Piedmont.

'That's my idea, and I'll make enough money to send you kids to college, too.'

My heart fluttered. College. I dreamed of going and reading all the books in the big library at the teachers college in Edmond fifteen miles away. My teacher took our class there on a field trip in the spring. I had never imagined there were so many books in the world. The tiny one-room library in our rural school had about fifty books, but at the college there were rooms and rooms filled with books on everything. Laurence taught me to read when I was four, he said. I couldn't remember not being able to read.

'What do you want to be, Baby?' Laurence asked me.

'Nancy Drew.' My brothers laughed. 'Well, maybe a nurse. Then I could help you when you're a doctor,' I said.

'Why not be a doctor?' Laurence said.

'Girls can't be doctors,' Hank said.

'Girls can be anything they want to be, Hank. I don't want you marrying some dumb hick and having babies, Roxie, savvy?' I knew he was serious when he called me 'Roxie' instead of 'Baby.' His voice was icy. That sound in his voice always scared me.

'Yes, Laurence.'

'That-a-girl, don't you forget you're going to amount to something. You, too, Hank, you're going to get out of here and not farm. Practice shooting baskets three hours every day, you promise?' At nine Hank was already a good ballplayer.

'Yes, Laurence, I promise.'

'Listen,' Laurence said. He rolled down his window and the volume of the wind's howl amplified. 'A coyote.' I couldn't hear anything but the wind and the engine. Dust filled the cab. Laurence pulled off the road onto the shoulder and stopped, cut the engine.

'Come on, Hank, let's go get that coyote or it'll be killing Daddy's sheep.' Laurence grabbed his .22 from the gun rack behind our heads.

'I'm scared, don't leave me alone,' I whined.

'Come with us,' Laurence said.

'Tag-along, tag-along,' Hank sang.

'Watch your mouth, boy,' Laurence said and boxed Hank on the side of the head.

Now I could hear the coyote howling. I walked behind my brothers. Laurence carried the rifle suspended, pointed ahead. We walked through a field of dry wheat stubble. The bright light of the moon made the field look golden. I imagined we were walking on streets paved with gold, like those in heaven.

Laurence and Hank stopped abruptly and I nearly ran into them. Laurence raised his rifle to his shoulder and aimed. I could see the coyote. It was sitting on its haunches and howling at the moon. A few feet away was the bloody, mangled corpse of a lamb. The dry, rust-colored leaves of a lone scrub oak rustled in the wind.

'Don't shoot, why do you have to kill him?' I pleaded and tugged on Laurence's denim jacket.

The shot rang out and the coyote's howl faded to a yelp then a whimper. Then the only sound was the wind. Laurence crouched by the coyote.

'Clean kill. Let's take him for the dogs to eat. Hank, you be sure and stretch that skin out tomorrow for it to dry. You can keep the bounty for yourself.' (My father would take the coyote's ears into town and collect the five dollars the county paid.)

They each grabbed a hind leg and began walking back to the road, dragging the coyote. We walked without talking, the wind wailing. The carcass left a narrow path as it flattened the wheat stubble. I walked on the path, looking into the marble-like eyes of the coyote.

'The lamb was already dead, so why'd you kill the coyote? He was just hungry,' I said, whimpering.

Laurence stopped and turned. 'What you got to understand, Roxie, is that once an animal kills like that it'll kill again and it's got to be done away with.'

Six

Fields of Clover

Happy heels clicked on my walk

And a blue-eyed woman
with a bag of lemons
rang my bell ...

Blue eyes
handed me the bag
laughing silky smooth
Imagine me an Okie, she said
with my own lemon tree ...

WILMA ELIZABETH MCDANIEL,
from 'A Woman with Lemons'

After Laurence left in 1946, Mama mourned, Daddy grew even more quiet, Hank and I felt more vulnerable, and Vera flourished.

'Come with me, Baby, and I'll show you all the things in my treasure chest,' Vera would say.

'Baby, you've seen that old stuff. Stay here with me and I'll draw you maps and teach you the capitals of all the states,' Laurence said.

That's how it was until Laurence left home. Vera would tug on my left arm, Laurence on the right. I had seen inside Vera's treasure chest many times but never tired of it, and she was always adding new things, a pretty button or doily, a set of napkins or something else she made in home ec. Some of Vera's teenaged girlfriends had cedar chests, but Daddy said they cost too much so Vera's treasure chest was a big wooden box that Daddy made from orange crates. He called it her 'hope chest,' for hoping to marry, he said, but there wasn't much there for starting a home, more just a collection of her most precious things, and her locked five-year diary in which she wrote every day.

I had always chosen Laurence in those tugs-of-war over me when he and Vera were teenagers and I was six or seven years old. I was sure if I failed to choose Laurence he would reject me and never again read to me or teach me or let me follow him to milk the cow. I simply assumed that Vera would never reject me, but she always ran off crying when I chose Laurence over her.

'Bug-eyes,' he would holler after her.

Vera did have huge eyes like big marbles, the only one of us kids with blue eyes like Daddy. Laurence also called Vera 'nigger lips,' because she had full lips like the stars in the movie magazines she kept in the treasure chest. I always wondered why Laurence chose Vera's most beautiful features to poke fun at, because everyone knew she had stunning eyes and sensuous lips, but the taunt always worked and I think she really thought her eyes and lips were ugly.

Only after Laurence graduated and escaped to California did Vera no longer have to compete for my attention (although I awaited the mail daily for a letter from Laurence). My world was now more organized by women with Vera and Mama working hard to socialize me properly. And Vera also worked hard at being my role model. Once Laurence was gone, she insisted on her rights. She demanded and got her own room in our tiny house by threatening to leave home. Mama and Daddy slept on the divan in the living room that year and Hank and I shared what had been Laurence's bed. No one dared enter Vera's room without her invitation. Nearly every day she would take me into her domain to inventory her treasure chest. She even let me hold her diary, run my fingers over the red lizardskin cover and open it with the tiny gold key she kept on a chain around her neck. We pored over her scrapbooks, so neat and organized chronologically, and over her high school yearbooks with loving notes from all her friends.

She came into her own at school. Vera was medium height but a fast basketball player and good shooter. She starred in school plays and excelled in all subjects – especially home economics and typing. No one could out-type her and she dreamed of being an executive secretary. Our age difference of nine years precluded competition or jealousy, so we never quarreled and she was exactly the kind of big girl I wanted to become. Popular girls were fair and round, not angular, their hair naturally curly and shiny – and most important, they were either first-string basketball players or cheerleaders or both. There was little hope for me considering my skinniness, sickliness, darkness and stringy hair, but Vera encouraged me by reminding me of the story about the ugly duckling, so I kept hoping.

Even after Vera graduated and moved to Oklahoma City to go to business school and work, she still had a big influence on me and she came home nearly every weekend. At first she boarded with a family but had now moved in with a roommate at the YWCA in downtown Oklahoma City. For nearly two wonderful years, until she married when I was twelve, I had adventures, thanks to Vera, that no other kid in Piedmont could imagine.

One day in September at noon recess a few months after Vera had graduated and moved to the city, I was playing red rover with a dozen other kids when a small airplane appeared in the bright blue southeastern sky and floated closer and lower until it landed on the rodeo grounds southwest of town. We rarely saw airplanes in the sky and none had ever landed in Piedmont. I stood motionless and gazed southwest, then noticed that all the other children were doing the same. The plane was visible at that distance, about a mile away. I could see two people climb out and walk toward town but I couldn't tell what they looked like. I hoped that plane would stay until school turned out so I could go see one up close for the first time.

About ten minutes later, still during recess, two strangers walked toward where I played in the schoolyard. Then I recognized one of the strangers as Vera. She wore fancy brown jodhpurs and tall riding boots that weren't cowboy boots and a big brown leather jacket like fighter pilots wore. She had on dark glasses. The young man with her was dressed similarly and wore a cap and goggles.

I ran to my sister, who was beaming and glamorous. All the children gathered around and gawked. The big girls and boys and the teachers came out and greeted Vera. I had never been so proud.

'Can I go see the airplane, Vera?' I pleaded.

'That's why I rode out here, to show you an airplane,' she said, and led me away from school to go look at it. None of the teachers tried to stop us.

I never saw that boyfriend again. Vera always had a boyfriend after she moved to the city. Until she met the man she married she dated a half-dozen quiet young men. She always brought them out to meet

us. I think one requirement Vera had to date a man was that he have
a car – or an airplane – so she could visit home, and be willing to
bring me back and forth to visit her.

Those happy times were actually few and far between, and the
world just did not seem right without Laurence. I was fragile and
plagued with chronic asthma. I remember one day when my mood
was dark as the low menacing storm clouds in the sky. I crouched on
one of the half-dozen cellar doors in the field south of the red brick
school building, staring out over the deep green field of clover and
beyond to the red earth that rolled on to the distant horizon. Only the
day before, during recess, I had run through the clover looking for
lucky four-leafs never found. Now I was sick. Echoes of laughter and
shouts of joy wafted around me. I could see my schoolmates running
through the clover, stopping, searching, running on. They carried
baskets or paper sacks. It was the Good Friday Easter egg hunt, an
event I looked forward to all year long.

My teacher had made me stay behind, close to the cellar in case a
tornado formed out of the storm clouds. I had come to school that
morning wheezing. The teacher said that going on the egg hunt could
bring on an attack, and if a tornado blew in and everyone had to run
for the cellar I might get left behind.

The kids over thirteen had hidden the eggs for the hunt and were
free for the afternoon. Most were in the gym shooting baskets. Some
boys played horseshoes and some of the older girls walked around
outside, talking and laughing. I knew I wasn't being punished, but
tears burned my eyes as envy overcame me.

The gym door flew open and my brother Hank burst out, falling to
his hands and knees on the concrete sidewalk. Three big, blond boys
came out after him, laughing and pointing at him. They were senior
basketball players. Even though they were distant I could hear their
words blown by the wind.

'Get up, chief – or are you going to run home and tell your squaw
mama on us?'

'I ain't telling nobody,' Hank said.

The three big boys grabbed Hank and dragged him around the
building out of my sight. I shot up from the cellar door and ran. I
skidded to a stop as I rounded the school building. One boy was
holding Hank from behind in a bear hug while the other two were

forcing his knuckles up and down against the brick wall.

'Hank, I'm here, what do you want me to do?' I yelled. I ran and tackled the leg of the boy holding Hank. 'Stop it, leave my brother alone.'

The boy kicked me off and I crumpled like a dry leaf in the red dirt. Hank turned his head and looked down at me, his face twisted in pain.

'Go away, Roxie, you're sick.'

'They wouldn't hurt you if Laurence was here,' I said, choking with asthma.

'Laurence ain't here. Go home, Roxie.'

I spent more time with my mother than my father or my brothers and sister, because I was sick. I remember those days when I would be home alone for days with asthma. Mama propped me up with pillows on the divan because breathing came a little easier sitting up than lying down. I distracted myself from the painful wheezing and dry hacking by listening closely to the radio. Oral Roberts was preaching and faith healing. Mama mailed him a dollar bill from her egg money every month that she made from selling her homemade bread, eggs and fresh-churned butter. She was also trying to save enough money to take me to his church in Tulsa that he might heal me of asthma. I was not very interested in Oral Roberts. His preaching made me worry about Daddy and Laurence, who did not believe in God. According to Oral Roberts, they would surely burn in hell.

I was waiting for the Campbell's sweepstakes announcements. Mama had entered the sweepstakes, writing in twenty-five words or less why she loved Campbell's soup. I was the one who ate the soup, tomato, the only food I could get down while suffering from asthma, and I drank the Lipton tea made with a tea bag as advertised on the *Arthur Godfrey Hour*. Later in the afternoon Mama and I listened to *Portia Faces Life,* and I dreamed of being like Portia, a woman lawyer, unmarried, independent.

During World War II, country music came to us for a half hour on Saturday nights on Oklahoma City's WKY with NBC's truncated broadcast of the *Grand Ole Opry* from Nashville. Cousin Minnie Pearl, Roy Acuff, Pee-Wee King and Eddy Arnold entered our humble living room and allowed us to know we were a part of, and one

with, our kind of people in a faraway place in the old homeland of
Tennessee. Listening to Roy Acuff pour his heart and soul into 'The
Great Speckled Bird,' about a beleaguered and downtrodden people
('our people') who would triumph in the end, gave us hope as no
Sunday sermon could.

After the war ended, the airwaves swelled with 'our' music. We still
had our thirty-minute Prince Albert–sponsored *Grand Ole Opry,* but
much more. Every station played Little Jimmy Dickens singing about
being poor and rural – 'Country Boy,' 'Out Behind the Barn,' 'Sleeping
at the Foot of the Bed,' 'Take an Old Cold Tater and Wait' – validating
who we were, instilling pride in our kind. Hank Williams brought us
'Jambalaya' that told of other poor, rural people like us down in the
bayous of Louisiana. Bob Wills sang to Daddy's part-Texas heart with
'San Antonio Rose' and 'Mexicali Rose,' and my heart skipped a beat
when his 'Take Me Back to Tulsa' throbbed out of our little radio.
Then along came Kitty Wells and Patti Page, who brought a female
perspective with their answers to Hank Williams's honky-tonk angels
in 'The Wild Side of Life' and 'The Tennessee Waltz.'

Country music included gospel songs. Red Foley gave us 'Just a
Closer Walk with Thee' and 'Peace in the Valley.' After old-time country singer Stuart Hamblen was saved by Billy Graham in Los Angeles,
he wrote and sang 'It Is No Secret' and 'This Ole House,' which
Rosemary Clooney took to the top of the pop charts.

I'm now convinced that this music was delivered to us, drowning
us in song and belief, helping keep us docile, especially the angry and
dispossessed who had gone to California. It helped keep us women
religious while it comforted and encouraged our men, who boozed it
up and slugged it out in taverns over cheating hearts.

We poor rural whites were no longer foot-soldier Indian fighters,
and were not easy to silence if we got mad. What we had was oral
history, a powerful memory, so the music, a part of that history as
well as how we told it, absolutely seduced us.

Mama liked the music but thought that all of it except gospel was
sinful. Yet she also had secular ambitions. Mama's goal was to be
appointed postmistress at the Piedmont post office, so she applied
when the old widow postmistress died. She didn't get the job, but in
1950 she served as the local census taker. Daddy griped but let her
use the pickup. Mama dragged me along that summer to every house

in town and throughout a ten-mile radius of the countryside.

Mama had many ways of making money, which she squirreled away clandestinely to buy things for us kids – comic books and movie magazines, soda pop and candy, class rings and Easter dresses, home permanents, and cartons of cigarettes to send Laurence, and smokes for herself, too. She smoked Kools, always secretly, even though everybody knew she smoked. Once on a Sunday morning just before we went to church, which was three blocks away, Mama set our outhouse on fire, and the early arrivals at the Methodist church across the road from us came and put it out with their Sunday jackets. Hank and I were embarrassed, but not one of those country gents who snuffed the fire said a word about its origin.

Mama baked bread to sell and kept chickens and sold the eggs. She had learned many things in the girls' home, one of them being wallpapering, and was much in demand, especially during the summer months. Hank and I served as her apprentices. Mama also came to be known in the town, which was bereft of doctors, as something of a miracle worker. She made her rounds giving diabetics their shots, treating pneumonia, scarlet fever, measles, mumps, ulcers. Each patient paid her what they could, usually in kind, with a dozen eggs, or a fresh-killed chicken, or some hand-me-down clothes.

Mama had encouraged Laurence to become a doctor, probably a dream she had for herself. But Daddy mistrusted doctors, seeing them as crooks who charged too much. Daddy trusted veterinarians. Sometimes it seemed to me that he simply valued the health and lives of animals more than people.

Daddy disapproved of what he called Mama's 'faith healing.' He sniped at her, 'You care more about strangers than your own family, gadding around in the mud and snow doing your voodoo.'

One winter day a little girl walked up behind me as I sat alone by the window of the sixth-grade classroom looking out at the other children playing at recess. The little girl hissed in my ear: 'Your mama's a witch.'

I turned, wheezing, and rasped, 'Is not, take it back.'

'Is too, my mama says so, and I won't take it back.' The little girl skipped away. I cried silently and the wheezing grew worse.

Yet children loved Mama, not as a mother-figure, but more like another, older, child. She always had a trail of kids following her.

After school and on Saturdays and all summer long, our home was open to all kids. Clusters of children would gather around the kitchen table gobbling the goodies and listening to Mama's fantastic made-up stories, which involved gremlins and fairies, princesses and princes, pots of gold at the end of rainbows, trolls under bridges, and wolves, and buried treasure in the countryside. She would shoo all the children away before Daddy came home, and he never knew about our after-school adventures.

The first summer after Laurence was gone Mama started a Cub Scout troop. She sent off for certification and got it, and they sent us two guidebooks. Six boys and six girls, eight to ten years old, including me, Hank and two of our cousins, made up the troop. Mama took us hiking, naming the birds and plants, explaining how to avoid rattlesnakes or what to do if bitten. She read to us from the Scout guidebook about good citizenship and behavior, how to be strong and brave, how to be 'big boys,' as the guidebook read, and never cry.

The Scout book I liked best was *Daniel Boone, Wilderness Scout*. It had special meaning to me because Mama had scouting in her blood. She claimed Daniel Boone as an ancestor, as do many families of the trekking frontier culture, I found out later.

Our Cub Scout troop went along for more than a year before a Scout supervisor got around to visiting. Mama lined us up in our yard for inspection. Someone took a picture of us, which I still have. There are twelve children, six boys and six girls. Hank holds up his basketball. I am on the end of the front row, hair in pigtails, biting my lower lip, chin tucked in. I wear a plaid coat that comes way above my knees, bare legs, brown-and-white saddle oxfords and anklets. My mother stands in the back row, a head taller than the tall boys. She looks so young and pretty and so happy.

'What have we got here – little girl visitors?' the Scout Chief said. We glanced at each other and shuffled our feet.

'No sir, the girls are members too,' Mama said proudly, her eyes sparkling.

'This will not do. Girls belong in the Brownies,' he said.

'What's Brownies?' Mama asked, her smile frozen.

'Brownies is the little Girl Scouts, like Cub Scouts only for girls,' he said.

'Well, we're just a small town here and we do everything together,' she said. The Scout Chief said he wanted to speak to Mama alone and they went inside the house. We all sat down on the ground, pulled out bags of marbles and waited, the boys shooting marbles and us girls playing jacks.

After a while Mama's voice boomed, 'Just get out of here, then. We don't need you. I'll take a shillelagh to you.'

The man shot out the door, ran to his car and peeled out, leaving a cloud of red dust behind. Mama came out dabbing her eyes with a handkerchief. I thought the man had hurt her, and ran to her.

'I'm all right, Baby, but that man says we're banned, that we can't have boys and girls together, and he took the guidebook and the Daniel Boone book,' she said.

The children sat looking up at her. My cousin Lee Ann broke the silence: 'Well, we don't need his ole books, Aunt Louise. We got you.'

Her face brightened. 'Let's hike down to the creek.'

We continued our banned Cub Scout troop. But I missed the books, especially the one about Daniel Boone. It was the story of the brave hunter charting the Indian roads through the eastern mountains and leading the settlers Moses-like out into dangerous Indian country, Kentucky and the Ohio territory, a few years after the American Revolution. Mama had stressed the part of the book where it said that Daniel Boone was never an Indian hater even though he killed Indians to take their land; she said that the Indians were like the wild animals he loved and killed.

Mama's sympathy for the Indians never went much further than her admiration for Daniel Boone and the Scout guides. On the other hand, she did marry my father, a committed hunter. Daddy would come home nearly every day with a squirrel, possum or rabbit he'd shot while making his fuel deliveries. He dressed them outside and fed the guts to the dogs. Mama wouldn't touch wild meat until it was skinned, cleaned and dressed. Then she would fry it up for dinner, though she didn't eat it herself, and neither did I, but then I didn't eat much of anything except Campbell's soup.

I remember one Saturday when we were in El Reno. Hank and Daddy were in the barbershop while Mama and I went to the dime store to buy a window shade. I had wandered out of the dime store while Mama was looking at shades.

Outside the door sat three old Indians, a woman and two men, whom I had noticed when we went into the store. I stared at the Indians. Their long, black hair was matted, and their tattered clothes were almost in rags. They shared a dirty worn quilt that was so thin it looked like it was about to fall apart. The January day was sunny, the sky such a bright blue it hurt my eyes, but it was freezing cold and the north wind whipped up newspapers lying on the sidewalk.

I stood in front of the Indians. They showed no signs of acknowledging my presence, staring straight ahead, looking through me. I felt invisible and free to study them. I had never been that close to a real Indian, not, like my mother, assimilated or intermarried. They were smoking – the men hand-rolled cigarettes, the woman a corncob pipe she puffed on without touching it with her hands. I saw the objects dangling from their ears, and the holes in their ears that the objects hung from. The earrings were long and slender, brown, black and white. Porcupine needles, I realized. They were beautiful. I had never noticed that porcupine needles were pretty even though I picked them up nearly every day. I could not reconcile the rags on the Indians and the beauty of their earrings.

The Indians shared a dirty old liquor bottle, passing it from one to the other, each sipping and handing it over. They were so silent that I wondered if they had voices. Although Daddy had related conversations he'd had with Indian cowboys he'd worked with, I had never heard a real Indian talk. Our school played two basketball games each winter with Concho, the nearby government Indian boarding school, but the Indians never spoke. I thought about the time when Laurence made a run to dunk the ball and the Concho Indian players ganged up on him and broke his collarbone, and I remember the whispered discussions between Mama and Daddy and Laurence at home that night that it had to do with their perception that Laurence was an Indian boy pretending to be white.

I wanted to say something that would get their attention so that they would speak, so I could know if Indians had voices. But I couldn't think of what to say and I knew that children were not to speak first to old people. 'Speak only when spoken to,' Mama always said. It was disrespectful to interrupt the thoughts of old people.

The Indian woman took one of the porcupine needle earrings out of her ear and extended it to me. It happened so suddenly that I simply reached out and accepted it. The woman continued to stare ahead as if I were not there. I held the beautiful object in the palm of my hand and gently wrapped my cold fingers around it. At that moment Mama jerked my arm and dragged me away. I stuck my right hand that held the earring in my coat pocket, already trying to figure out where I might hide it safely. As I looked back at the Indians one of the old men held up his hand, palm outward.

'Why don't they talk?' I asked.

'They don't speak English,' Mama said.

'What do they speak?'

'Indian.'

Mama stopped and turned to me. 'Now don't you ever, ever try to talk to an Indian again. They have diseases and they're dirty.' I had never imagined you could catch a disease by talking.

'You said Daniel Boone liked Indians,' I said. I was almost crying because I didn't understand what Mama was so mad about.

'That was different. The Indians in his time were proud warriors. These around here are just old dirty, drunk Indians.'

Mama was more or less isolated in that narrow, white community of Piedmont. Her best friend was also mine, a widow woman born in 1879, ten years before the Oklahoma Run, which her family joined. We called her 'Aunt' even though she wasn't related. In fact I had two great aunts and a great uncle on my father's side in town, but Aunt Fanny was better than a real aunt or even grandmother to me.

Aunt Fanny lived right behind us in a nice, solid frame house, much larger and better furnished than our tiny house, and it was always scrubbed and immaculate, even though it didn't have indoor plumbing. She allowed Daddy to run his sheep on her yard and on a large empty lot she owned. Everyone else in town thought we were crazy having sheep; no one else owned them, and it was said that only the lowly Indians and Mexicans out in New Mexico and Arizona ran sheep. Aunt Fanny had grown children, and grandchildren; one of her daughters was married to the biggest wheat farmer in the county, heir to one of Piedmont's founding families. Fanny was skinny, white-haired and asthmatic, the only asthmatic in town besides me. She made me feel special for having asthma.

'It means you're descended from kings and queens,' she said, claiming that asthma was an inherited disease of royalty.

Aunt Fanny kept a stack of *True Romance* magazines under her bed and would pull them out for me to read aloud to her. I didn't understand everything in the stories but was fascinated by the lives of the city people in them, especially wild girls who smoked 'reefers' and drove fast cars. And Aunt Fanny told me old-time stories, but especially over and over the story of finding her husband hanging from the barn roof twenty years before.

'He must've been sick and not wantin' to tell me or he wouldn't have killed hissef,' she said.

'I bet he caught cancer, Aunt Fanny,' I said.

The old woman was precious to me because I wanted a grandmother who would love me, and maybe Mama needed a substitute for the mother she never had, so we adopted Fanny. I hated my real grandmother. Daddy's mother made no secret that she disliked me and Mama. After Grandpa Dunbar died four years before I was born, my grandmother lived in San Antonio, then moved back to the Rio Grande Valley, where her daughter and family and two sons and their families lived. Every six months she visited Piedmont, where she had lived half her life. She stayed with her brother and his wife and with her two sisters and their husbands in town, and sometimes a night or two with us although she did not like to because she couldn't stand to be around Mama. She called my mother 'trash' and 'half-breed' to her face. She extended her spite to me because, she said, 'You're just like your mother.' She doted on my brothers and adored Vera, who she claimed looked exactly like her and was named after her.

Grandma Dunbar refused to claim me as her grandchild. More than once she hissed at me that she didn't believe Daddy was my real father, that Mama had 'run around' in San Antonio before becoming pregnant with me and that my real father was probably a 'bloodthirsty Comanche,' or perhaps a Mexican – just as bad in Grandma's eyes.

Except for Daddy, all Grandma's other children owned their own homes and nice cars, and she blamed Mama for Daddy being a failure: 'Crazy,' 'wild,' 'low class' and 'red dirt' were some of the accusations she hurled at Mama.

One terrible time when Grandma Dunbar was visiting, Mama came down with a terrible attack of her chronic skin inflammation, which she called poison ivy. Her eyes swelled shut and every inch of her body was puffed and sore. Mama tried every remedy she knew and covered her body in pink calamine lotion, but nothing worked. Then her throat swelled shut and she couldn't eat or drink water. Finally Daddy became scared and took her to the hospital in the city. Grandma was visiting and Daddy asked her to stay with Hank and me while they were away.

For two days I had to suffer Grandma's meanness. At breakfast the first morning Hank and I sat waiting while Grandma fixed food. I was hungry because I had been upset about Mama being sick and couldn't eat the evening before. I had cried myself to sleep. Grandma whistled to herself while she cooked. The bacon smelled delicious and made my stomach rumble. She brought one plate piled with bacon and two fried eggs, biscuits and gravy and set it in front of Hank. I looked up at Grandma but she walked away and poured herself a cup of coffee.

'Grandma, can I have an egg? I like it fried hard,' I said.

'*May* I, not *can* I, and do you know how to say "please"?'

'Yes, ma'am, please may I have an egg?'

'No, dirty little girls don't get eggs. I'm going out to feed the chickens.'

Daddy never challenged his mother. He said she had never been quite right since the Ku Klux Klan had terrorized them and beat his father half to death. After Grandpa died she converted to the Church of Christ and became a fanatic Christian, but even Mama's nearly equal Christian devotion didn't win any points with Grandma. Only recently, Daddy told me that his mother had married his father when she was thirteen. During the following twenty years she had over a dozen pregnancies.

Maybe the connection seems too literal, but it was right around then that Daddy told me that he'd give me all the black sheep for my very own. I believed he was trying to atone for Grandma Dunbar's cruelty. At least one, sometimes two black lambs were born every year and they were my pets: 'Sometimes their mamas and the other sheep don't like them,' he told me. I adored them, though, and fed them with a bottle until they grew old enough to be sold for meat. The point is that their wool wasn't valuable. Kipling's story 'Baa, Baa Black Sheep' was one of my favorites.

But my father never did back my mother when Grandma Dunbar

attacked her. Mama's only weapon against the world was her darling son Laurence. Once he was gone, Mama and Daddy didn't fight as much, but they hardly ever spoke to each other at all. They would use Hank and me as intermediaries.

'Roxie, tell your mother the water's boiling,' Daddy would say, with Mama right there in the kitchen.

'Hank, tell your father that kerosene tank is getting low,' Mama would say when Daddy was not three feet from her.

The two of them were marching out of step toward a bleak future, and so it was tension that filled our small living space, not laughter, or love. But they both worked hard and incessantly. Daddy was always the first out of bed, at five, inky dark outside in the winter. Still in his long johns he started the kerosene stove in the living room, then the cooking stove in the kitchen. He dressed in the kitchen and sat down by the stove in the front room to pull on his socks and boots. I slept in the living room and woke to watch him pull on his long stockings and attach them to garters, then pull the lace-up work boots on. Out into the cold Daddy plunged, to feed his sheep after a usually unsuccessful attempt to rouse Hank to help him. By the time he returned at six, Mama had slipped out of bed, dressed, rushed to the outhouse to smoke and back to the kitchen. The smell of bacon frying and coffee boiling was the only alarm Hank needed to roll out of bed. He trekked out to the toilet.

I knew the minute my feet hit the floor in the morning if I could go to school that day, as I was practically disabled by my asthma. If I couldn't make it to the outhouse and had to use the slop bucket in the kitchen instead, I was home for the day. Daddy drove off in his gasoline truck at seven, dropping Hank and me, if I could go, at school.

The arrival of Laurence's weekly letters and pages of colored-pencil drawings were Mama's greatest treat, and mine, too. For me he drew clouds with their names, the heavens with the names of stars and planets. He sent lists of words in Gothic German script, and in Spanish, Latin and Greek with their English meanings, dates and facts of history, maps of parts of the world with their capitals, lists of presidents, skeletons with the names of bones, drawings of monkeys getting bigger and standing up and then being human with tens of thousands of years written above their heads, topped by the word 'evolution.' He wrote me that I should memorize everything he sent, and I did. In each letter he told me how I must plan to go to college, and he counseled Mama to encourage Hank and me.

Mama began writing. The first time I stayed home and discovered her new pastime, I was confused and felt lonely. She didn't even turn on the radio and almost forgot about eating at noon. Mama had always written many letters, but this was different. Mama's lean, muscular torso hunched over the long table in the front room was unfamiliar to me. I watched her profile, brown-leathered skin stretched over a high forehead, a prominent jaw, tensed long brown neck, her black hair cut short and frizzled from a permanent. Her large, strong right hand calloused on the side of her middle finger from writing, she scrawled large letters with a pencil in a lined Big Chief tablet. She stopped every half hour or so to sharpen her pencil with a paring knife and dashed to the outhouse for a cigarette. She filled pages and pages.

'What are you writing, Mama?' I asked.

'Just a story,' she said.

It turned out that Mama was sending her stories to Laurence. And then a letter came from him urging her to send her stories to the newspaper, saying she was a great writer.

'I think I just will,' she said.

And she did. That was how she came to be the 'Piedmont Reporter,' with a column, 'The Piedmont News,' in three weekly newspapers in the nearby towns of Yukon, Edmond and El Reno. Finally, my mother was able to create her own niche in that small, white, rural world where she had not been entirely accepted, and she was happy. She did about what she wanted and lied to Daddy about her excursions to cover events, and she instructed Hank and me and our cousins to not tell on her. Mainly these deceptions had to do with her using the car. Fortunately, the odometer didn't work and she always put gasoline in to replace what she used running around the area collecting news items and visiting.

Although Mama took me along with her on these trips, she really turned over my socialization to Vera, whose lessons are still imprinted in my mind, such as my compulsion to always leave some food on my plate.

'Leave some food on your plate, else people will think you don't get enough to eat at home,' Vera said.

I stared longingly at the last bite of the best hamburger I'd ever eaten and tried to figure out the logic of my sister's warning.

'Who will think that?' I asked.

'The waitress,' she said.

I looked around the crowded coffee shop served by one waitress, a middle-aged white woman, and wondered how she could keep track of which people ate all their food and if she reported her findings to someone. I was also confused because Mama's dictum was to 'clean up your plate' and to think of all the starving children in Africa that the preacher told us about when he was asking for money for missionaries. I never could clean up my plate at home and often didn't eat more than a bite, but one thing I could consume without effort was a hamburger and malt. When Vera had asked me what I wanted to eat I didn't hesitate. Always before when I had visited her in the city, we had eaten in the YWCA cafeteria and there were no waitresses. I couldn't remember worrying about leaving food on my plate but supposed that was because there was no waitress to see. Vera's mission there was to teach me to eat with a fork instead of a spoon and how to cut meat up into bites instead of plopping it on a piece of bread and eating it with my hands, as we did at home.

We were in the upstairs coffee shop of Katz Drugs on Main Street in Oklahoma City, two blocks from the YWCA. It was my first time at Katz's and it struck me as a wonderland. Many of the diners were black but they sat in a separate section and were served by another middle-aged white woman. I asked Vera why they were separated from us and she said she didn't know. That surprised me because Vera knew so much about the ways of people in the city. She did say she got teased about being named Dunbar because a black (she said 'nigger') school in Oklahoma City was named that. I was thrilled that a whole school had our name and wanted to go see it but Vera said it was in 'nigger town,' on the east side and white people didn't go there.

The waitress slapped down a pale green piece of paper and Vera studied it carefully, then dug in her purse for her billfold. She clutched a dollar and the check and got up to leave. I noticed a dime she had left on the table and picked it up.

'Vera, you dropped a dime.'

'No, Roxie, that's for the waitress. It's called a tip.'

My neck burned with embarrassment and I felt like a dumb hick. Vera's tone of voice implied that anyone should know what a tip was. Vera was teaching me many new things, bringing me to the city to stay with her. Her room was on the ninth floor of the YWCA and we rode an elevator, my first, to get there. The room was small, nearly filled with two twin beds. Vera had me stay with her only when her roommate, also a country girl, went home for the weekend. I thought the room was beautiful. From the large window I could look down to Main Street and watch the people and cars rush past. Across from the Y was the huge, glistening Municipal Auditorium and City Hall.

Vera's room had two sinks and down the hall was a spotless, cavernous room with flush toilets, bathtubs and showers. A little further on was a beautiful 'parlor,' as Vera called the big room with a grand piano and deep, dark divans and chairs. All the floors had their own bathrooms and parlors. On the second floor was a big indoor swimming pool and downstairs a cafeteria where Vera usually ate all her meals except for those rare occasions when she ate out. The YWCA was a dream world filled with beautiful big girls. I was determined to live there one day.

Once I looked up the Dunbar school in the Oklahoma City telephone book. I wanted to see it in writing. To my surprise there were a dozen listings for Dunbar, all on the northeast side, which Vera had said was 'nigger town.' Later when we were in the twin beds, lights flashing, horns honking down on Main Street, I asked the question I had asked my mother so many times: 'Why is everyone but us named Dunbar colored?'

'What makes you think that?' Vera said.

'I looked in the telephone book and all the Dunbars live in colored town, and I never met anyone else outside our own relatives by that name,' I said.

'It's because the Dunbars were Scotch-Irish and owned a lot of slaves in Virginia. The slaves always took their masters' names,' she explained – the same answer my mother had gaiven me years before. I asked the same question I had asked my mother:

'How do we know our people weren't the slaves instead of the masters?' I asked.

'Don't be silly. Go to sleep,' Vera said.

I lay there wondering how we could ever have owned slaves. Scarlet O'Hara's life was as far from me as the man in the moon's was. But that Scarlet and I both came from slave-owning families is what made me able to identify with her, that and her descent into poverty and her scratching her way out of it. So if we'd been wealthy plantation owners at one time, then our poverty now was noble because it was undeserved, caused by forces outside our control.

And Vera was another Scarlet, clawing her way out of rural poverty. After completing business school, Vera realized her dream and became the executive secretary for one of the biggest grafters in Oklahoma, a contractor made wealthy by building a housing development that was named Midwest City next to the newly constructed Tinker Field, a U.S. Air Force base east of Oklahoma City. Thanks to the postwar boom, he had struck it rich by winning a military contract. Our perennial senator, oil man Bob Kerr, made certain that Oklahoma secrued plenty of federal contracts.

Vera came home most weekends, now laden with gifts for all of us. She gave me my first baby doll and later a fancy doll, a birthstone ring, green cowboy boots, an overnight case – precious, lovely things. She bought us all winter coats and shoes, even a waffle iron and a set of silverplate tableware and china for Mama. She must have spent nearly all her money on us. Vera still took me with her to stay at the YWCA, and once she took me to her office.

'See, everything is red – the telephone, my IBM typewriter, my chair and desk lamp,' she said. Red was Vera's favorite color and she had red shoes, and a red winter coat and cap. I was impressed with the fancy office and dreamed of growing up and being exactly like my sister.

For the first time I caught a glimpse of how real rich people live. Vera's boss had a huge ranch adjacent to Midwest City, where he kept a herd of Shetland ponies. Vera took me there to see them and I fell in love with the dwarf horses and wanted one for myself more than anything in the world. Her boss offered me one as a gift but Daddy put his foot down: no Shetland ponies in his domain. Or perhaps no handouts.

Then Vera got married. She was twenty, and I was eleven. She had a June wedding right out of *McCall 's,* paying for it all herself. It was the biggest wedding ever seen in Piedmont. I was the flower girl. Vera bought me a dress to wear, and Daddy a new suit to give her away in. John, the groom, was a quiet, thin, red-haired young man from a small eastern Oklahoma town, working his way through an accounting degree. Vera had chosen her patterns of china, crystal, sterling.

Daddy bought Vera a cowboy clock for her wedding – the kind of 1950s retro collectible that now sells for a couple of thousand dollars – or maybe he won it in one of the shooting matches he entered, or bartered for it. The clock itself was a small part of what was really a large bronze statue of a cowboy, hat and all, on top of a fancily saddled horse. The clock was inlaid into the side of the horse. The cowboy statue was mounted on a bronze base that was covered underneath with green felt. I thought it was really ugly, and Vera, of course, hated the thing, although she made no comment when Daddy proudly presented it. I think she was too surprised about receiving anything at all from Daddy, who never gave gifts under any circumstances. Vera kept the cowboy clock in a hall closet with the broom and vacuum sweeper, and took it out to put on top of the television console only on the rare occasions when Daddy visited her new home.

Following the Perfect Wedding, the couple moved into their perfect little house, a two-bedroom, white brick house with a tiny front lawn, back yard – a model house in Midwest City, the suburb her boss had built. Vera furnished it in the latest style with blond oak and all the modern appliances. Their life was fixed and neat. They were among the new young suburbanites.

I still visited Vera, now in her new home, as I had at the Y, but I was bored there. That suburb was so quiet, and all the houses, all the yards, even the people and dogs, looked the same – young married white couples with cocker spaniels and well-kept lawns. There was a small shopping center a mile away but it was frequented by the same bland people who lived in the suburb and it had no soda fountain. When I was there I was always the only teenager. And Vera became very impatient and strict in her lessons for me. Everything had to be spotless, not a speck of dust or a smudge on a window. It seemed I only ever visited on Saturdays, housekeeping day.

Soon I replaced Vera as my surrogate mother with someone else, Laurence's new wife. Laurence didn't warn us beforehand, but when he showed up, he had a big surprise with him when he came home from California to visit after he finished Compton Junior College (with an AA in 'police science,' he planned to join the Los Angeles Police Department). He brought a bride. Jan had just turned sixteen and Laurence nineteen. Her father was a carpenter, a Dust Bowl Okie who had migrated to Los Angeles and met Jan's Okie mother there. Laurence and Jan met in Gardena in south central Los Angeles, her hometown, where they both worked in the same drugstore and where her parents worked in the legal gambling joints in that then Okie, now African-American, township.

The night after Jan and Laurence rode in on the Greyhound bus, Laurence's old buddies gave them a charivari, which we pronounced 'chivaree,' an old Scottish ritual that everyone in rural Oklahoma practiced, whether Scotch, Irish, Polish, Czech or German. The organizers did different things depending on the situation. If the couple had a house ready to live in, the hosts invaded it and messed it up, stripping all the cans of their labels, dismantling the beds, putting the furniture on the roof. Since Jan and Laurence had no home that could be invaded, they took Jan hostage and made Laurence strip and sit naked on top of a telephone pole all night while they threw rocks at him. They let me stay with Jan in the Methodist church basement where they held her. I tried to comfort my new sister-in-law but Jan was terrified and hysterical. I had taken the custom of charivari for granted until I saw how an outsider hated it. Now I felt ashamed of the backward ways of my people when Jan kept screaming, 'You no-good country hicks, let me go! And let Laurence go!'

Jan stayed with us for six months after Laurence was drafted and stationed with the early 1950s US occupation in Japan. Although it was an easy post, he could not afford to support a family there. I adored Jan, but Mama didn't approve of her. Jan was gorgeous – voluptuous and olive-skinned, with dark eyes set in high cheekbones, and wavy black hair to her waist. She had a Cherokee grandfather and looked Indian, and she was proud of it. To me, Jan was Debra Paget, Ava Gardner and Dolores del Rio rolled into one – the most beautiful woman I'd ever seen. She let me comb her shiny hair and touch her face. She let me watch her take a bath in the zinc tub on Saturday nights. I had never seen a naked adult before. Jan hugged and kissed me and calmed and soothed me when I was having asthma attacks. She had a little brother my age whom she had babysat while her mother worked, and she missed him. She called me her first baby.

Jan told me about gambling casinos in Gardena, about all-night parties on the beach, about dancing at the Palladium, the movie stars she had seen, especially about Sammy Davis, Jr., her favorite entertainer, whom she'd seen in clubs, and she told me about riding the ocean on boards. I longed to be transported to that magical place.

I thought Mama treated Jan much like Daddy's mother had treated Mama. It pained me to see it, but Jan was so different from anyone people in Piedmont had ever met that maybe Mama didn't know what to do except try to change her, as she had changed herself. Jan was bold and talked and laughed loudly. She had never been inside a church. For her, sex was an appropriate topic of conversation. She smoked and drank bootleg whiskey openly. Mama was ashamed of Jan, and she did not relent until Jan changed. Within that six-month stay, Mama transformed her. First went her long hair and scarlet lipstick, then the bare-shoulder dresses and shoes with ankle straps, then the thin gold ankle chain and the earrings in her pierced ears. She still smoked, but only in the outhouse like Mama. Soon Jan looked almost dowdy but nothing could camouflage her glow. One thing she refused to do was go to church. And it wasn't just Mama who was worried about that. I feared for Jan's salvation. Even after giving up so much of herself and that faraway place that drew me, and I suspect Laurence, to her in the first place, Jan still didn't win Mama's approval. No woman was good enough for her son.

Seven

Buried Treasure

Jan opened my eyes to a world beyond Oklahoma, and then she was gone, back to California with Laurence. But just at that time I got a real glimpse of life outside Oklahoma. It was during the one and only family vacation of my life – to visit my birthplace in San Antonio and my grandmother and Daddy's sisters and brothers on the border with Mexico.

I was twelve, and thrilled I actually crossed an international border and entered a foreign country.

In 1923, Daddy's parents and a half-dozen children of the ten still at home moved from Oklahoma to the Texas Rio Grande Valley on the Mexican border. Daddy was a teenager and hated leaving his beloved hometown of Piedmont, the only home he had known. Although he later came to love *El Valle*, at sixteen he'd run away from home, working on ranches in Texas and Oklahoma as a line rider, better known in lore as a cowboy. And I suspect that he had a relationship with his powerful father much like the one he later experienced with Laurence. Most of Daddy's brothers and sisters remained in McAllen or settled in San Antonio, where they raised their families and prospered moderately. One uncle became a US border patrolman in McAllen, a *migra*, as the Mexicans call that despised *tipo*. Daddy's oldest sister and her husband owned and operated a modest citrus orchard in McAllen, hiring Mexicans who crossed the border daily to work and returned home in the evening. Another uncle became a veterinarian like my grandfather, in San Antonio, and later moved to Oklahoma City; and yet another managed a Sears store in San Antonio. One of my older cousins became a local star as a country singer – Udell 'Dell' Dunbar – on the radio in San Antonio.

The Texas relatives were our 'rich' kin – that is, they had indoor plumbing, carpets and drapes, and new cars and pickups. They would trek back to Piedmont and stay with us, nostalgic for the old rural life, but they tired quickly of our primitive living conditions, especially the absence of plumbing, and would scurry back to their comfortable lives. Every November, Daddy made his pilgrimage alone back to south Texas to visit his mother and brothers and sisters, but mainly to hunt deer. He always came home with a buck tied to the hood of the car, our meat for Thanksgiving and Christmas feasts.

It was Thanksgiving 1950, when our family – except for Laurence who was in California – went south. The five of us crammed into Vera's new Ford (she left her husband at home). Our two days in San Antonio we went to the radio station to hear my cousin 'Dell' Dunbar singing live, dressed as if he were performing at the Grand Ole Opry, even though only his voice came over the airwaves. We also accompanied our relatives to a Church of Christ service, the church of my grandmother and several of her children. It was the first time for me inside that denomination. They allowed no musical instruments nor singing, and the men and women sat separately, following Paul's orders in the New Testament. I couldn't wait to get out of there.

But for me the big moment was when Daddy and Mama took me to northeast San Antonio, Culebra Street, to show me where I was born. The building that had been the feed store my grandmother owned was now a tavern. 'You can tell your friends you was born in a beer joint,' Daddy joked. Mama frowned.

I experienced strange sensations about the cold, rainy and, to me, ancient city I found myself in, the place of my birth. San Antonio was two centuries old, and strange with its crumbling Spanish buildings;

I had never seen anything more than sixty years old, so San Antonio scared me. And it seemed like a foreign city, with Spanish the language most heard on the streets, spoken by people who looked like the Indians in Oklahoma. When we visited the Alamo, I felt as if I were in another church of sorts, a monument to my Anglo-Saxon, Scotch-Irish ancestors who drove out the infidel savage Mexicans. I have to say that I did feel proud.

We drove to McAllen on the border, which, without ancient sites, seemed more familiar. And across the Rio Grande from McAllen was Reynosa. Except for the border that separated the two towns, they seemed to merge into each other. But crossing that bridge over the Rio Grande led to another world.

I had never been outside Oklahoma, in fact I had never been outside my county and the two counties adjacent to it in Oklahoma. I was an avid reader and knew a lot about faraway foreign places, but not Mexico. I expected it to be unfamiliar, of course, the language for sure. What I did not expect was the terror I felt walking down Reynosa's shabby main street.

We drove down the nearly empty, palm-lined wide main street of McAllen, and a few minutes later parked and walked along a narrow Reynosa street that teemed with people and animals. The unmuffled giant blue buses roared and belched diesel, parting the masses, leaving clouds of smoke and dust in their wake. Everyone, it seemed, was either buying or selling something, mostly food, chickens in every stage – from life to death to fully cooked – caramel and chocolate candy, corn on the cob dipped in fresh cream, tortillas, and all kinds of produce I had never seen before: mango, papaya, avocado, black beans, jalapeños, cactus. The vendors were mostly Indian-looking women wearing aprons, and the buyers were mostly Indian-looking women wearing aprons; the latter were maids for rich Americans, Vera whispered to me.

Chaos. It was my first experience of chaos. I'm certain I did not know the word at the time, and perhaps not having a word to describe the scene made it even more frightening. I wanted to leave, and my fears doubled when I noticed that my mother and father, by then in their early forties and married for twenty-five years, appeared much younger. Both of them laughed and bargained with the vendors, Daddy rattling away in Spanish, which I'd never heard him speak and did not know he could. They fit in and appeared happy together for the first time in my memory, but they seemed to have forgotten me. My fourteen-year-old brother Hank was dressed like the Cisco Kid from the black cowboy hat to black cowboy boots he'd bought when we stopped in Waco, and he strode confidently through the crowds, head and shoulders taller than anyone else.

Vera, my self-appointed protector, stayed by my side trying to explain things to me. She and Laurence had been there several times before I was born and she did not seem afraid.

'I want to leave,' I said to Vera, trying not to betray my fear.

'Are you choking up, Baby?' Vera asked.

Asthma. The second she mentioned it I began wheezing, my old friend/enemy on tap to get me out of a bad situation. Asthma is a real and life-threatening disease, but, I learned later, it can be triggered by stress. Vera ran to Mama and told her we would go to the car and wait. And there I sat, on the edge of the teeming chaos, waiting, wheezing.

That was the first time I remember being conscious that my asthma was part of how I dealt with problems and reality and it made me suspect that I might be a little bit crazy – 'tetched,' as we said. On the other hand, I felt a certain sense of pride, of having been blessed with special powers.

After returning from Texas, I began to have experiences such as knowing things before they happened. I recall the first time well. It was the night before Easter Sunday when I had a dream, and the next morning I heard that Travis Brown, my brother's best friend, had died. I had dreamed every detail except one – the identity of the dead man. In my dream the face was smashed and bloody, the car totaled, the place familiar, just down the road from the Bohemian Hall. I found out who had died a few hours later at breakfast on Easter Sunday morning. Daddy had come home from delivering papers at seven that morning. At three every Sunday morning he drove to Yukon to pick up bundles of the Sunday *Daily Oklahoman,* which he then delivered to all the subscribers in and around Piedmont. At the Brown farm he learned the bad news.

'There was ole Pop Floyd's marshal car in their driveway with its red light flashing,' Daddy said, 'I knew right then that something terrible was wrong and was thinking maybe it was about Travis, that he'd been in a fight over at that Bohemian Hall and landed in jail or the hospital. But then I seen Eula Brown or I heard her. You know how she's like the blamed Rock of Gibraltar, but she was yelling so that the dogs started to howling. Cleo, he just stood there shaking like he'd been struck by lightning.'

Daddy told us what Pop Floyd had reported. 'He said it musta been about three in the morning and raining hard. Travis had been carousing in the Bohemian Hall more than four hours, drinking and dancing. Maybe they'll close that danged joint down. Travis hit the creek bridge head-on, Pop Floyd says probably going a hundred miles an hour.'

Big tears rolled down Mama's cheeks as she listened to the story. 'Poor Eula, Jesus help her, poor Eula. I need to tell Laurence, it's going to break his heart.' She cranked the phone and asked the town operator to put through a call.

I stared at the uneaten biscuit and bacon on my plate, trying to block out remembering the dream, everything just as Daddy told it. I was sure my dream had caused Travis to die. Only God and Jesus knew about it, and only they could tell me what I might do not to kill again.

'Murderer,' Mama shrieked, and I was sure she had figured it out, but no, she was railing about the devil of drink and dancing that drew a beautiful boy into the den of iniquity, then cast him out into the storm. Satan was the murderer.

'Is Travis burning in hell, Mama?' I hadn't even thought about the fate of Travis's soul, only his permanent absence.

'I believe that boy made his peace with the Lord the second before dying. I believe the Lord forgave him. He was a good boy and Jesus knew that. I think Travis is in heaven.'

I excused myself and ran to the outhouse to vomit. I prayed to Jesus that he take Travis to heaven, explaining that it was my fault that he died, and that I would do whatever Jesus wanted to make up for it, if only he would save Travis from fire and brimstone.

The Wednesday after Easter they buried Travis Brown. The whole town crowded into the Baptist church to pay their respects to their favorite son, their golden boy. Then a caravan of cars led by the black hearse snaked for three miles northwest on the damp, dark red roads to Matthewson Cemetery. The mourners trudged quietly up the man-made hill, the only sound their footsteps crunching the red shale of the path and the wind singing in the cedar trees. A gray dome of receding rain clouds touched down on the horizon of flat red earth in every direction.

The funeral wasn't my first but the first one for a person I cared about. I was sad, and scared, certain I might slip and tell about the dream I had Saturday night, the night Travis died, his head broken and shattered. I thought it most likely that I had caused Travis Brown's car to swerve off the highway into a creekbed nose-first. Travis's handsome face was damaged beyond recognition, Mama said, and that was why the casket remained closed.

Travis was one grade behind Laurence, but they had been best friends ever since they started school, and also rivals. Laurence al-most always won because he was older, but after he left Travis soared, unchallenged. He was the town hero, a boy so handsome and per-fectly built, so polite and well behaved, so intelligent and amusing, that he was loved by everyone. He had been the only person who could cheer up Laurence when the dark cloud of anger engulfed him.

Travis was like another big brother, and his sister, Mary Jane, was in my grade and my best friend. At least once a week when I wasn't sick I would ride the school bus with Mary Jane to the Brown farm and stay all night. Travis never let up entertaining us with games and puzzles and tricks and stories and pranks, all the while doing his chores around the farm.

The Browns owned a 160-acre tract that had been in the family since Travis and Mary Jane's grandparents on their mother's side had homesteaded it in the Oklahoma Run in 1889. The Browns were from an old settler family like ours, but unlike us they still owned the land and made their living working it. They planted most of it in wheat to sell and the rest in alfalfa for cattle feed. They kept a dozen milk cows and a whole colony of hogs. Eula Brown's vegetable gar-den was one of the biggest around. They weren't rich, though; the Brown house was only four small rooms with no plumbing, but their barn was huge, with stables for cows and horses and a hayloft. It was a favorite place for us to play. Travis had secured a thick rope from the eaves above the hayloft and we would swing off the loft like Tarzan, landing in a pile of hay below.

I was going to miss Travis. I stood close to Mama, shivering in the spring wind. Nearly all the women and girls, including me, wore our Easter outfits. Mine was the yellow organdy Mama had ordered from Montgomery Ward, and last year's white ballerina-style slippers that were now too small and hurt my feet. I envied Mary Jane, sitting with her mother and father in the only chairs. If Mary Jane were to find out about my dream I knew I would lose my best friend.

Now Billy Bragg, the clubfooted preacher's son, blew 'Taps' on his trombone. Everyone in the Baptist preacher's family played an instrument, making a little family orchestra with piano, trombone, violin and xylophone. But now only the trombone filled the air. Tears brimmed in my eyes as the sad notes floated past me in the wind and seemed to echo off the prairie. Billy started playing 'Higher Ground,' and the preacher lifted his arms for us to sing along.

> Lord lift me up and let me stand
> By faith on heaven's table land
> A higher plane than I have found
> Lord plant my feet on higher ground

Mama whispered to me that Mrs. Brown had requested the song because it had been Travis's favorite hymn. Unlike Laurence, Travis had been a regular churchgoer.

Now I knew I had some sort of ability but did not know if it was a gift from God or the mark of the devil. I feared being discovered, for I was certain Mama and the preacher would think I was possessed by the devil. Then I learned to divine water. Despite the preacher's warning that only God could make miracles, invoking Exodus 20:4 against witching water – *Thou shalt not make unto thee any graven image, or any likeness of any thing that is in heaven above, or that is in the earth beneath, or that is in the water under the earth* – I took the risk. Everyone believed it was possible to witch water and ignored the preacher.

'Hold the sticks and relax. Don't look at the ground and try not to think about anything. Find a spot on the horizon and stare at it. Then walk slowly, holding the sticks angled to the ground.'

My second cousin Warren was teaching me how to find water with

witching sticks. He was my great-aunt Flossie's only child and had a
talent for witching water, so he started a well-drilling company and
was making money 'hand over fist,' as Daddy said, adding, 'Money
begets money,' meaning that Aunt Flossie had bought Warren his
drilling equipment and a truck for him to go into business.

That summer, Warren took me with him around the countryside
as he went about identifying places to drill. Finding water in western
Oklahoma was something of a miracle and Warren was considered a
sage at it. He had an idea that I might have the knack for witching
and could help him.

'How do the sticks know when there's water?' I asked when I saw
the sticks in Warren's hands cross and he marked a big X with white
chalk on the red shale. The sticks were just plain thin elm branches,
like long twigs. I thought witching sticks held some kind of magic.

'The sticks don't know nothing. It's your own mind that knows
and that's because your body knows. The human being is eighty
percent water and water attracts water. You let your body and mind
go and they'll know when there's water,' he said.

'But why do you need the sticks then? Why do they cross like
that?'

'It's my body makes them cross, just happens. Anybody can do it if
they just concentrate. Trouble is, people got too much on the mind.'

Warren was a big dark man, good-looking like Cary Grant. But
unlike the other big boys in town he had never played ball and hated
everything about horses and rodeos. When he was young, and a rich
only child, the other boys called him a sissy. Now he was twenty-four
and a bachelor still living with Aunt Flossie in the big white house
down the street from ours. Uncle Guy had died the year before.
Warren didn't have many friends and some of the town kids were
scared of him. But I liked him. He always gave me candy and I liked
him more that summer he decided to teach me how to witch water.

'You can do it, you got the knack for concentration, probably you
being sick so much and all,' he said.

His words thrilled me. Again I realized that my asthma could be an
advantage, that weakness could be a strength, that I was special in a
good way. All it had meant before was that I couldn't play ball or play
hard at anything or ride horses.

I concentrated. We were out on a red shale rise near a neighboring town, on the acreage of some farmer I didn't know who had hired Warren to witch and then drill. It was a hot July morning, and still. Warren said it had to be still to witch and there weren't many days without hard wind. The early morning hours were best, before the wind woke up and descended like a fury.

I stared at the horizon where a green alfalfa field began and found my spot. There was a jersey cow over there. I picked a brown spot on its side hoping it wouldn't move, and I walked stiff-legged, the tips of the sticks about three inches from the ground. Warren stood perfectly still. The only sounds were crickets chattering and the crunch of shale under my sandals.

A funny thing happened to my vision as I stared at the brown spot on the cow. It was as if that spot became the whole world and I was inside it, a vast reddish-brown space not much different from the land, but there was nothing else there. I forgot what I was doing and as if in a trance I walked slowly as I would blindfolded to pin the tail on the donkey.

I felt the sticks tug on my arms, tugging them downwards. It was the smallest motion but jolted me back to life.

'Bingo! You did it, Roxie.'

Warren took out his chalk and marked a big X on the red shale. A week later he struck water drilling on that very spot and treated me to a ride to the City. I never went out witching with Warren again because I was entering my teen years and thought of that phase as juvenile, and Warren himself married a lovely woman from the City who took me under her wing, and she discouraged the practice of witching.

I always hungered to go to Oklahoma City and took every opportunity to do so. Once or twice each summer, while Daddy was at work driving the truck, Mama would take Hank and me to the City. She was afraid of driving in traffic, so we'd leave the car at the crossroads of the Piedmont Road and the Northwest Highway and flag down the Greyhound with 'New York' on the front coming from the west; the ones going west said 'Los Angeles.' I loved the refrigerated bus with its overstuffed seats and tiny toilets in the back and dreamed of going to the ends of both routes. Riding high above the highway thrilled me, like being in Daddy's gasoline truck but without the heat and fumes and noise. The bus dropped us at the shopping center on the northwest edge of the City where there was a C.R. Anthony clothes store and a Kress variety store. Those trips were kept secret from Daddy and were supposedly for the purpose of buying Toni permanents, Jergens lotion, and sewing things for my mother – really only an excuse for going to the City.

And there was one special occasion every August that took us to the City – the state fair. Hank would take his best ewe or ram to show off and try for prize money. We stayed with Mama's sister, who lived in a mobile home not far from the fairgrounds. One year the state fair was more special than usual. Always there was a Saturday night program that cost extra and Daddy would never let us go. But that year the Weavers were to perform. My father and everyone else loved their hit song, 'Goodnight Irene.'

'Sometimes I live in the country, sometimes I live in town, sometimes I take a great notion to jump in the river an' drown,' Daddy sang while cleaning his gun or tinkering with the car engine.

For once Daddy took us to the show. The summer night was soft and warm. I felt wrapped in velvet sitting in the outdoor coliseum. I had never seen so many people in one place. But they were familiar, country people just like us. Daddy said that city people didn't go in for the state fair because they didn't like animals. The men and boys wore overalls, the women and girls feed-sack dresses. Some of the teenaged boys wore crisp blue jeans, and all the men over sixteen wore freshly blocked straw hats, it being summer – in winter they would wear blocked felt hats. From up high where we sat, there was a sea of straw hats all around the stadium.

The stage was far, far away so when the three men and one woman of the Weavers came out they looked like people on television. But the sound was loud and clear, unlike television or radio. The Weavers sang a long time and ended with 'Goodnight Irene.' The tall, skinny banjo player named Pete Seeger invited the audience to sing along and we did, over and over, into the inky night. 'Goodnight Irene, goodnight Irene, I'll see you in my dreams.'

Little did we know then that 'Goodnight Irene' was written by a black Louisiana convict, Huddie Ledbetter (Leadbelly), and was being sung by people who would soon be blacklisted as communists.

Partly due to this rise and fall of the Weavers, among other experiences, I began confusing fallen women and communists and Satan, and they all seemed somewhat preferable to the supposed God-fearing pillars of the community. Darla was a case in point.

Just recently Vernon Rose died at age seventy. My father sent me the obituary, as he always does when someone from Piedmont dies. That is the main reason for communication between us. I read the obituary carefully, remembering Darla, Vernon's first wife. There is no mention of Darla in the obituary, although their children, Mary Alice and Virgil, are listed among Vernon's survivors. But in the long obituary, eight years of Vernon's life are missing, the years between his senior year at Piedmont, when he eloped with Darla, up to his second marriage, which lasted until his death. I hadn't known what happened to Vernon, but the obituary said that he had been a pillar of the community in a nearby larger town, owning a prosperous hardware store, serving as a Baptist deacon and president of the Chamber of Commerce and Kiwanis Club, among a dozen community activities.

When Darla Cross and Vernon Rose ran away to get married in Arkansas – where the legal marriage age was sixteen as opposed to eighteen in Oklahoma – it was a big scandal in Piedmont. But I thought they were another Romeo and Juliet. I had read the Shakespeare story. Darla and Vernon didn't die, though, but it turned out about that bad.

The couple came back home after they eloped and lived with his parents out west of Piedmont, farming. The town women even gave Darla a wedding shower. I couldn't imagine Darla as a farmer's wife. Darla was petite but with a figure out of a movie magazine, like a smaller Jane Russell. She showed off her figure by wearing tight sweaters cinched with a wide belt. Her hair was long and black, coarse like a horse's mane, and always wild. I thought she was like the famous literary horse, Black Beauty. Her eyes were green like a cat's, like Vivian Leigh as Scarlett O'Hara. She wore heavy pancake makeup and bright red lipstick. What I liked most about her was that she had dark skin like me. Some people said she had Mexican or Indian in her, some said Gypsy. When I listened to Hank Snow's 'Mexicali Rose' I thought of Darla.

Even though she was sexier and flashier than any other girl in school, Darla's family belonged to the strictest church around there, the Free Methodists. Her parents were very old and probably never knew how Darla looked at school because she changed on the bus and in the bathroom at school, then changed back to go home. Everybody knew about it and some of the other high school girls did the same thing.

Darla was popular. Not only was she basketball queen, crowned by Vernon, the basketball captain, but she played a mean game of girl's basketball herself, as a fast, sharp-shooting guard. Darla and Vernon were two years older than Laurence and seemed like royalty in our little school. Every chance I got I spied on them at recess and in the halls, holding hands, stealing kisses. There was no doubt in my mind that Darla was the most beautiful girl in the world.

Why they eloped was a much-discussed mystery. I heard Mama and my aunt whispering that probably Darla was 'in trouble,' but the months passed and there was no baby. I would see Darla with her mother-in-law when they came into town to buy groceries on Saturdays. Darla was still beautiful but the tight sweaters were replaced with print house dresses, her hair was cut short, and the makeup was gone.

Then Darla and Vernon surprised everyone by adopting a little boy they named Virgil. I overheard Mama saying to my aunt that she thought Darla couldn't have babies because she had got rid of the one she eloped for, and that's why she adopted a child. I didn't fully understand what she was talking about. Virgil was two when they got him from the Baptist orphanage in the City. He had a shock of bright red hair and the bluest eyes. Darla said she just fell in love with him on a visit to the orphanage.

But then only a few months after little Virgil came to live with them Darla got pregnant. Mary Alice was born before Virgil turned three.

'Darla took them kids and flew the coop. Old man Felker says Vernon was beating her and she went and ran off,' Daddy reported one Sunday morning after he'd finished his paper route.

'Lordy be, I can't believe it. He seemed like such a good boy, that Vernon,' Mama said.

Darla was gone. Both the Rose and the Cross families were tight-lipped about what had happened. The whole affair from elopement to two kids to Darla running off took less than two years. But soon

Darla reappeared in town to go to church and visit her parents on Sundays, and she let Vernon's family see the kids. No one knew for sure what was going on but there were rumors that Vernon wanted Darla back. He kept on farming and some people thought he might kill himself for losing Darla. But Darla didn't go back to Vernon and he didn't try to kill himself.

Darla became a beautician in Oklahoma City, working in a salon in the shopping center on the northwest edge of town where Mama would take Hank and me. We would go over and visit with Darla. She was back in tight sweaters, with wild hair and makeup and lipstick, and just as stunning as before she married Vernon.

Our lives became intertwined for some time. When Virgil was about five and I was ten, Darla and Mama made a deal that Virgil would stay with us that summer. Darla put little Mary Alice with her grandmother. Darla said she wanted the kids to be in the country and not home with babysitters. That arrangement turned out to last for three summers, until Darla married Oliver, the bald old man who owned the beauty parlor where she worked. Oliver drove a black Cadillac Fleetwood with pushbutton windows and air conditioning. He owned several businesses in the city and some oil wells. My father always referred to him as a 'sugar daddy.'

I did not particularly welcome little Virgil in our home. I was long accustomed to being the spoiled baby, and I hated the attention Mama gave him. She doted on Virgil and plied him with candy and toys, which Darla paid for. Poor little boy: most of them ended up in my possession. For once I got a taste of the power of being an older sibling. I was merciless, yet the little guy adored me and looked up to me, which made me even more tyrannical. Daddy was mean to him, too, mainly playing tricks and teasing him about being a city boy.

Virgil had the palest skin I'd ever seen and he couldn't be out in the sun for more than ten minutes without burning beet red. He reminded me of a white rabbit. Daddy got him a straw hat that was too big and slipped over his eyes, but he loved that hat. The clothes Darla brought out were crisp new shorts and fancy little suits and ties and white shirts, and shiny leather shoes. Daddy bought Virgil some bib overalls and cowboy boots and he loved them.

After Darla married Oliver they moved into a small house not far from the beauty shop. Before that, Darla and the children had lived in a room in the back of the beauty parlor. I became an on-call babysitter for them. They would come out in the Cadillac to get me on Saturday and take me back on Sunday. Darla still worked in the beauty shop, and I spent Saturdays with her watching the kids while she worked. She still had her little room and bath there, and the kids and I would watch television.

I spent a lot of time in that beauty shop with Darla, and she would give me money to take the kids to the drugstore next door to buy comics and candy, and money to buy whatever I wanted for myself. She always did that when a man came in the shop. I knew what a prostitute was and guessed what 'pimp' meant because I had read *From Here to Eternity* – secretly, of course. I guessed that she was doing tricks in the back room and that Oliver knew about it and took part of the money. For reasons I don't understand I wasn't shocked, probably because I liked Darla, and I admired the prostitute in *From Here to Eternity*. But I never told Mama or anyone else what Darla was up to.

On Saturday nights, Darla and Oliver always went out. There was a movie theater a block away from their house and Oliver would give me money to take the kids to the movies and for popcorn and Cokes. Oliver and Darla returned in the early morning hours, sometimes after the sun was up. They were invariably drunk and fighting when they came in and it usually ended in blows that woke me. I would lie wide awake and still, hoping the children wouldn't wake up. On Sunday mornings I would sometimes find Darla still dressed up, in the kitchen fixing breakfast for the kids, and with one or two black eyes. She never talked about it.

One Sunday morning at Darla's, she called me into the bathroom and asked me to unzip her dress in the back. I did and before I could get away she turned toward me and shed her bra and out fell big foam falsies. Darla was as flat-chested as a boy. I stared and she laughed.

'Men are easy to fool, Roxie. They don't care if it's real or false long as they can show you off,' she said. She liked the song 'It Wasn't God Who Made Honky Tonk Angels,' Kitty Wells's answer to Hank Thompson, who sang, 'I didn't know God made honky-tonk angels.'

Darla seemed confident, but prostitution even in Oklahoma was fraught with danger. I realized that while I was working for her, when they found a woman's head down by the creek south of Piedmont. Some young couple I didn't know from Yukon, out late on a Saturday night, were necking in his pickup when they decided to take a blanket and find a nice spot under the full moon to smooch. On their way back, they crossed the dry creek bed and the girl stumbled over what she thought was a rock. She fell down and twisted her ankle. Lying on the rough shale she found herself face to face with a woman's head. The young couple ran in horror and reported the find to Pop Floyd. The next day Pop Floyd called for a citizen's posse to search for other parts of the body.

My brother and I and two cousins monitored the activity all the next day as they searched. Every time Pop Floyd caught sight of us he yelled, 'Get out of here, you tykes – this ain't no job for chillun.' Like all the kids we were scared to death of Pop Floyd, and we scrambled away but found new hiding spots to watch from. I was nervous about rattlesnakes because we were crouching in the tall jimson grass. We usually ran fast through the grass in summer but now my curiosity triumphed over fear.

The searchers didn't find anything that first day but sometime later a hunter found a left hand when his dog went to pick up the dead squirrel he'd just shot and came back with the hand in its jaws. With that hand and the teeth they tried to find out who the woman was but couldn't. An artist made a drawing based on the head and put it in the newspapers. The drawing showed a pretty blonde woman. They said her eyes were cornflower blue and her hair was natural blonde but peroxided even blonder. They thought she was no more than twenty years old. The hand didn't have a ring on, so what with the bleached hair and no wedding ring, they decided she had been a prostitute and was probably murdered by a man who took her out. I wondered what Nancy Drew would think of that. It seemed to me if the woman had a ring the murderer might have stolen it, and maybe she had a husband that had killed her. But mainly I thought of Darla and how she might end up that way.

After the authorities had decided that the dead woman was a prostitute who had sold her body and probably deserved to get killed and cut up, the search was called off. The newspaper said no one had come forward to report a missing woman, which they said corroborated the police theory that the woman was a prostitute, probably from Texas. Anyway, the newspaper said, the police couldn't go around identifying women's body parts or they wouldn't get anything else done, because they were always finding body parts of women like that.

The Baptist preacher warned us in his sermons that summer that we might find body parts and shouldn't go near the creekbed where the head and hand had been found. He was always griping that the kids in town ran too wild, and he looked straight at my mother when he said it. It was well known that Mama was always taking a horde of kids out to search for buried treasure. Mama told us stories about bandits and cowboys on the Chisholm Trail, stories Daddy had told her, and, long before that, about Coronado's soldiers who had crossed through there (I'm not sure how she knew about that). Mama was convinced that there must be gold and jewels hidden somewhere or just interesting things that those long-ago people had lost, like jewels and gold watches stolen by bandits or, from the Spanish era, a golden cross, a jewel-laden spiked helmet or a silver stirrup. We never came up with any of those items in our searches but we didn't mind; we were thrilled by Mama's stories about bandits and cowboys and Spanish soldiers and forgot about really finding buried treasure.

The preacher railed: 'One day, mark my word, one of your children will find a small box and in that box will be a finger of that devil woman and that child will be cursed. Don't let your children go gallivanting about and, children, do not ever open strange boxes.'

His words terrified me: *A finger in a box.* I could not imagine anything scarier than that. Mama changed our area of search for treasure to the north side of town but I was still afraid.

After that I felt more a hostage than a participant in our treasure searches.

'You are going whether you like it or not,' Mama said.

'I don't want to,' I said.

'You're not sick. You run around in those fields just fine with Hank,' she said.

'That's different,' I said.

Sometimes Mama won and sometimes I succeeded in not going treasure hunting, but in either case I never really won. Mama had a chart in her mind and on that chart she dispensed black marks and gold marks, which she said God in heaven was keeping account of, and she actually said, 'You get a gold mark,' or 'You get a black mark' and kept track of our scores in her notebook. She said that when the roll was called up yonder, God would have that list and judge us accordingly. She quoted from Revelation 20: ... *and the books were opened, which is the book of life: and the dead were judged out of those things which were written in the books, according to their works ... And whosoever was not found written in the book of life was cast into the lake of fire.*

I always received a black mark if I refused to go treasure hunting with my mother and the other kids, but even if I went I chalked up at least one black mark, if not several, for my attitude. The other children who trailed Mama into the fields to look for treasure also received her marks, but nearly always gold ones. Hank never received black marks and he easily got out of going treasure hunting so he could practice shooting baskets.

My resistance to Mama's excursions galled her, somehow as though I was judging them and her. I think I had never really liked the game, and now I was afraid of what I might find. I remember knowing that the excursions were for Mama, not for me, not for the other kids, although they greatly enjoyed sharing the experience. How I hated to pretend I was having fun, going ooh and ah. The other kids from town adored Mama and her games. I became bored and angry and sulky. I was by then into my teens and rebelling and surely this upset Mama, who had been my greatest idol for years. A few years later my father would accuse me of driving Mama to drinking because of my behavior. And maybe it was so.

'You better straighten up, Roxie.' Mama grabbed my thin arm hard and twisted. 'I mean it.' Her eyes were fierce, full of anger.

'I'm not doing anything wrong,' I said.

I had found a protected crevice in a gulch and squirmed into it. I wasn't sick and not really hiding. Mama and the kids were busy counting white chalk formations on the red shale walls of the gulch and I could hear them yelling out numbers. Mama claimed to be keeping track in her head and the winner was to get a gold mark. But I knew it was rigged, that she would choose her favorite kid of the day to award. I knew I couldn't win no matter how hard I tried because she would never bestow a gold mark on me. I think it was Mama's way of trying to teach me to be competitive and probably she thought she was acting for my own good. Unfortunately, this kind of normal conflict between mother and daughter would never be transcended, as it had been with Vera.

'Let go, you're hurting me,' I whined. Tears welled in my eyes as the pain in my arm became unbearable.

'You get out there with the others,' she said. She let go of me and stalked away. I sulkily trailed behind, hating her, hating the God who was recording my behavior in heaven, according to my mother's reports.

Dorothy and Donna, who were sisters, one a year older and one a year younger than me, won that day and many other times. Their father, like mine, drove an oil truck – Sinclair, not Mobil – and they too were poor. But they were fair-haired and cute, especially Dorothy, whose blonde curls were thick and wavy. I sat behind her in school from first to seventh grade, until she jumped ahead to ninth grade, which was high school at the other end of the building. I would stare at that hair, longing to have it, longing to have her freckles and even to wear glasses like she did. Mama always held Dorothy up to me as the model daughter I should aspire to be. Dorothy herself was always nice to me, and I played with her and her sister in their attic room for hours on end. But I was jealous of Dorothy. I wanted to be the kind of girl my mother wanted.

However much my mother tried to distance herself from me, I was the only one in the world who witnessed much of Mama's secret life. Mama was a snoop and that embarrassed me terribly. She found every imaginable excuse to go inside people's houses and invade social affairs to which she was not invited. When she won the census-taking job when I was eleven, the opportunities were vast. And when she started writing her newspaper columns she had an even better excuse for crashing private showers and bridge parties. Maybe her probing was more than nosiness and she wanted to educate me about how people unlike us lived, especially the local rich people.

My mother was not what you'd call socialized. For the first sixteen years of her life before she married, she had seen only extreme poverty, even as a foster child. Poor families signed up to take in foster children (then as now) because they received money from the county for it, and needed the labor of the children. Mama just couldn't get enough of how the rich lived and tried to expose me to it, not as a criticism or warning but, on the contrary, I think to inspire me to find a place in that better world. For all her belief in the golden gates and a better place beyond, I think she wanted her kids to find the beyond in real life.

The house Mama most wanted to see was south of Piedmont a few miles. James Schmidt, the richest man in Yukon, owned a whole section there that he called his 'farm,' although no known farming went on. He was already seventy when I started the first grade in Piedmont, and was the self-made entrepreneur we were all told to emulate. He was born in Prague under the Austro-Hungarian empire, his family overland merchants. They emigrated to the United States when he was a boy and his family made the 1889 Oklahoma Run, winning a homestead near Yukon. He must have had a natural head for business, for he soon established the largest independent flour mill in the Southwest in Yukon, then organized Yukon's first bank, then bought up half of the town over the next few years.

But Mama was not particularly interested in the Schmidt mansion in Yukon; the one she wanted to get inside was his country home just outside Piedmont, that house nestled down on the creek in the woods so it was invisible from the Piedmont–Yukon highway, the house surrounded by an electrified chain-link fence and gate.

There was no way Mama could just barge into that house as she did other houses, like the one built by the Yukon dentist, our dentist. It was the first 'California-style' split-level house in Oklahoma, so reported the Sunday paper. One day she gathered up Hank and me and drove directly there. We walked up to the door and she rang the door bell. The dentist's wife, an attractive blonde with two toddlers hanging onto her skirt, opened the door. Mama said, 'Good morning, we came to see your beautiful home,' and just went right on in, me trailing behind. Amazingly, the dentist's wife became a hostess, offering Mama coffee and Hank and me soda pop, and she took us on a tour of the whole house. I left still confused about the difference between a two-story house and a split-level one; the only difference apparent to me was that the split-level house was a glass house that could easily be shattered in a bad storm.

What everyone in Piedmont knew about the mysterious place near our town was that the rich man kept his mistress there, and that was what interested Mama. No one had ever seen Miss Stuart in person

but she was known to be his mistress. As a Catholic he could not
divorce his wife, so he kept Miss Stuart sequestered in that house
nobody ever visited.

To this day I do not know how Mama gained entrance to that
house but I remember the visit vividly. I must have been twelve at the
time. Mama was already writing her columns, so probably she simply
called Miss Stuart on the phone and talked her into letting us in.
Mama's favorite Bible saying was Acts 10:34: 'God is no respecter of
persons,' meaning that no one is any better than anyone else whatever their station in life. As a graduate student in the mid-sixties I was
taken by Jacques Lacan's observation that a man who thinks he is a
king is crazy, but a king who thinks he is a king is even crazier,
recognizing it as Mama's folk philosophy. She was no respecter of
important personages.

There was a phone intercom at the electrified gate to Schmidt's
estate. Mama announced who she was and the gate magically
opened. She drove our beat-up pickup down the gravel road for
about half a mile, and there it was, the forbidden house, a rambling,
beautiful natural stone structure, one story high, and large enough to
have occupied a full block in Piedmont. Miss Stuart stood at the door
to greet us. A black Lincoln sat in the driveway.

I was shocked seeing Miss Stuart. When Mama explained to me
that she was a 'kept woman,' and I'd heard others speak of her that
way, I imagined a sexy movie star like Jean Harlow. But the woman
who welcomed us into her home was old, old enough to be my
grandmother. Her hair had that blue tinge of well-off older women.
Her face was wrinkled. She had spent her entire adult life, thirty-five
years, as that rich man's mistress. Later, when I read Steinbeck's *East
of Eden*, I connected the errant mother with Miss Stuart.

Mama didn't seem impressed or surprised by anything we saw
there or what Miss Stuart had to say. Being a natural-born investiga-
tive reporter, she already had Miss Stuart nailed just to gain entrance
to the house where she was kept and where no person other than
Schmidt was known to have entered.

Miss Stuart was the perfect hostess during our two-hour visit. She
treated Mama and me with utmost respect, giving us a tour of the
dozens of rooms with their plush, off-white wall-to-wall carpets and
velvet sofas and chairs, the color scheme being shades of cream to

dark brown. Then she settled us in the living room, a remarkable place. There was a man-made lake and the entire wall of the living room was glass and faced the lake, the water sloshing against the glass. I spent nearly the whole hour there trying to figure out why the house didn't float away.

I listened carefully to their conversation. I am amazed even now how Mama could get people talking; she would have made a great psychiatrist. The best-known gossip mongers in print and on the radio at the time – Louella Parsons, Hedda Hopper and Walter Winchell – were great in Mama's eyes.

'What is he like, really like, you know?' Mama asked Miss Stuart.

'He is sweet, the most gentle man in the world. I know some would condemn him for maintaining two families, but he never lies to his wife or to me. He is a great man,' said Miss Stuart.

'What is that helmet on the wall there? It looks like a conquistador helmet,' Mama said.

'That is an exact replica in pure sterling of Kaiser Wilhelm's helmet. You know he was a great admirer of the Kaiser and opposed America's entry into the Great War against him,' Miss Stuart said.

Mama went on and on with her questioning, and Miss Stuart spilled out her heart about how hard it was to be only a mistress to the only man she had ever loved. And so my mother even got in to see the kept woman of one of the county's richest citizens.

My mother respected poor girls who 'made good,' like Miss Stuart or Darla or my sister Vera. Just as Shirley Temple's image had haunted my older sister's childhood, Anita Bryant's haunted mine. Later, of course, both became better known for their politics, but during my childhood they were the models of what every mother seemed to want her daughter to be. This was true even among African-American girls my age, I was surprised to discover while reading former Black Panther leader Elaine Brown's memoir, *A Taste of Power.*

I knew Anita Bryant was the girl Mama wanted instead of skinny, sickly me, and she tried her best to remake me into Anita. Tap dancing lessons or even tap shoes were out of the question financially, but perhaps my hair could be curled and, if Mama could get me to eat, dimples might appear. Alas, my straight hair refused to hold a curl and my body rejected heavy food.

How did I know about Anita Bryant and Ronald Reagan in my

isolated condition? My Aunt Flossie purchased the first TV set in town, a huge console with a tiny screen. On Saturday evenings she allowed our family and some other relatives in town to invade her spotless living room to sit on the floor to watch *GE Theater,* hosted by Reagan, and *Sooner Shindig,* a local show starring Anita Bryant. I adored the handsome, amiable, silver-tongued Reagan, who was Daddy's age, and the dimpled, curly-locks Anita, who was my age. The heroes Laurence had given me, Belle Starr and Billy the Kid, were replaced by rich and proper heroes who wouldn't live by the gun and die young.

'Didn't you have any good female role models?' my daughter asked me once when I shocked her with the information that I had nearly worshiped Anita Bryant.

I told my daughter about certain teachers, and women who smoked in public, and the wild women living and dead I had admired. Then I remembered Aunt Ella, the one real living woman who showed me that a girl could grow up and be or do anything she wished without killing anyone or becoming a prostitute.

Aunt Ella was not my blood relation, but the wife of my mother's oldest full brother. My uncle was posted in the Aleutian Islands off Alaska when he died, a lifer and officer in the army, and close to retirement. Aunt Ella and their two young sons were living in Whittier, in south central Los Angeles, in the home they owned. Left a widow in her mid-thirties, she never married again. She raised her boys and also took in Laurence when he came to Los Angeles after graduating from high school. Aunt Ella raised two sons and, once her boys were in college, sold her house and bought a VW bus. That's when I first met her.

In that prehippie–era bus, Ella installed a narrow bed, a pedal Singer sewing machine and a typewriter, and she spent many of the following years crisscrossing the continent, a woman alone, visiting relatives and camping in her favorite national parks.

Fortunately for me, Aunt Ella chose to stop at our place for a week or so every summer for several years when I was a teenager. To me, she was a beautiful and exotic woman, and I was certain that she was a magician or some kind of positive otherworldly persona. She had waist-length, shiny auburn hair (with the help of henna), which she kept in tied-up French braids during the day, but let down at night.

She allowed me to brush her silky hair at bedtime using her sterling silver hairbrush, for me a privilege and an ecstatic experience.

While I brushed Aunt Ella's hair, she told me stories about faraway places where she and my uncle had been based during his army career. She told me mainly about a beautiful tropical island called Hawaii, about its tragic history, about the violent overthrow by the US government of its native queen, and about the beautiful and hospitable native Hawaiians.

Only recently I learned from Aunt Ella's granddaughter that Aunt Ella had been what then, during the McCarthy era, was called a 'comsymp' or 'fellow traveler,' because of her outspoken adherence to the ideals of humanistic socialism. Maybe I absorbed some of those ideas from her; I already had plenty from my father's stories of my Wobbly grandfather. But what I remember Aunt Ella for was her brazen independence. Not until I was through with two marriages, in my late twenties, would I discover the thrill of self-sufficiency and independence, and I've never been willing to give it up for anything else advertised as good for women since.

Eight

Becoming a Girl

us men don't have to
look no certain way

like a woman does …
you take Buck Owens
why he looks just right

if you put that face on a woman
they'd run her out of town

WILMA ELIZABETH MCDANIEL,
from 'K-Mart Sage'

'Please don't wreck it or Mama will whip me,' Prissy whined.

'I'm not going to hurt your precious bicycle,' I assured her.

'You don't even know how to ride,' she said, gulping a sob.

'Do too,' I said.

But she was right. I was twelve years old and had never ridden a bicycle. Prissy's was the first one in town. She was ten and tiny, an only child and only grandchild, doted on by them all. I liked her mountains of new dolls and toys that she let me play with.

The bicycle Prissy got for her birthday was the biggest toy of all and I intended to learn how to ride. It was a small girl's bike, a shiny royal blue. I had watched Prissy being taught by her father to balance and pedal and was confident I would learn fast.

I took a deep breath, mounted, my feet dangling on the ground because the bike was too short for me, and I mumbled a quick prayer for Jesus to keep me and the bike upright. And I took off slowly, wobbly, but I kept going and it became easier, smoother. I was a natural-born bike rider.

'Where you taking it?' Prissy squealed after me.

'To Meyer's for a pop – meet me there,' I yelled into the wind.

It was approximately four city blocks to the store and slightly downhill from Prissy's house. The bike picked up speed and soon I was sailing through the hot summer wind. It was my first experience of my body moving free and fast and singular. As I neared Meyer's store it dawned on me that I had no idea how to stop. Peddling backwards did not cross my mind as a possibility. Taking my feet off the pedals slowed it down but not much. My mind raced as I got closer to my destination and I made a decision: I would run into something to stop. I wasn't going very fast when I turned the bike toward the brick wall of Meyer's and hit it head on.

The bike wasn't badly damaged, just some dents that Daddy was able to hammer out before Prissy took the bike home. And I suffered no more than a skinned elbow and knee and shin. But after that Prissy refused to let me touch her bike and Mama told me to leave the child alone.

So began my campaign to acquire my own bicycle, an impossibly expensive item. Hank wanted one, too, so we begged and begged. One day Daddy came home with what looked like a bunch of junk, but, when sorted out, constituted the parts and wheels required to construct two bicycles. Daddy could make anything or fix anything. He had searched junkyards until he found all the necessary parts, and with his tools and welding iron and rubber patches and some silver paint he created two perfectly workable, but extremely ugly, bicycles. Hank's was really tall with a bar across the top. Mine was shorter and without the bar but my feet couldn't touch the ground when I sat on the seat. It didn't matter.

Hank and I were whirling dervishes on wheels. For the first time I could keep up with my brother. We perfected daredevil tricks from standing up on the seat to riding backwards and we rarely ever touched the handlebars. That bike of mine was fast and smooth, perfectly balanced, and I didn't care a bit that it was ugly. New bicycles started turning up all over town that summer, and Daddy even made a couple more for our cousins who couldn't afford them, but none matched mine for speed.

Jenny Lou Shannon, the richest kid in town, being the granddaughter of old James Shannon, who owned one of the stores and a lot of wheat land, got the slickest new bike but she always wanted to ride

mine. We traded bikes a lot although I preferred my old nag. Jenny
Lou was a year younger than me, so I had no trouble talking her into
forming a girl's bicycle club. I don't recall why we excluded boys or if
it was their choice not to be in a club with girls. Eight girls including
Prissy gathered in the shade of the Methodist Church steps across
from my house to found our club. I was elected president by accla-
mation and Jenny Lou was the treasurer, her task being to get money
for us from her grandfather. But as president and oldest I insisted on
keeping the money and records.

What we had was the kernel of a girl's gang. We were inseparable
that summer and ran wild, or rode wild. I suppose our mothers
tolerated our all-day absences, relieved that we kept our distance
from the boys. We didn't even think of boys except to challenge them
to races, which I always won.

Since Piedmont had only one block of paved street and we were
forbidden to ride on the nearby highway, we perfected dirt-biking.
We even rode across rough shale countryside. The new bikes began
falling apart and Daddy was forever fixing them, making them uglier
and uglier with welded spots. He patched our tires until they were
mostly patches and pumped them with air with his tire pump. But
my bike never broke down.

I was always the leader on our rides – all the other girls had to
imitate whatever I did. When I let go of the handlebars and folded
my arms, they were supposed to do the same but not one of them
ever succeeded without crashing. Besides me only Hank could do
that trick.

Toward the end of summer, I had accumulated about twenty dollars in dues and quarter contributions from Jenny Lou's grandfather.
And Jenny Lou and I put on a carnival in her yard that made a few
dollars. Without discussing my idea with the members I decided to
invest the money. I had found an advertisement in *The Farmer Stockman* for rosewater-and-glycerine salve, a treatment for aching muscles. My idea was to buy twenty dollars' worth of the ointment for the
members to sell in town. I figured that with a hundred tins of salve
we could triple our treasury. That way, I reckoned, we could buy new
tires and other parts and paint for our bikes, and we could offer prize
money for competitions.

Maybe I thought I couldn't convince the others of my scheme, or maybe I thought I didn't need their permission, for by then I was reigning queen and dictator of the bicycle club and none of them ever challenged my decisions and orders.

I bought a money order at the post office and sent off for the salve. I made sure I was the one to pick up the mail every day so I didn't tell my mother or anyone else. I planned to get the tins and distribute them to the girls and we would fan out to sell them.

'What is this, Roxie Amanda Dunbar?'

I could tell Mama was mad when she used my whole name. She stood in the middle of the living room with a square box in her hands.

'That's for the bicycle club,' I said.

I had picked up the box early that morning and hid it under my bed. I planned to take it to the bicycle club meeting scheduled for that afternoon, at a time when Mama took her nap every day.

But it was not to be. After extracting the whole story from me Mama marched me to the post office and made me watch her mail the box back to its source. Then she went to the meeting with me and made me tell the story and apologize and promise to pay back the twenty dollars and resign.

'Storying is one thing and thieving another. There'll be none of that in this house.' Those were Mama's last words on the subject and the end of the club. I still rode my bike everywhere, but the others quit and their bikes rusted in their yards. Even Hank abandoned his for rodeoing. I missed my bicycle club.

Soon I too abandoned my bike and tomboy ways in an attempt to become a proper girl. Then there were the usual crushes on boys, one after another, none of them from our town. First came Don Shannon, a grandson of old man Shannon. Don was four years older than me, in Piedmont for the summer to learn to be a butcher. He paid no attention to me. Then there was my first real boyfriend, Billy. I met him at the skating rink.

Every kid in Piedmont caught roller-skating fever, already a national craze. The place where we skated was at the Edmond National Guard armory, which turned into a giant skating rink on Saturdays. It was free, and Hank and I and our cousins next door would ride to Edmond with Daddy and spend the whole day roller-skating. Most of the kids at the skating rink were children of Edmond poor whites, some from the tar-paper shanty town nearby. I didn't know how to roller-skate when I first started going and one little boy a year younger than me took upon himself the job of teaching me. Billy was a virtuoso skater but a wild boy. He was Irish Catholic and had nine brothers and sisters who lived with their mother on welfare in the shanty town. He didn't know what had happened to his father. He confided in me that he had stolen his skates.

'From the hardware store?' I asked, impressed.

'Naw, off a rich kid,' he said.

One time Billy and his big brother arrived in Piedmont on horses to visit me. That's when Mama put her foot down: 'Stay away from white trash like that Billy Hinkley.' And I minded her.

I formed a new crush immediately and forgot about Billy. Daddy was president of the Piedmont rodeo club, and the club officers met at our house all that fall and winter to plan the spring rodeos. One of the new officers Daddy recruited was a Texan who worked at Deer Creek, the SOHIO refinery between Piedmont and Edmond. That oil worker, Sam Black, had a sixteen-year-old son, Michael, who came along with his dad to the meetings. I fell in love with Michael Black the instant I laid eyes on him.

It was one of those getting-dark-early evenings in the fall when they came to the first meeting. Michael was the best-looking boy I'd ever seen. He was tall and slim, and wore all black, including his cowboy boots and a perfectly blocked black Stetson. I could almost imagine him as a gunfighter with a silver-inlaid gunbelt and a pearl handled revolver, silver spurs on his boots. He did have a silver buckle on his wide black belt. Michael reminded me of my then-favorite singer, Lefty Frizzell, whose 'If You've Got the Money I've Got the Time' I couldn't get enough of. I read about him and saw his picture in a country music magazine at Meyer's store. Lefty's father had been an itinerant oil worker like Michael's and had also moved all over Oklahoma and Texas. Lefty was Laurence's age and was dark with curly hair, thick straight eyebrows, thin lips, aquiline nose and a long, fine-boned face, almost pretty. Later I found out that Michael even played the guitar and sang.

Mikey, as his dad called him, never paid any attention to me that whole fall and winter. I could see that he regarded me as a skinny kid who was no more account to him than our spindly furniture. But I awaited the monthly meetings and daydreamed of Mikey that whole time.

And I had crushes on Audie Murphy and Mario Lanza, mooning over their pictures in *Photoplay* and listening to Mario Lanza singing on the radio.

My final crush on inaccessible boys during that time was a college boy. I met him when I visited my Aunt Ruth, one of Daddy's sisters, the summer before I turned fourteen. Aunt Ruth lived a hundred miles north of us in Stillwater, home of Oklahoma A & M College, now called Oklahoma State University. She was a single mother with two grown sons. Aunt Ruth had always worked since her husband abandoned her for another woman when the children were young. She was a devout Baptist. Seven years older than Mama, Aunt Ruth had taken on the role of civilizing her when she married Daddy, first by getting Mama to become a Baptist.

That summer Daddy put me on the Greyhound bus in Edmond to stay with Aunt Ruth for a month. She was working as the house-keeper and cook for the firemen's school at the university. It was a regular firehouse and the only one for the city. There were both journeymen firemen working as teachers and students doing their degrees in fire engineering. Aunt Ruth had her own small room and bath on the second floor of the firehouse, next to the dormitory where the student firemen lived and the huge kitchen Aunt Ruth reigned over. I slept on a cot in Aunt Ruth's room. I was an instant little sister or niece to those eighteen-year-old fire engineering students.

LaRay Reynolds was from Cheyenne, Oklahoma, a plains town west of Piedmont. He took me under his wing as his little sister, and he taught me to slide down the fire pole and let me ride in the fire engine. He even told me about his girlfriend back home and read her letters to me and showed me pictures of her, a gorgeous blonde cheerleader.

I soon realized that the reason for my visit to Aunt Ruth's was for her to help me learn to be a girl. I think it may have been Vera's idea because Aunt Ruth was Vera's favorite aunt and had taught her how to cook and clean and iron and sew, things Mama did well but would rather just do herself than teach. She would always say that she had to work 'like a Turk' when she was young and she didn't want us to have to.

Aunt Ruth tried her best to instruct me in cooking, and I did learn to make a perfect gravy and how to cut up and fry a chicken, and I learned to iron. I especially liked practicing ironing because the ironing board was at the window overlooking the firehouse where the fire engineer trainees milled about. I could watch LaRay's every movement.

I'd been there a week when I got into trouble and got sent home. During Aunt Ruth's long afternoon naps I explored the sprawling college campus with its old, dark brick buildings. I especially liked the huge new student union, a fantastic three-story brick building with a terrace on top. Inside were multiple parlors, library rooms, music rooms and a television room. Not having a television at home I hungered to watch TV.

There one afternoon while watching *American Bandstand* I met a dashing older boy. Shelby was nineteen, having just finished his first year as an engineering student and had stayed for summer school. He was from Chattanooga, Tennessee, and had an accent similar to ours but different, too. I had never met anyone from east of the Mississippi, from the old country where my ancestors came from. Shelby chattered on about 'Yankees' and I figured out that they were the same people we called 'Easterners.' He said there were too many Yankee teachers at the college. I thought Shelby was very worldly and charming so when he took my hand I didn't mind, nor when he stroked my knee. Just as Shelby put his right arm around my shoulder and his left hand reached under my skirt there was an explosion in the television room, a door slamming so hard and loud that everything shook.

And there was Aunt Ruth standing in front of me, her neck and face red as a fire engine.

Whack! She hit Shelby across the side of the head and he bolted. The door slammed and the room shook again.

'You little no-good dirty tart, piece of trash,' Aunt Ruth said as she grabbed my arm and dragged me away.

Everything happened fast after that. Soon I was on a Greyhound headed home. When I got to the Edmond bus station Daddy was waiting, his truck parked out front. He didn't say anything but I knew Aunt Ruth must have called him. We drove home, Daddy talking as usual about the weather and who owned what land along the way.

Mama was waiting in the yard. I could tell that Aunt Ruth had talked to her, too.

'Come help me pick some tomatoes for supper,' she said.

There in the garden by the side of our house, both of us squatting and squeezing tomatoes for ripeness, Mama said, 'Roxie, you don't want to be saddled with a baby, so don't go playing with fire. You understand? Don't let any boy touch you anywhere 'cause the next thing you know you get in trouble.'

That was about the extent of my sex education, so many things remaining mysterious. One morning in Sunday School not long after I'd been baptized, a third cousin my age was absent. Bonny had never missed Sunday school as long as I could remember. I didn't see her much except on Sundays because her family lived in the country southeast of Piedmont just over the Canadian County line in Oklahoma County, and she and her brothers and sisters went to a nearby rural school. But they always came into Piedmont for church.

I can't remember how we were related, or on which side of the family, but they were more or less hillbillies. The father was skinny and grizzled and played the fiddle and drank the home-brew corn whiskey he distilled (and sold it, too). His mother, who lived with them, smoked a corncob pipe and dipped snuff. It was Bonny's mother who brought her brood into Piedmont for church on Sundays. She was saved and wanted to make sure her kids were good Baptists.

We went out to their house a few times for Sunday dinner. I thought it was a magical place, with a tree house, a porch swing and a teeter-totter, all made by Bonny's father. The place was surrounded by a dozen disabled cars and pickups and there were more mongrel dogs than I could count. I liked it when Bonny's father got out his fiddle and played 'Turkey in the Straw' and got all of us tapping our toes, even Mama.

'Where's Bonny?' I asked Mary Jane when we sat down for Sunday school that day. Boys and girls were separated in Sunday school and there were eight of us twelve- to fourteen-year-old girls in my class.

'I don't know, but my mama said something bad happened to her and she went away,' she said.

I was worried about Bonny. I heard the other girls whispering about her. Then our Sunday school teacher, the preacher's wife, came in and the whispering stopped.

'We won't have our regular Bible lesson today. I want to tell you what happened to our Bonny and that will be the lesson,' she said.

All of us looked at each other questioningly. I wanted to get out of there and not hear what the teacher was going to say, although I had no idea what it might be. I stared at the empty chair in the circle where Bonny usually sat. She was skinny and had pigtails, reddish hair and hazel eyes, eyes that looked almost red. She was quiet but a great playmate because she was fearless and climbed trees like the boys, giving me nerve to follow her. I remembered that she hadn't been baptized yet, or even gone forward to be saved. I supposed there wasn't as much pressure on her since her family didn't live in Piedmont and they came to church only on Sunday.

'Bonny is in trouble, she's going to be an unwed mother. She's in Arkansas with her aunt and will stay there,' the preacher's wife said.

A baby! Bonny was thirteen, my age, and thought boys were stupid. How could she be having a baby? I didn't know much about how it happened but I did know a boy was required.

'Now what I want to explain is how you girls must be careful at your age not to flaunt yourself in front of your men. It's the worst kind of sin to tempt your father. He can lose control as Bonny's father did and commit a terrible sin, but it's your fault for leading him to it,' the preacher's wife said.

Bonny and her father had done it. I didn't know that was possible or ever happened. I felt sick to my stomach.

'May I be excused, please?' I asked as I ran out of the room to the bathroom. I didn't wait for permission. In the bathroom I cried instead of throwing up.

Later Mary Jane told me that what happened to Bonny was called incest. She said her mother had told her, and that it had happened between Bonny and her father for maybe two years. Mama didn't tell me anything and I didn't ask.

No one ever spoke of Bonny again.

Clearly the wages of sin were very high, and I was scared. Yet I stubbornly resisted being saved and joining the church, though not for lack of belief. It was customary that the children of regular Baptists 'go up front' to be saved the month before entering the ninth grade. You were instructed to wait for 'the call,' but the call was supposed to come at that particular time. The Sunday my time came I balked. To make things worse there was only one other Baptist my age, so Mary Jane went to the front alone. The preacher's wife and another woman came to me as the congregation, standing, sang 'Bringing in the Sheaves' over and over. Each gently took one of my arms, Mama nudging me from behind. I shook my head. My feet were lead. I had not felt the calling. The preacher's wife hissed in my ear: 'You can't refuse God's call.' I couldn't budge, and I could think of no excuse for my behavior.

For weeks after that they came for me each Sunday. The preacher and his wife came to our house to pray with me and Mama. Mama would say daily, 'How can you do this to me?'

'I haven't had the call,' I said. I really believed that I had to receive 'the call.'

'You're just stubborn and God will punish you for it,' Mama warned.

Finally I caved in and went forward. I didn't feel the call, only pressure, but once I was walking toward the pulpit and the preacher's outstretched arms I was overcome with emotion, which I interpreted (and remember) as 'the call.'

Being saved didn't make me a full-fledged Baptist. For that I had to be baptized, immersed in the tank behind the pulpit. The church would be darkened on a Sunday night, with only the baptismal lighted, the pews packed. The preacher and the 'candidate' both wore white gowns. I was determined not to do that. I didn't like watching the ritual and was terrified of having my head held under water even for a few seconds; I was certain I would die of an asthma attack.

I simply couldn't do it so I refused for months. Everyone talked to me about it – teachers and girls at school, Sunday school teachers, the preacher and his wife, my sister, Mama. Again I caved in. The baptismal experience was more embarrassing than frightening because I was older than the others being baptized, except for one old grizzled convert. But I was happy and proud to be a full Baptist.

Then, as a matter of course in the community, I joined the Rainbow Girls the summer before I turned fourteen. Vera persuaded me to do it and Mama was for it, too. Daddy didn't object even though he despised the Masons. Apparently, I was the only person in the family who knew his views of the local Masonic lodge. Vera had already joined years before and all during high school devoted considerable time to Rainbow Girls activities. She eventually attained the highest office, Worthy Advisor, and thereby received her pot of gold.

For each step in advancing as a Rainbow Girl the member received a colored bar, the colors of the rainbow. These were affixed to an Eye of God Masonic pin, the same symbol that's on the back of a dollar bill. When the colored links were complete, a pot of gold smaller than a dime was affixed at the bottom. That pin was one of the precious objects of Vera's I loved to touch, and I watched it grow to completion, three inches long.

The DeMolays were the boys' Masonic auxiliary, but for some reason there was no chapter in Piedmont, so several boys in town joined the one in Yukon. The Eastern Star, the women's auxiliary, was very active, and they were required to be wives or descendants of Masons. So the Eastern Stars were the non-foreign-born, non-Catholic elite of Piedmont. Although she never admitted it, Mama probably longed to be an Eastern Star because nearly all the Protestant women in the area, except for our relatives, were Eastern Stars. But there was no way she could be, having no known Masons in her family and not being married into a Masonic family.

Rainbow Girls were supposed to be related to a Mason, too, but there were exceptions and Vera was one. When a girl was very popular, and Vera was, they would recruit her. I was invited to join because I was Vera's sister.

Although I was flattered when asked to join, I hesitated, but after an imaginary conversation with my grandfather, I concluded that I would not be dishonoring his memory. I'm certain that social climbing was a major factor in my deciding to become a Rainbow Girl as well as Vera's insistence, but mainly my motive was to discover the secret ceremonies.

Vera and the other Rainbow Girls refused to murmur a word about what they did in the Masonic Hall one Saturday afternoon each month at their meetings. They were sworn to secrecy and could discuss it only with each other or a Mason or an Eastern Star. Hard as I tried to pry information out of Vera, all she said was that there was nothing scary or painful about it.

I had another qualm about joining. My classmate and friend Lorene was Catholic and was thereby automatically excluded from a Masonic organization, and she was contemptuous of what she called the 'prissy' girls who joined. But when I talked to her about my joining she encouraged me so that I could find out the secrets and tell her. I promised I would, and I did.

The big day came for my initiation, a summer Saturday afternoon. Vera came out from the city to bear witness (Mama was not allowed to attend). The visitor seats were filled by former Worthy Advisors and Eastern Star ladies. It was an all-female affair and Masons were not allowed, just as women were not allowed in Mason's meetings. The Rainbow Girls officers wore net formals in pastel colors, except the Worthy Advisor, who wore a white net formal. The visitors and I, as the initiate, wore regular churchgoing clothes.

I trembled with nervousness because I had no idea what to expect and was surprised that so many people were there. Vera would tell me nothing despite my pleas.

'Just do as you are told,' she said.

There were a half-dozen 'stations' I had to pass through with the lowest officer, called Faith, as my guide. We stopped at the station of Hope and of Charity, all the time Faith rattling off long speeches about seven golden candles, seven stars, seven churches, seven angels, seven thunders, seven woes, three gates, a lake of fire, and lambs, which I recognized from Revelation. I was astonished that the girl playing Faith had memorized nearly the whole book, and it didn't occur to me that I would be called upon to do the same if I were to become Faith. The words were pretty familiar, though, because Mama knew every verse by heart.

An hour or so passed as we visited the stations with Faith's mesmerizing voice the only sound. Then Faith led me to the front of the long hall where the Worthy Advisor and the Associate Worthy Advisor sat on throne-like chairs occupying a low stage. Their faces were grim. Even though I had known those girls all my life they seemed like strangers now.

Faith abandoned me in front of the Worthy Advisor and returned to her station. Another girl appeared at my side. She had been sitting on a chair in the middle of the room, off to the side of the circle of 'colors,' the rank-and-file members who had not yet attained an office, some of whom never would. She was Proctor and produced a wooden box with a hole in the top. Each officer held in her hands a white marble and a black marble. The Worthy Advisor spoke. The voice coming out of that grave presence startled me and I jumped.

'Each officer has a vote. One black ball and you will never be a member of the Rainbow Girls,' she said. 'Your fate is now in the hands of God.'

I didn't know what God had to do with it, but I supposed He had shared my records from his 'Book of Life' with the officers. I panicked. I had not expected a judgement and assumed that it was only a ceremony.

My ears pounded as I stood there waiting while the proctor took the box to each officer and finally to the Worthy Advisor herself. With a terrible scowl on her face she dropped a ball in the box and it clinked against the other ones. The sound echoed. I was certain that she, at least, had blackballed me.

The proctor counted the balls. I couldn't see them. Time stopped and it seemed to take forever. I was resigned to my fate and tempted to bolt rather than be humiliated in front of the elite of Piedmont, embarrassing my sister. All my bad deeds rushed through my mind, and I thought of my mother and her accumulation of black marks against me.

Then I heard applause and looked around. Everyone was standing and smiling at me. The Worthy Advisor had made a sign they all understood after the proctor reported her findings. I had passed.

After a long-winded, memorized speech by the Worthy Advisor about the duties of a Rainbow Girl, she swore me to secrecy, my hands on a large white Bible held by the proctor. I didn't feel a pang of guilt when I swore never to divulge the secrets even though three words pounded in my mind: 'I will tell.' I thought of Grandpa Dunbar. That would be my revenge.

A full set of Rainbow bars with a pot of gold at the end was not my fate. I think I managed only two before I left Piedmont. The secrets were disappointing, most of them obvious from the initiation alone. I knew we weren't getting the whole story, that the Masons possessed secrets of the cult that were never divulged to the girls and women of the auxiliaries, and that included something about white lambskin

aprons and the blood of a lamb. However, I did attain the first office
of Faith and was the guide for the new initiates the following summer. Memorizing most of Revelation was hard work. But I got my
first formal evening gown to wear while carrying out my responsibility. Shopping for it was a ritual itself, with Vera as a kind of worthy
advisor. The formal could be white or any pastel color, and I fell in
love with one that the saleswoman called 'periwinkle blue.' It had a
strapless satin bodice with a long satin skirt covered with multiple
layers of delicate, lacy net. But Vera said it was too expensive, so I
sulked and told her to pick out one herself. She chose a plain, white
net formal. When I look at the old photographs of me in my first
formal, I now think I look like a very pretty young woman, but I was
not alone in believing I was ugly.

Mama thought I was ugly – I looked exactly like her – and she was
still trying hard to improve my appearance, to remake me into something like Anita Bryant, with curly hair and dimples. She took me to
Yukon and spent her hard-earned egg money on a permanent. Nothing could be done about my skinniness, black eyes and dark skin,
but at least my hair could be changed – my straight, fine hair. Curlers
with wires to an electrical contraption bound the chemicaled strands
of hair. I could smell my singeing hair and the chemicals, a sickening
odor. Mrs. Smith, the beautician, darted from my torture station to a
separate space in the rear of the long storefront room where two
caskets sat: Smith Beauty Salon and Funeral Parlor. Did they know
the difference between the dead and the living? Did they treat them
differently? Mrs. Smith was tending the hair of corpses while she did
mine. I gasped for air and wheezed. Mama returned just as I was
about to risk jerking my hair out by the roots to get away from the
machine. I was released from the metal, electrified curlers. My hair
was frizzy but it didn't last long. Later Toni home permanents were
invented, and Mama never gave up trying to transform my hair, and
her own.

The other problem was my dark skin. One day I came home and
found something unfamiliar on my orange-crate dressing table. It
was a small, black porcelain pot that fit in the palm of my hand. I
opened it and inside was a gritty yellowish cream, a skin-bleaching
cream. Mama never said anything about it and I didn't ask, but I used
it until it was gone without any noticeable result. I turned to God to

lighten my skin, praying fervently for a miracle.

Around my thirteenth birthday, already shaken by the mystery of menstruation, I noticed a round white spot no bigger than a thumb-tack on my chin. It had either appeared overnight or else my first exposure to the summer sun had made it visible. It must have been sudden because my skin even without sun was darker than that of anyone else in town. True to my nature I panicked, believing it was an act of God and surely punishment for something I'd done wrong – a lie, even a white lie, or talking back to Mama – or for something I had not done that I should have, such as not praying enough or not sincerely enough. But in the back of my mind I was certain that the punishment was due to my fervent prayers that my dark skin would turn light. I stopped the prayers and censored the wish that had become so much a counterpoint to my every waking thought that I could not always preempt it. Each time the wish popped up I asked for God's forgiveness.

The spot was easy to hide with my hand. I developed a thoughtful pose holding my chin. After a while Mama grabbed my hand away and said only men held their chins like that, but she didn't appear to notice the spot. No one did. I began to think I was imagining it. One day the white spot turned vivid pink after I'd been in the sun. A blister rose on the spot during the night and when it healed the white spot was gone, just vanished. Overjoyed, I prayed for hours thanking God and promising never again to wish to be different in any way, and that I would even consider becoming a missionary, although I tactically considered that I should hold that bargaining chip for a later, bigger deal with God. After all, He'd withdrawn the white-spot punishment. I promised to memorize Psalms.

Toward the end of summer I woke to a new phenomenon – a narrow, white ring around each of my eyes, making me look like a raccoon. At first I didn't relate the new development to the chin spot. Vera, out for Sunday dinner with her husband, took me off alone and asked me if I was shaving my eyebrows. It was an accusation, really, and obviously absurd. I said I wasn't. She said I should stop doing it.

Next my lips were ringed with white, then my ears; a spot ap-peared on the center of my throat. My hands and feet acquired white-ringed fingernails and toenails, my knees and shins developed perfectly round, symmetrical white spots. Every scratch and bruise turned white. Memorizing Psalms had not worked.

I had never sunbathed like the other girls because I was already darker than anyone else, and in my summer shorts, barefoot, I turned even browner without wishing it. 'Dirty brown,' Mama called my coloring – her skin was the same color – not the honey gold of suntanned blondes. But I took to sunbathing because I found that when the white spots were burned they would often disappear. But radiation did not arrest the white-spotting over my entire body.

Vera took me to a dermatologist in the City who gave the affliction a name, 'vitaligo,' a defect in the melanin that destroys pigmentation. 'Only a cosmetic problem with no cure. It will continue until all your pigment is gone, take maybe ten years, twenty. Meanwhile, you will be spotted like an Appaloosa, the prettiest kind of horse there is,' the doctor said. (Only since Michael Jackson admitted that he suffers from vitaligo and was not bleaching his skin have I been able to explain my own loss of pigment and receive comprehension: Oh, yes, that Michael Jackson disease.)

Mama gave up on making me pretty and began cautioning me that I would not be able to depend on beauty to get ahead. Getting ahead was something she believed in and encouraged fervently. Her directives remained open-ended and vague, a vast space I filled in with various ambitions, among them to become a movie star, a long shot with my appearance. That did not keep me from peering for hours at the faces in the movie magazines, which only reinforced my frustration. Another option was sports, including the rodeo. My asthma locked me out of that possibility.

One day Mama sat down beside me while I stared at a picture of Ingrid Bergman in *Photoplay,* and told me: 'You're never going to be pretty, so you'd better use your brain.'

I took her message to heart and immersed myself in school.

My homeroom class was, fortunately, unusual. For one thing it had the smallest number, only three students. All the other grades were at least four times larger. One of my teachers said it was because of the Dust Bowl when people weren't having babies, when men were gone looking for work, but that made no sense to me since the several grades before mine were larger and their births dated back to the Dust Bowl, too. Why in that year 1938 so few of us were born remained a mystery to me.

The other peculiarity of my grade was that we three were girls. All the other grades were evenly divided between boys and girls. Since my class was so small it was merged for most subjects with the grade above so we were always ahead of our age in our studies. And we three classmates – me, Mary Jane and Lorene – were famously teachers' pets. It was likely a good thing for me that the class was small and that it was only girls, although I wasn't conscious of it then.

All my grade school teachers were women. Except for the first grade teacher and the typing teacher, they were usually at Piedmont for only one year. Some of them were hardly more than girls themselves, nineteen and twenty years old, studying for their teaching certificates at the state teachers college in Edmond. They left for better jobs once they finished their degrees. From the first to the eighth grade my world was made up of my girl classmates and the women who were our teachers, almost like an all-girls school. I learned to type in the eighth grade. Typewriting was the second important skill I learned, after mastering the bicycle. Just as with my bike, I learned quickly how to be fast and shot ahead of my classmates in a short time; again, I could compete and win. Mastering typing also bestowed on me an amazing sense of freedom, far more powerful than I'd felt mastering bike riding. It took me a while to realize that it was not only the skill that made me soar and brought me to the typing room before and after school and during lunch hour and recess, but it was also what I was typing. I was writing stories. Soon I started a two-page school newspaper that I wrote, typed and ran off on the ditto machine. About then, the summer of the coronation of Queen Elizabeth, I acquired a pen pal in Birmingham, England, and wrote to her daily. I was after all my mother's daughter.

Graduating from the eighth grade was a grand moment. The whole town came out that Tuesday evening for graduation. Seniors and eighth-graders were honored on the same occasion, except we eighth-graders did not wear black caps and gowns like the seniors. The Sunday before was Baccalaureate, a solemn religious affair, the only Sunday of the year when the congregations from the Baptist and Methodist churches, and even from the tiny Free Methodist church out north of town, and even the sinners, backsliders, unbelievers and Catholics gathered in the school auditorium to hear the Baptist or Methodist pastor preach. The graduating seniors decided on which preacher would preside and that year it was the Baptist preacher because his son was a graduating senior.

Only three of us, Mary Jane, Lorene and I, were graduating from the eighth grade. The big question as always for graduations was who would be valedictorian and who salutatorian and who would receive the prestigious American Legion award for good citizenship. Each of the three of us had all As throughout grade school, but I was the only one who had straight As with no minuses, so I was valedictorian.

I longed for the American Legion award but was certain I wouldn't be chosen. It was not based on scholarship, but rather on character and patriotism, and was given by the American Legion post in Yukon based on essays written by the candidate. Two years before, Hank had won the award. Now it was between Mary Jane and me, for everyone knew Lorene didn't stand a chance, being Catholic and Polish. Knowing she was out of the running, Lorene had written a mean essay praising Adlai Stevenson, who was running against General Eisenhower for president that year. She even wrote that Eisenhower was a fraud playing the moderate since he had chosen Richard Nixon for his vice-presidential candidate, whom Lorene called a fascist. At the time I had no idea what she was talking about.

My essay was an admiring portrait of Andrew Jackson as the father of democracy. Mary Jane's was about how children should obey their parents, and she won. The award always went to the most athletic and popular girl or boy, and that was Mary Jane in our class.

I finished that school year on top of the world: I had managed, despite asthma and vitaligo, to find my niche in the community at the top. I was a good Baptist girl, a Rainbow Girl, the smartest girl and the best typist. I had arrived and felt confident. Now I would be in high school and read Shakespeare, act in school plays, perhaps even make the basketball team, because I was growing out of my asthma. But the ominous summer that followed my graduation foreshadowed a bad time ahead.

Nine

Plagues

but war is always with us
and you gird up
and move on to other arenas
fake diamond strikes
bonanzas of pure gold
that will turn green tomorrow

WILMA ELIZABETH McDANIEL,
from 'Fronie Lost the War'

The summer of 1953, when I was fourteen, children were dying all over the United States and all over the world, the radio said, not just in western Oklahoma. That summer, Becky, a second cousin my age, disappeared one day. They said she was in a hospital in the City, inside an iron lung that breathed for her. Months later she returned in a wheelchair, her legs withered and white as a catfish belly. They said she would never walk again. They said it was the disease that President Roosevelt had had and the reason why he'd been in a wheelchair. Mama had survived polio at thirteen. The state authorities had taken her out of a foster home and put her in a hospital, then a girl's reformatory. Mama told me how dreadful polio had been, but she survived with only a twisted spine and a limp. She had a theory that the germ lived in water and that summer she would not allow Hank and me to go swimming in the pond, or even go outside the house much.

It was a boring, dry, restless summer.

That summer of polio was also a time of the locusts. They darkened the sky at noon one day and then swooped down into the corn fields and the wheat fields, leaving only stubble after feasting for three days. Mama invoked Revelation 9:3: *And there came out of the smoke locusts upon the earth.* A stranger in a dark suit came to the town and all the farmers gathered to hear him tell about DDT. He was from the government. Daddy spoke up at the meeting and said that any-thing that would kill dogs and cats, as the government man warned, would kill children, too. But most of the farmers ignored him and carried away cans of the liquid that smelled a little like kerosene.

The Baptist preacher warned us that the polio and the locusts were like the plagues in the Bible, that they were just the beginning, that the people had fallen into wicked ways and vice was rampant, that Jehovah was punishing the people for turning against Him. So when a Bible salesman came to the door one day that summer, Mama was willing to do anything to prepare for the apocalypse. She used her egg money that usually went for schoolbooks and new shoes to buy a thick white Bible with colored pictures. The salesman and Mama kneeled and prayed together. I did not like the pictures in that Bible, of swords and blood and angry faces, God's face in the sky.

Daddy said the preacher was wrong, that locusts are always some-where eating crops and that they arrived in cycles like bad blizzards or swarms of tornadoes, that God had nothing to do with it because there was no God. His words frightened Mama even more.

Because of the polio and the locusts, which meant that the farmers would have no crops to sell and no cash, the Gypsy circus did not come that summer. Ever since I could remember the Rolando family had trundled in with two trucks and set up a big top. They had a Bengal tiger in a cage and monkeys that did tricks. There was a fat lady and a trapeze couple. Rolando himself was a magician who made white rabbits disappear and put his wife Gloria in a wooden box and sawed through it without hurting her. Rolando also threw knives at Gloria, making a perfect outline of her slender body on the sheet of plywood behind her. Hank tried to get me to play Gloria to his Rolando, but even though Hank was deft with his Bowie knife I wouldn't play that game.

The tent revival didn't come that summer either, so there was no camp meeting, no voices in the night singing, 'Shall We Gather at the River' and 'The Old Rugged Cross.'

And the threshing crew did not come for there was no wheat to thresh. Every summer the combines – huge motorized contraptions – would arrive with truckloads of young men and some families. They would camp with the machines in the fields they were working and come into church meetings and go to the circus. Some of the young men in town would sign on to go with them to Kansas, Nebraska, the Dakotas and Montana, and end up in Saskatchewan, as Hank would the following year.

That summer of 1953, no strangers came around except the government man with poison and the Bible salesman. But the radio brought us other news of impending disaster, the plague of communism. The Red Menace was everywhere, and it didn't help to have a Red in the family tree. I was scared, even if no one else was. And the execution of the Rosenbergs terrified me.

I remember that day, June 19, 1953, well; Mama's birthday was the day before, and I hadn't even made her a card because I was sick. At six in the evening the sun glared hot, close to a hundred degrees. I lay on the divan in the living room. I wheezed and struggled for air, too weak to swat the flies that buzzed around my head. The asthma attack had started around noon, caused by the blowing red dirt.

I stared at the torn screen door. My eyes shifted to the stained ceiling where rain had leaked in and left brown spots. Now the stains were drought dry, but a month before spring tornadoes had brought torrential rains that left teats of water hanging from the ceiling, the water pinging into the tin pans Mama put on the floor. My eyes settled on the worn green linoleum on the floor, scuffed and dusty, then to the green plastic curtains, torn and coated with a film of grease and red dirt. Everything around me was ugly.

I heard Mama banging around in the kitchen cooking supper. Daddy had come in, railing against the drought: 'Blamed corn's drying up and blowing away, derned locusts, hotter than Hades out there.' He stretched out on the double bed that filled the bedroom. I could see his scuffed lace-up boots and hear his snoring. His log-sawing alternated with the chirp of crickets and the song of a mockingbird.

Hank crashed into the room from outdoors, dribbling his basketball. He turned on the chipped plastic Philco radio and hunted for a baseball game. He switched stations and found no game, only news, so he abandoned the blaring radio and dribbled into the kitchen.

'Beans again?' I heard him whine.

'I bought you a Milky Way, hon',' Mama said.

Hank dribbled out the front door, candy bar already half-eaten.

I concentrated on the words coming out of the radio. The man spoke of electric chairs – two thousand watts, he said – for a couple, Julius and Ethel Rosenberg, in a place called Sing Sing. He said their heads were covered with leather hoods and that the woman wore a dark green and white polka-dot dress. He said the electric chairs were made of oak, my favorite tree because it grew from a tiny acorn. I imagined giant carved oak chairs decorated with light bulbs, thrones for a king and a queen, in a room full of songbirds. But then the radio man explained how long it would take for the couple to die in those chairs. He said that Sing Sing was a penitentiary.

I tried to figure out how light bulbs might kill. Our house was hooked up to electricity, one wire that entered through a hole in the wall and was attached to one light bulb and to the radio. There was nothing else that required electricity. Electricity fascinated and scared me, like lightning or magic. So, I thought, maybe electricity could kill somebody. I imagined the Rosenbergs lit up like light bulbs, glowing, slowly burning from the heat. I thought it would take a long time to die that way. Our light bulbs died after two months.

My mind turned to the real question: Why were they burning those people alive, like they had Joan of Arc?

Suddenly Mama and Daddy stood in front of the radio, their necks craned. I hadn't even heard them come into the room. The radio man said, 'The convicted communist spies are considered traitors by all patriotic Americans.' Mama cupped her face in her hands, Daddy braced his hands on his hips. They scared me with the scared looks on their faces. I gasped for breath. They stood as if frozen for what seemed like a long time. Then Mama glanced my way and must have detected the alarm in my eyes. She nudged Daddy and he switched off the radio. They went to the kitchen to eat.

Mama darted into the room with a cup of hot Postum, which she thought relieved asthma, and she placed a hot, dampened Vicks-saturated towel on my chest. I braced myself and caught a sliver of air, then used that precious commodity to aspirate, 'What did they do wrong?'

Mama knitted her brow and narrowed her eyes in that way that said I shouldn't ask.

'They're communists, Reds, like the devil,' she said.

I didn't understand 'communist,' but I knew about the devil and I knew that he was red.

Mama hurried back to the kitchen. I heard Daddy's voice: 'Them Russkies likely drop an atom bomb now.'

'The greatest sin in America is our disregard for God. God may allow Russia to destroy America. Russia will get it in the end, but she may destroy America.' The handsome, famous Billy Graham preached to a packed stadium at the Oklahoma City fairgrounds. The last time I'd sat in those bleachers was four years before when I heard the Weavers sing 'Goodnight Irene.' The audience looked similar, mostly rural people, but unlike before there were many blacks and Indians in the crowd, and more women than men. I was there with my mother.

'You have a moral disease, and that moral disease is sin. The root of all the world's ills is sin and sin has separated us from God. And men must pay the penalty for breaking the law of God.' He said that the polio and the locusts were realization of prophecies from the Bible and communism was just as much a disease as polio, all brought on by our sins, and that the execution of the Rosenbergs was a purification.

Mama loved Billy Graham. He was in his early thirties then and so good-looking with his golden pompadour, chiseled face and piercing blue eyes. Mama cut out pictures of him from magazines and newspapers and pasted them in a scrapbook. But that was the first time we'd seen him in person. She was enraptured. So was I, almost hypnotized. The pianist started playing and the preacher led the crowd singing 'Stand up, stand up for Jesus.' That was the call.

'I beg you to come now before it is too late. Stand up! Leave your seat and come forward! Come quietly up and say, "Billy, tonight I accept Christ."'

Mama and I were already saved, but he also called for those of us who were saved to come forward and rededicate our lives to Christ.

After one verse of the call song, a single woman in a house dress descended the steps and stood on the grass beside the stage, then a young boy, then a black woman with a baby, then a stream of people that turned into a flood. That's when Mama and I rose from our seats and went down front.

Standing beside the stage, we could see Billy better under the bright lights. He paced, crouched, pointed his long index finger, sweat glistening on his broad forehead. I stared at him. He reminded me of the African lion in the zoo, the king of the jungle, pacing, roaring, more powerful and beautiful and purer than any other living creature.

Mama tugged my arm. The new converts were streaming inside the huge white tent behind the stage. She wanted to take a look inside and thought Billy might come there after he finished preaching. But he didn't. There were other preachers there. They directed the women and men to different sides of the tent. We sat down on the folding chairs. There were small pencils and cards on the chairs and we were supposed to write our names and addresses and mark the choices:

1) Acceptance of Christ as Savior and Lord
2) Reaffirmation of Faith
3) Assurance of Salvation
4) Dedication of Life

We checked all four and Mama wrote on the cards that we were already saved and baptized. A few days later we each got personal letters from Billy Graham blessing us and asking for money. Mama sent in five dollars for us and showed the letters to everyone in town.

That fall I entered the ninth grade – high school – and was relieved to leave that nightmarish summer behind. But another disaster was not far away, one that would change the course of my life, as my mother turned into a hopeless alcoholic. I'm not sure when or how she broke her teetotaler fanaticism and took that first drink, but I remember when I discovered that she was drinking.

It was early November 1953, and after a long Indian summer a chill was in the air. I sat by the school bus window staring out at the star-studded black sky. Next to me was Phil, a new boy in town, recently orphaned when his parents were killed in a car wreck. He had come to live with a great-aunt. Phil was my boyfriend, my first. Phil and I rarely exchanged words and no kisses, only hand-holding. He was an outsider, tagged as an egghead. He wore thick, horn-rimmed glasses and always carried a science book but commanded a certain amount of respect because he was a hotshot basketball player. We were on the school bus, the boys' and girls' basketball teams, twenty-seven of us – first and second strings, plus four cheerleaders, the coach and bus driver – traveling ten miles east to Deer Creek for a game.

I was worried. Hank and I had been home alone for two weeks. Mama and Daddy had driven to Los Angeles to visit Laurence and Jan and their two-year-old son. Jan was six months pregnant. They were due home any moment because Daddy had to be back at work on Monday. He'd sacrificed his annual deer hunting to please Mama, he said, and she would surely never hear the last of his 'throwing it into me,' as she always accused him. All that violence was simmering, and sitting next to Phil I couldn't help but think about car wrecks and parents dying.

From the back of the bus came sounds of couples smooching, chief among them my brother Hank and my best friend Mary Jane. They had started going steady at the beginning of the school year. Hank was a senior and the best basketball player in the history of the county and was headed for All-State and an athletic scholarship. Mary Jane was short, muscular and quick, the best female basketball player in the county. And she was Shirley Temple cute, with naturally curly hair, sparkling blue eyes and dimples. I was on the second string of the girls' team, more an honorary position than anything else, a tip of the hat to Hank's status, and to my older brother and sister before us.

The girls' game was first. We won, but I spent the entire time on the bench. I made my way to the locker room, which smelled of sweat. I was clean and dry as a bone. I changed my basketball shoes for my nearly new brown penny loafers that Daddy had bought me before they'd left for California. As I hung the blue and gold satin basketball shorts and shirt on a hanger I smelled my mother, that combination of Avon floral sachet and Kool cigarettes, but also something alien, sour or sharp that I couldn't identify. I turned and she was extending a white box and smiling. I took the box and opened it to find a pleated half-slip, of the most delicate robin's-egg blue, the most luxurious item I'd ever touched.

'I bought it at the gift shop on Catalina Island. We went over there on a glass-bottom boat,' she said. I loved the slip and pulled it on over my shoes.

'It's so pretty,' I said.

'There's something else there,' Mama said. I dug below the tissue paper and found a crested white wool cardigan, just what I had been wanting. I put it on over my dress. I wanted to hug Mama but we never hugged each other in my family.

'Thank you, Mama. It's beautiful,' I said.

Something was wrong, I felt it – a look in Mama's eyes, a certain excitement, the way her face was flushed. I thought about that look and the odor on her breath all the way through the boys' game and on the bus ride back.

At home that night I identified the source of the odor. I found a strange item in the icebox, an unlabeled bottle of dark purplish liquid. I had never seen or smelled wine, or any other liquor except near-beer, but that liquid looked exactly like the Welch's grape juice I loved and craved and hardly ever had because it was expensive. One whiff and I knew it was something else.

From that evening on, I don't believe I ever saw Mama sober again, although I never saw her take a drink during the horrifying year and half that followed until I fled.

Ten

She-Lion

we put our fingers
in our ears
and ran faster to
get away

WILMA ELIZABETH MCDANIEL,
from 'A Mother's Night Prayers'

My mother was never sick during my childhood. She claimed never
to have had a headache or a cold in her life; she never even took an
aspirin, which of course as a sickly child made me feel like a whining
wimp. Mama was a *macha*. During World War II, when medicines
were reserved for military use, Mama developed gum disease and had
all her teeth pulled without anesthetic, proudly claiming that she had
not felt the pain. Later that extraordinary resistance to pain nearly
cost her her life when she suffered appendicitis; her appendix burst
but she felt no pain to warn that she was ill.

I'm not sure I believe that part; it happened after I had escaped,
after she had kicked Daddy out, when she was all alone in the house,
and drunk. It may have been the gin that dulled the pain that time.

I had no way to describe what was happening to my mother, or to
me. The word that came to mind was 'crazy' but the one time I
spurted it out Daddy shouted, 'Don't talk about your mother that
way.'

Yet as Mama's craziness escalated, so too did her independence,
and I paid attention to that. She began working as a full-time assis-

tant editor for the Yukon newspaper and continued her regular 'Piedmont News' columns in the Edmond and El Reno papers. She bought herself (us) a refrigerator – we'd always had a nonelectrical icebox – then a TV, both being objects of modern civilization much opposed by my father. Hank and I came home from school each day to an empty house and watched the Mickey Mouse and Eddie Fisher shows on TV. Sometimes we tried to cook supper so it would be ready when Mama and Daddy got home, Kraft macaroni and cheese or a can of chili. Two or three nights each week Aunt Fanny would bring a pot of stew or beans and a pan of cornbread. We had been spoiled by Mama and resented her not being there to serve us hand and foot.

Just after Hank graduated from high school in the spring of 1954, Mama insisted on buying the house next door, larger and nicer than our flimsy box. It was owned by one of our former landlords, whose tenants we'd been on a farm outside town. The place had running water and a bathroom, two bedrooms, a whole separate dining room, a big kitchen with a propane stove and a pantry, a spacious screened-in back porch, and a cellar – we'd always had to run to neighbors' cellars during storms. Daddy gave in and bought the house. For Mama, buying our former landlord's house seemed a sort of emancipation. For me it was the first time I had my own room. For all of us it was our first indoor plumbing.

We moved to that house during the summer between my sophomore and junior years, the summer I worked as a live-in babysitter for a Czech veterinarian and his wife in Yukon. Mama got the job for me. During that summer I visited Mama at the newspaper office nearly every day. She was always tottering but acted more or less under control while at work. I was home that summer only on weekends, when I got a taste of what was to come.

That summer of 1954, I also ended up watching the Army-McCarthy hearings on television. Laurence wrote from California and said he wanted me to pay attention to the hearings, something he said might be hard for me to understand but to try. He said there was an investigation of army people who were traitors and that the man who uncovered what was going on was a great man, a US senator from Wisconsin named Joseph McCarthy.

Laurence had written about that man before, and I had heard my parents discussing him, saying he had to do with movie stars and some other people who were traitors, and that John Wayne and Ronald Reagan were on the senator's side and helping him. Laurence sent a newspaper clipping with a list of movie stars and entertainers who were communists, and on that list were the Weavers.

I figured McCarthy had something to do with the Rosenberg execution the year before because he had written that the Rosenbergs were evil people, communists who had given the Russians secrets about the atom bomb. I had asked Daddy if those communists were like his father and he hit the ceiling.

'Your grandfather was a man from here, not an Easterner. He was a hunter and a farmer and he fought for people on the land,' Daddy said. But I heard the fear in his voice just as I had seen it in his and my mother's eyes when the Rosenbergs were executed. We had a Red in our family tree, everybody knew that; my father was named after the most famous of them. I don't recall ever being told directly, but I caught on that I should not ask about or brag about my grandfather the Wobbly any more.

I could understand why Laurence liked Senator McCarthy. To me, the senator seemed the smartest, handsomest man in the world, and he had a beautiful voice, how I imagined Clarence Darrow would have sounded. He made everyone else around him seem small and weak. He would look a little like John Wayne, I thought, if he dressed up like a cowboy. Almost as handsome and impressive was the young lawyer who was on the senator's side. Roy Cohn wasn't that much older than Laurence, and he had big dreamy eyes.

Dutifully I sat in front of the television in the darkened living room of the young Czech couple in Yukon while their little boy slept or played in the back yard. I tried to follow every word. I felt very important carrying out such a hard assignment from Laurence, much harder than learning the words he regularly sent me to memorize. After a week of the hearings, I became afraid because I could see that those were not just words being exchanged, that a terrible danger loomed on the horizon related to the atom bomb. I hadn't understood before why people were talking about building bomb shelters. Now I knew. And I knew that there were secret communists all around. I realized that was why they had executed the Rosenbergs. Communism was presented as a disease, a virus that could cripple a person's mind, but worse even than polio because it could poison everyone else around, even if they didn't catch it themselves, and there was no vaccine to prevent it except for extreme caution, suspicion and vigilance. I accepted the diagnosis as well as everyone else in our family and community.

After the Supreme Court decision to desegregate schools that year, billboards sprouted all along the roads and highways saying 'Impeach Earl Warren' and 'Earl Warren Is a Communist.' Mama became obsessed with communism and integration. Her boss and mentor, the editor of *The Yukon Sun,* sang loudest in the choir of hundreds of local anticommunist and anti-integration newspaper editors.

When the McCarthy hearings ended, I drowned my worry and confusion in movie magazines and Johnnie Ray songs on the radio, and flirting with the cute boy who delivered groceries. There was nothing I wanted more in the world than to be and look like a teenaged girl who'd stepped off a page of *Seventeen.* One way I found to feel normal was to act above it all – more in the know, what would later be called 'cool.' I was more a typical fifties teenager than I could have realized then. Lorene felt the same and we grew even closer that summer, talking on the telephone and writing letters. Lorene was a social and physical freak, too, being Polish and Catholic and tall and politically informed and radical.

Our cool act was given a boost when Lorene's cousin from Los Angeles visited. Mickey was our age, but he had been raised by his Okie-Polish parents near the defense plant where they worked in Orange County. He even used the word, 'cool,' and people around Piedmont were hicks, except for Lorene and me.

Although Jan had told me stories about surfing and beach-blanket parties and dancing at the Palladium, I had been too young then to appreciate the excitement. Mickey was a surfer with bleached (green-hued) hair and his lean, perfect body was the color of clover honey. Mickey played us his surfing records and taught us to dance surfer-style. Of course, dancing was forbidden by the Baptists, but I didn't tell anyone at church about my other activities, and my parents didn't seem to care what I did or who I was with.

Mickey had traveled by Greyhound over Route 66, but he already had his driver's license and Lorene's father let him drive their car. They would pick me up every evening in Yukon and we were off to the roller-rink or a drive-in movie, and on weekends to the stock car races and swimming pools.

Teenage normality, as I envisaged it, ended the Sunday after Mickey rode into the sunset aboard the Greyhound, back to paradise. Before Mickey left, Lorene had turned sixteen and got her driver's license. That Sunday she drove, alone, into town from their farm after church, to take me for a ride. Two miles north of Piedmont we crashed when Lorene lost control of the car as it skidded over the dry red shale road and we plunged down an embankment nose first into a dry creek bed. I raised my left arm to cover my face and soared though the windshield, shattering it. The first thing I noticed was that I was alive and the second thing was that my left arm was dead. I was covered with blood, my white blouse and shorts saturated and sticky. I climbed out of the windshield and immediately the blood dried and caked on my arms and hands, on my face, in my hair. My left arm was hanging, bloody, half severed at the elbow.

'I will never be able to type again,' I said out loud. Lorene didn't have a scratch but was wailing and crying and pounding her head against the steering wheel, saying, 'I've killed you, you're my best friend, oh God forgive me.'

I comforted Lorene as calmly as I could and persuaded her that we had to walk to the next farm to get help because it was doubtful that any car would pass by during Sunday noon mealtime. It was a day in a scorching hot August, but I felt cool, even cold, shivering. My teeth chattered uncontrollably. We walked more than a mile to the next farmhouse and interrupted the family's Sunday feast. The farmer, a deacon in my church, put us in his pickup truck and dropped me off at home, then took Lorene to her farm southeast of Piedmont.

I stood in our back yard, asking myself: 'Am I invisible? How long have I been standing here like this?' The shock slowed the world down to slow motion. I observed the scene and it seemed almost normal, like a Norman Rockwell painting on the front of *Look*: Laurence and Jan and their three children, who now lived in Oklahoma City, had come out for Sunday noon dinner, arriving after I left. Now, in the mid-afternoon, Daddy was churning ice cream in the yard, my three-year-old nephew perched on top of the ice cream maker to steady it, just as I used to do at his age. Daddy sat in a chair brought out from the kitchen and cranked with effort. I could tell the ice cream was nearly ready because he strained to turn the handle. Daddy's lips moved – he would be telling stories about cowboy days to his grandson, stories I knew by heart.

Mama sat on the porch steps playing with her youngest grandchild, smiling, doing patty-cake.

'Why don't they notice me?' I asked myself. I could not hear any sound at all. Lips moved but I could hear no voices. Everything was so vivid and bright, blades of grass sparkling, leaves on the trees glowing, shiny black horseflies circling the ice cream churner. It crossed my mind that maybe I wasn't really there at all, but dead, and that my spirit had returned to tell them goodbye but they could not see me.

Then I noticed that Laurence and Jan were missing. I thought to myself that they must be inside the house quarreling. The first thing Jan would want to do when they arrived each Sunday to visit was to leave. I told myself that they must be inside the house and could save me. I was hurt and needed help. I thought I was bleeding to death.

'What happened, Roxie?' I heard a familiar voice and the sound came back on, voices, Mama's laughter, the baby crying. Jan had grabbed the baby from Mama, and ran to me; now Jan stood in front of me, reaching out to hold me.

'Be careful, you'll get bloody,' I said and collapsed into her arms.

The next thing I knew I was lying down in the back seat of Laurence's black 1949 Ford coupe. I felt no pain, only deadness in my left arm and hand. Laurence was driving fast, which he always did, and Daddy rode shotgun.

'Slow down, boy, or you'll get us into another wreck,' Daddy said.

'The baby could lose that arm and she's lost a lot of blood,' Laurence said and didn't slow down.

'Where's Mama?' I asked.

'Stayed home,' Laurence said.

I cried softly, feeling sorry for myself, like a child, thinking: 'Mama doesn't even care that I'm hurt and may die or lose an arm, she doesn't even care.'

Many times when I am with one of my older brothers or my sister, I intend to ask whether or not our mother beat them as she did me. Perhaps I have asked them but I cannot recall ever receiving a clear answer. I don't remember her beating them and she never laid a hand on me until she started drinking.

And when she started attacking me, I concluded that she hated me. I reasoned how this could be so: Mama was only thirty when I was born, the last child. She could not have wanted me. I asked myself: Did she make me sick with asthma so she wouldn't hurt me? Had I been a boy would she have wanted me or loved me more? Did she make me sick, and then when I was no longer sick or she couldn't make me sick any longer, was that when the hate for me came out? However I reasoned it, I thought I must somehow be to blame.

I tried to convince myself at the time she was hitting me that it was simply because I was there, not because I was me and she hated me. Something inside me told me that she knew what she was doing and why. It was because she hated me, because I was unwanted, because I looked like her and she hated herself.

The first blow came when I returned home from Yukon to go to school. I had a boyfriend but not for long. It lasted about one month and ended on my birthday. I sat at the kitchen table in the corner in the strange new home, looking out the window. From that window I could see a strip of the Piedmont–Yukon highway, see the headlights of cars coming into town. It was nearly midnight and I had been sitting there watching for five hours, waiting for Ronnie, my date, to appear.

It was September 10, 1954, my sixteenth birthday. During the time I had sat there waiting, Mama and Daddy fought. Mama passed through the kitchen, where I sat, a dozen times on her way out to the garage to drink and smoke. She did not seem to register my presence. Around nine, Daddy slammed out and took off to the City to drink and dance. Then around ten Mama blacked out on her bed. They hadn't remembered it was my birthday.

I kept the lights off in the kitchen so I could see the headlights on the highway. Now and then I would see a car and wait, holding my breath, to see if it took the route Ronnie had used on our previous three dates.

The new Southwestern Bell rotary dial telephone was right beside me on the wall. I had never called Ronnie but always waited for him to call me. I knew his number by heart and took the phone off the hook several times to dial, but didn't.

Ronnie had been out to our house for dinner and ice cream the Sunday before. Mama took a picture of him in the yard. I held the picture while I waited. He wore new white buck shoes, new Levis, and a black crinkled-nylon, see-through, short-sleeved shirt without an undershirt, shirt tail out – the current boy's style. He was five-foot-nine and compact, a shortstop on Yukon's high school baseball team, beginning his junior year like me. He had hazel eyes set in a baby face and close-cropped curly black hair. I thought he looked like Audie Murphy in my favorite movie, *Sierra*.

I thought about the Sunday before. It was then that we agreed he would take me out on my birthday. Everything had seemed all right. Mama wasn't sober but she didn't make a scene, and I didn't think Ronnie guessed she was drunk. Daddy had been friendly to him, and Hank, a freshman basketball star at Oklahoma City University, which seemed to impress Ronnie, was home for Sunday dinner.

I had met Ronnie while working in Yukon that summer. His father owned a grocery store and meat market on Main Street, and Ronnie was the delivery boy. He drove his own cream-colored, low-slung Hudson, all souped up and detailed. Every weekday afternoon at three, that cool, ghostly car would enter the alley behind the house where I lived in as a babysitter. It would stop and the boy, whose name I did not yet know, would get out and unload three or four boxes of groceries at the back door of the coffee shop that faced Highway 66. I would watch him from the kitchen window. Then one day I got brazen enough to be outside hanging wet clothes on the clothesline. He noticed me and said hello. The next day I was out in the yard even closer to the fence by the alley, and he asked me if I lived there, and I said no.

'You related to the Kraviks?' he asked.

'No, I'm from Piedmont, taking care of their little boy while they work at the vet clinic,' I said.

My heart pounded like it wanted to jump out. He was so cute and cool. His car radio blasted out Chuck Berry and Little Richard.

Each day we talked over the fence for a longer time. That started only two weeks before I had to leave and go back to Piedmont to school. On my last day in Yukon I told him I was leaving and he asked me for a date for the next weekend. The next Saturday he came to Piedmont to take me to Yukon to the movies. Afterwards we parked off the highway in a grove of cottonwood and kissed for a long, lovely time. He never tried to go any further than kissing on our three dates in those two weeks.

I had no reason to think Ronnie would stand me up on my birthday. I thought he must have been in a car wreck, but in the back of my mind I knew it was over for reasons I could not imagine. Tears rolled down my face and splattered on the oilcloth on the table.

Two weeks passed with no word from Ronnie: I never saw nor heard from him again. And then Hank came home for a weekend and took me to Yukon to the movies. In the lobby after the movie, when I was waiting for Hank to come out of the men's room, Ronnie's best friend walked up to me and said hello.

'How's Ronnie?' I asked.

'He misses you,' he said.

'He stood me up and never called or anything,' I said.

'Well, you can thank your mama for that. She went to the store and told Ronnie's dad he'd better see to it that Ronnie married you,' he said.

Humiliation washed over me. Hank came out and I left the boy without a word. But the ache that nearly made me double over was not only from embarrassment, or the loss of my boyfriend, but also because I believed that my mother wanted to marry me off to get rid of me.

I hit her back once, only one time. Again she tried to match me up with a boy. It happened during basketball season in 1954, the beginning of my last school year at home. I was a junior, and as the junior class we were in charge of the candy and pop concession at ball games and at noon in school every day. Juniors ran the concession to make enough money to pay for the Junior-Senior banquet at the end of the school year. There were only two of us, Lorene and me, in our class by then since Mary Jane had moved to the City, so it was a lot of work, buying the candy, peanuts and pop, banking the money and keeping accounts, setting up the concession and running it. I'd given up trying to play basketball, but Lorene was on the girls' team.

I was sitting alone behind the concession stand, reading a book. There would be little business until halftime. A boy who was from Mustang High School, the opposing team that night, came out of the gym door and sat on the corner of the concession table. I can't remember his face or looks at all except that I didn't like them. He looked older; maybe he had dropped out or graduated from high school. I remember his smirk, a kind of knowing grin. I told him he was missing the ball game after coming such a long way to see it.

'You're better to look at than any ole game,' he said. He reached over and put his arm around me.

I jerked away as if a snake had touched me.

'Get away from me, you creep,' I said. I'm sure my eyes were filled with murder. His smirk turned to surprise. He stood up and faced me. I was on my feet now.

'Hey, you ought to tell your mother not to lead guys on to you,' he said, and slunk away.

I left the concession stand unattended and shot into the gym to find Mama. I found her watching the game, sitting on the front row under Piedmont's goal, yelling and weaving in her chair. I grabbed her arm.

'Come with me,' I said.

She stumbled along beside me. I held her forearm hard and squeezed, nearly dragging her, as she had done to me so many times when I was little. I got her into the empty hall near the concession stand so I could keep an eye on it.

'Did you send that creepy boy out to flirt with me? Did you?' I demanded, still squeezing her left arm.

She grinned, a sickeningly lewd grin. 'Yes, I did. Time you had a boyfriend. You didn't like him?' she said.

'Don't you ever, ever do that again,' I said.

She hit me so hard – a punch, not a slap – that I thought my jaw was broken. Without any reflection I hit her just as hard in the jaw, the first time I had ever struck another human being in my life.

From my blow, Mama fell against the table but straightened up and walked away.

'You'll pay for that,' she said over her shoulder and went back into the gym.

And I did.

It wasn't just Mama; Daddy drank, too. He and Mama would fight, and he'd take off to Snug Harbor, a bar at Lake Overholser on the edge of the City. Then he bought the town beer joint in partnership with a woman he'd met at Snug Harbor. Jealousy drove Mama to harder drinking. She bought her gin from the bootlegger and was often arrested. No one ever said anything about Mama's drinking and arrests, as if it weren't happening.

And I was alone. Hank was at Oklahoma City University; Mary Jane and her family had also moved to the City; my boyfriend from the year before, Phil, had left Oklahoma to live with other relatives and, after an exchange of letters, we lost touch. Mama had driven Ronnie off and I didn't have a boyfriend. Lorene was still my friend, but I couldn't tell her what was happening at home. I felt trapped alone with my parents, and scared for my life.

Nighttime was filled with terror that kept me awake and trembling. Mama and Daddy would fight all night after he stumbled in drunk, and she screamed accusations about his carousing. She accused him of hiding her bottle, and she frantically searched for it. In desperation she would wake me, pound me with chairs and lamps, accuse me of being in on hiding the bottle. I would curl up in the fetal position holding a pillow over my head, and check the damage in the morning sunlight.

I didn't tell anyone what was happening. I was ashamed and somehow felt I was at fault. I was afraid for my life. I dreaded going to Sunday school after the preacher's wife looked straight at me when she talked about The Fall and quoted Genesis 3:6: 'And when the woman saw that the tree was good for food, and that it was pleasant to the eyes, and a tree to be desired to make one wise, she took of the fruit thereof, and did eat, and gave also unto her husband with her; and he did eat.'

I thought my mother was a fallen woman and that everything in my life was falling apart.

Then I lost my one channel of communication, my pen pal, Shirley, in Birmingham, England. I would write her every day until I had filled both sides of two sheets of paper and typed it out and mailed the letter. And every week I received a thin blue airmail letter from her.

Shirley and I sent each other pictures, of ourselves, our dogs, our parents. And when Queen Elizabeth was crowned, Shirley was in the crowd at the coronation and sent me pictures. At first we postured and lied to each other. I portrayed my family as well off and made my father into the owner of an oil company and a great horseman, my mother into an elegant lady who spent most days at bridge club. Shirley described her father as a shipping executive but later admitted he was a dock worker. Her mother, at first portrayed as a society lady always giving teas and playing cards in a ladies' club, turned out to work in a laundry, leaving Shirley to care for her younger brothers and sisters. Both of us pretended at first that we had nannies and tutors, aping stories from the romantic English novels we read and shared.

Eventually, little by little, the truth emerged. It took about two years of peeling away the veils of pretension, and then we started pouring out our secrets to each other. I wrote Shirley long letters about my crushes, about my parents fighting, my skin defect, the rise and fall of my bicycle club, menstruation. Shirley wrote about her father being a socialist and a militant union man and I wrote about my grandfather being a Wobbly. Then when I started admiring Senator McCarthy I wrote passionately about the evils of communism. Soon Shirley wrote that her father had reformed and become fiercely anti-communist and had left his union.

Every letter, hers and mine, described the books we were reading, which were often the same, long discussions of the French Revolution based on our reading *A Tale of Two Cities,* about the Parisian poor from Hugo's *Les Miserables*, and the heroic poor in Dickens, with whom we identified. Our common favorite, though, like most girls our age in the English-speaking world, was Louisa May Alcott's *Little Women*. And *Black Beauty* expressed our spirit of alienation and innocent wisdom. Shirley didn't know about Nancy Drew and couldn't find those books in the library so I summarized them for her.

Our final letters crossed each other. My last letter told of my mother's drinking and my fear of her, about the wreck and how she had paid no attention. It was the first time I'd told anyone about Mama. I ended the letter with 'I will understand if you decide not to be my pen pal anymore.'

Shirley's letter arrived the day after I mailed mine to her. It said she was pregnant and was being sent to a government home for unwed mothers to have the baby. Her father had beaten her when he found out, and she had a broken nose. Shirley wrote that her father wanted the boy's name but she did not know for sure because, she wrote, she had slept with several boys and didn't want her father to know that.

She ended her letter with 'I know you are going to think I am a terrible girl. I didn't write you about sleeping with boys. I hope you can forgive me, but if you decide not to be my pen pal anymore I will understand.'

I suppose each of us felt the other had rejected her. I didn't think less of Shirley and wanted to write, but by then nothing seemed real and I was just hanging on. I suppose it was the same for her. For whatever reason neither of us ever wrote the other again.

School kept me going, especially drama, speech and typing, in which I won county and state awards. I was able to type nearly as fast as before I'd lost the use of the two fingers numbed by the injury to my left ulna nerve in the car wreck. I put out the school newsletter each week. I made straight As, but no longer bothered to get Daddy to sign my report card; I simply copied his signature and it was never questioned. Who would question a parent's agreement to straight As? After the experience with Ronnie I put the idea of boys on the shelf along with the dream of escape. Two years and I would graduate from high school. I was good at waiting: asthma training came in handy. I counted the days.

What actually saved me was my English, drama and speech teacher. Dr. Sylvia Mariner was a Californian and had a doctorate in philosophy from UCLA. (Twenty years later I would receive a doctorate from UCLA, still thanking Dr. Mariner.) When her Oklahoma-born army officer husband died, she arrived from Los Angeles to live in his family's old home-place outside Piedmont. She lasted only one year.

At the end of the school year, the FBI came through inquiring about her, hinting at subversive activities and Communist Party affiliation, and she was fired and moved away to take a university position in Texas. I did not know that until two years later when she wrote and explained it to me, and that knowledge was one of the turning points in my not buying the Red Scare anymore.

Dr. Mariner, as I always called her, never spoke about my home situation, but she took me home with her many nights. My parents never noticed when I was missing. I loved staying at her house. From ceiling to floor every wall in the front room was lined with books. She introduced me to John Steinbeck's *The Grapes of Wrath*, which I'd heard of but which was censored along with the movie in Oklahoma.

She said the book was about my own people, who were heroic. She
loaned me other books that were not allowed in our school library.
And she kept me busy in speech and drama. By choice, she said,
she'd never had children. She said that a woman's biology was not
her destiny. Dr. Mariner was impressed that my grandfather had been
a Wobbly, and she told me stories about the Okie migrant farm
workers in California. Edwin Markham's *The Man with a Hoe* was her
favorite poem and she had known Markham personally. She said I
should be proud of my roots whatever happened to my living family
members. At the end of the school year she gave me a sterling silver
acorn pendant and wrote: *Your mind is an acorn that will grow into a
giant oak*.

During that school year of 1954–55, when I was home alone in
Piedmont, everything changed, not just my mother. Today Piedmont
is a bedroom suburb of Oklahoma City, with gas lines and sewers
running out there. It's still a town with its own post office, and the old
main street is a ghostly version of what it was when I was growing up.
The buildings are boarded up, everything closed. A new business
strip has sprouted nearby along the highway, with a little store and
gas station owned by my second cousin, and a coffee shop and some
other businesses, including two real estate offices. But most of the old
houses in town are gone, including the two I lived in, replaced with
rambling brick ranch houses with manicured lawns. All the streets
are paved and named and they have some sort of town government.
The old Baptist and Methodist churches are gone, replaced by much
larger, modern sanctuaries. There's a new school and auditorium, the
old brick building having been demolished. Some of the old-timers
built a monument out of the bricks inscribed with names of students
who graduated from the old school. Hank had my name put on a
brick even though I didn't graduate there.

The changes that made Piedmont a suburb began during that
time, as if Mama's breakdown signaled the end of Piedmont as we
knew it, or so Daddy believed. That year, Southwestern Bell arrived
and installed a dial telephone system connected with Oklahoma City,
with SHerwood our prefix, replacing the old local system with its
central telephone office and crank phones, party lines and no privacy.

City families began moving out to Piedmont that year. The first
two were families of factory workers whose teenaged boys were in

trouble with the law. The fathers commuted the thirty miles to work and the boys entered our high school and became my friends.

I had more in common with Roy and Benny than with my old friends in town. Roy was in my grade, the first boy ever, and Benny was a year younger. Roy was something of a problem for Lorene and me at first. As juniors in charge of the refreshment concession we handled up to a hundred dollars in cash at times, and never less than forty dollars. Roy was a thief and always had his hand in the till. We had to watch him and could never leave him alone with the money. But once we understood that, it wasn't a big problem. Roy was a large boy, flabby rather than athletic, but he was stronger than either of us so he hauled the boxes of candy and pop. He had his own old car and he drove us to Yukon to make purchases and deal with our bank account. Roy drank beer and whiskey and smoked on those sojourns.

'Be careful once we get to Yukon or Sheriff Pop Floyd will get us, and he's mean,' I said.

'Yeah, he nearly killed my brother outside the Bohemian Hall once,' Lorene said.

Roy was careful in Yukon. Lorene and I didn't join in the drinking or smoking but we didn't mind, either. Roy didn't always show up at school and we would make excuses for him, saying he was picking up something for us. We did most of his homework for him, too.

When Benny moved to town he and Roy inevitably became buddies. None of the other Piedmont boys would have anything to do with either of them, calling them 'white trash' and other names. Lorene and I were their only friends. Benny seemed more dangerous than Roy. Roy was jolly and always laughing and good-natured like a big teddy bear, but Benny had murder in his eyes. He was wiry, about my height, with hair the color of copper, styled in a ducktail. His freckled face was thin and pointy and his small blue eyes were dead and icy. I thought Benny looked like Billy the Kid, although I had never seen a picture of him. Benny wore tight, faded jeans and tee shirts and black motorcycle boots; he was always neat and clean but always dressed the same. Roy was a slob, his shirttail always out, buttons missing, wrinkled trousers that were spotted or torn, and worn-out, thin-soled shoes.

Benny had a mo-ped that he called a scooter, the first one ever seen in Piedmont. He didn't talk much, and he never smiled, seemingly waiting for something, probably the day he could be free and on his own. But Benny never missed school and although he was twice as smart as anyone in his class he made Cs because of his bad attitude. Benny read voraciously, mostly Mickey Spillane, but he would read anything.

Both Roy and Benny were beaten regularly by their fathers, beaten hard, systematically, stripped, whacked with bullwhips and razor straps and two-by-fours; it was just a part of everyday life, usually around suppertime when their fathers came home from work. Their fathers would make them strip naked, tie their wrists above them, and methodically beat them. They told me about it and showed me their backs with deep cuts, and fiery welts that were often bloody. They said their 'hind ends' looked the same but didn't show me.

Hearing Roy and Benny's stories made me feel lucky for my own comparatively mild beatings. They were the only ones I could talk to about my mother. I was ashamed and didn't want the people in town to know. But my secret was safe with Roy and Benny since no one talked to them and they didn't tell their families anything.

After a short time Roy and Lorene and Benny and I paired off, taking nighttime rides on the country roads, Benny and I in the back seat. I expected something to happen, kissing at least, but it didn't. The boys smoked and drank, and we all talked about our dreams.

'I'm going to get out of this place, that's all I know for sure, get away from these prejudiced, peanut-brained, hicky Baptists,' Lorene said. She knew I didn't take her hatred of Baptists personally, that I knew it was wrong what they thought of Catholics.

'I'm going to be a reporter for a big newspaper far away,' I said.

'Like Brenda Starr?' Roy asked, seriously. Brenda Starr was a comic book character, a redheaded police-beat reporter who solved all the crimes.

'No, a foreign correspondent covering wars, like Ernest Hemingway,' I said. I had just read *A Farewell to Arms,* which Dr. Mariner had loaned me.

'Ain't no wars now,' Roy said.

'There's some in Africa, I think,' I said.

'I want to go to a big city, maybe New York – no, Los Angeles, yeah, that's it, work as a lifesaver on the beach,' Roy said.

'So you can ogle all the pretty girls in bathing suits?' Lorene teased.

'Naw, not that,' Roy said.

Benny was quiet as usual, so I poked him. We were sitting in the back seat of Roy's car, Benny staring out the window into the dark night.

'What do you want to do, Benny?' I asked.

'Get me a Harley, run with a club,' he said.

'Just like ole Marlon Brando in that movie,' Roy said.

'Something like that,' Benny said.

And Benny meant it. *The Wild One*, starring Marlon Brando, was then a big hit, and we went to see it several times. The semi-factual drama told the story of the 1947 Hell's Angels invasion of Hollister, California. For us, the Hell's Angels represented youth rebellion, something that could occur only in the promised land of California.

Benny grew on me. I decided I wanted Benny to be my boyfriend, and even began daydreaming that we might run away and join a motorcycle gang. He took me riding everywhere on his scooter. He would just appear in front of the house, or pull up beside me as I walked, not saying a word. I would climb on behind him and hold tight around his skinny waist, feel his taut muscles against my arms, feel the air in my face. Benny was never reckless and never tried to scare me on those rides. Sometimes we held hands in the back seat of Roy's car when we were out cruising, but no more than that.

One day Lorene told me that Roy and Benny 'liked each other.' I had been telling her that I wanted Benny to be my boyfriend, but that he was shy with me.

'They're different – they like boys, not girls, that way,' she said. I could not comprehend what she meant.

'You know, like in *From Here to Eternity.* They're queers,' she explained.

'Homosexual,' I corrected her. I had looked up 'queer' in the dictionary after I found it in *From Here to Eternity,* but the definition didn't explain anything. So I had asked Dr. Mariner what it meant. She told me about homosexuals and how she had many friends in Los Angeles who were homosexual, men and women, and how it wasn't nice to call them queers. But it never dawned on me that I would meet a homosexual in Piedmont, much less two.

'How do you know?' I asked Lorene.

'Roy told me,' she said.

We continued our foursome rides on country roads, and Benny took me on his scooter like always.

Right after the school year was over, before I left home, both families picked up and moved back to the City, first Roy's, then Benny's. I never heard from them, or of them, again.

The bathroom was where it ended, my life in Piedmont, when I was sixteen years old. The bathroom, the first one we'd ever had, was my refuge and my prison. It was the only room in the house that locked, and there was a window large enough for me to climb out if necessary. It was small but there was a straight-backed chair there. When Mama and Daddy would yell and scream and throw things I would take my book and quietly slip into the bathroom, latch the door and read. Or I would stand at the window, my arms folded on the windowsill, and stare out into the night or day, contemplating my fate, trying to block out the sounds of violence. Or I stood in front of the mirror staring into my face, not so much studying my appearance as making sure I was real and intact. Mama had broken my nose during one of her nocturnal attacks and it had healed crooked, so my face looked different on the right and the left.

I had to be alert to timing in the bathroom, to slip out before Mama might want to use it. She smoked in there, since she was still smoking secretly. Usually she went out into the garage to smoke and drink, but when she needed to use the bathroom she smoked a cigarette while she was in there.

That Sunday afternoon in late May was a combination of Memorial Day and Laurence's birthday. He turned twenty-seven and he and the family had come out for Sunday dinner and a cake Mama bought. School had been out for three weeks by then, and I didn't know what to do. I had no money of my own, and no transportation. There were no jobs in Piedmont.

I stood there that Sunday looking out the window south. There was a nice fresh breeze; it was still springtime. The sky was brilliant but the sun was not yet hot. Morning rain had settled the red dirt so the road that passed the house was deep red. I no longer believed the story that our dirt was red from the blood shed by the Indians, but that day I thought I smelled blood in the breeze rising from that red dirt.

The house was quiet. After dinner and cake Jan had put the children down for their naps on pallets on the living room floor and lay down with them. Daddy left in the car to go check on the beer joint. Laurence stretched out on the divan to sleep. Mama darted in and out of the house for a while to take nips from her bottle in the garage, then she settled down on her bed to black out.

I had locked myself in the bathroom to think, to try and figure a way out. I could see no way out. I had one full year of my sentence left to serve, until I graduated from high school. I had hoped Vera would invite me to live with her and her husband in their home in Midwest City so I could look for a summer job there. But suddenly they sold their house that spring and moved to a tiny apartment in Oklahoma City, too small for a third person. Living with Jan and Laurence was out of the question. They rented a three-room house in the city where the five of them were already crowded. And life wouldn't have been much better there. I often spent Saturday night with them and babysat so they could go out dancing and drinking, but they fought continually.

I heard Mama at the bathroom door. I had lost track of time while daydreaming at the window. Now I was afraid to open the door. She was jerking on the doorknob. I was trapped. I stood on the toilet and began climbing up to the windowsill to jump out. Then she jerked the door and the latch popped up. She grabbed me and dragged me down from the window and pushed me to the floor, stomping on my arms and legs, bent over me, flailing her fists at my head. I tried to curl up and cover my head but she was all over me and I was stuck between the toilet and the bathtub. That was it. She was going to kill me. I saw feet and then a form standing in the doorway. I caught a glimpse of Laurence's face. For a second I thought he might shut the door and leave.

'Help me,' I cried out. And he did. He grabbed Mama in a bear hug from behind and hauled her out of the bathroom, then came back.

'Get your things,' he said. 'You're coming with us.'

After my mother's death in 1968, my father wrote me that she had been 'like a she-lion' with us kids, that she would have died, or killed, for us if need be, or even 'slept with a nigger,' which apparently for him was a fate worse than murder or homicide, the ultimate evidence of self-sacrifice.

I've long known that Mama's violent, drunken assaults on me had nothing to do with *me*. She had every reason in the world to be crazy, having grown up a 'half-breed,' part Indian, part 'white trash,' impoverished and abandoned. I have always told myself that since all her other children were grown and gone, I was the only person around to attack when she needed to vent her rage at the world.

Eleven

Trying to Be a Typical Teenager

> When a mass cross-section of Oklahoma high school juniors
> and seniors was asked which living person they would like to be,
> the boys named Pat Boone, Ricky Nelson, and President Eisen-
> hower; the girls chose Debbie Reynolds, Elizabeth Taylor, and
> Natalie Wood.
>
> Paul Goodman,
> from *Growing Up Absurd,* 1956

I woke to a piercing screech. I opened my eyes and didn't know where I was. The room was dark. The high-pitched wail hurt my ears. Two crows must be at it outside the window, I thought. A shudder rattled my body. I flipped over and slammed into a damp lump. There was a crash at the foot of the bed and I bolted upright. A bulky silhouette against a dim light: Mama there to beat me.

But no. I heard a whisper: 'Roxie, it's all right. I stumbled. I came to feed the baby.' Jan's soothing voice. And I remembered where I was – in my brother's house in Oklahoma City, a Monday in June 1955. I was sixteen.

Jan picked up the squalling baby from her crib and came around to sit beside me as she nursed her. The starch of fear left my body and I limply lay back on the pillow. My three-year-old nephew, Hans, slept on peacefully beside me. On his other side was eighteen-month-old Henrik. Jan leaned over me, the baby tucked inside her left arm. She stroked my damp hair with her free hand.

'That was a pretty rough day yesterday. You all right?' I felt ten years old again, Jan comforting me during an asthma attack.

'What time is it?'

'Almost five. This little tiger is my alarm clock. Your brother leaves for work at seven. You sleep as long as you want.' She changed the baby and put her back in the crib and left, closing the door softly.

I needed to think about my situation. I stared into the dark, my mind blank. My eyes closed and I slept a dreamless sleep.

The window shade glowed from the summer morning sun when I woke. The smell of bacon frying caused my stomach to knot in pain. How long since I'd eaten? Twenty-four hours: a piece of toast the morning before. Hans stirred next to me. 'Mama,' he whimpered.

'I'm Aunt Roxie. Mama's in the kitchen.'

'God-damned son-of-a-bitch, Jan,' emphasis on the 'bitch.' Laurence's voice, with that built-in sneer. 'Get this god-damned dirty diaper out of the toilet.'

'I'm sorry, honey. I forgot.'

'You always forget.' My chest contracted. Hans trembled at my side.

'Your little sister's sleeping,' Jan hissed. Laurence shut up.

Laurence had been a stranger to me during the year since they moved back to Oklahoma. I hadn't been around him much since I was little, when I thought he could do no wrong. Now, at twenty-seven with a wife and three children and a low-paying job in a credit investigation company, he seemed like a walking time bomb. Jan had become a cowering shadow of herself, slumped, the sparkle gone. She tiptoed around him to keep him calm, and kept the children from annoying him. Jan had told me that Laurence was always nicer to her when she was pregnant. Maybe that was why she stayed pregnant most of the time. She also told me that he'd never once hit her or the kids, adding 'sticks and stones.' But I thought his words must hurt. His only peaceful moments seemed to be when he sat close to his phonograph listening to Mozart. He annoyed me with his contempt for rhythm and blues and his lectures on its invalidity as music: 'The saxophone does not even exist in classical music.' He had taught me to like classical music, but I hungered for rhythm and blues. Little Richard, Chuck Berry and Ruth Brown transported me and made my miserable home life more bearable.

After Laurence left for work, Jan piled the dishes in the sink, changed the two youngest, and set the boys in front of the television.

She held Hana, the baby. We sat nearly all day at the kitchen table, Jan chain-smoking and drinking coffee. We talked about Mama. Jan seemed relieved to be able to tell someone her feelings and theories about Mama; I certainly was. She had theories from the popular psychology books she read. Jan read a lot, and said she would always be grateful to Laurence because he taught her to love reading and classical music.

Jan told me how Mama got drunk for the first time out in California, and how she thought that was the beginning of Mama's binge that became a long, steady drunken state.

'We always had a jug of burgundy and we were all sitting around our trailer house drinking one afternoon, and your dad started teasing your mother about being a teetotaler. So she took the dare and chugalugged a glass of wine. I guess she wanted to piss him off. Those damned Baptists, they make it so a person has to be either a teetotaler or a drunk.'

But Jan thought there was more, that when three of Mama's children were gone and with me nearly grown, she lost her reason for living and turned to the bottle as a lover, a companion. And Daddy compounded her depression; Jan thought Mama felt rejected because he himself was going through a middle-age crisis and was attracted to younger women and started having affairs. Jan said Mama was at the age of 'the change of life,' and that's when women felt they were no longer attractive.

'We'd better call Vera and Hank to tell them what happened,' Laurence said when he came home.

Over coffee around the kitchen table we had our first sibling conference ever (and the last). Vera announced that she was divorcing her husband of five years, revealing that he was a gambling addict and had embezzled money where he worked. (Knowing that my brother-in-law, the goody-two-shoes Sunday school teacher, was really a gambler and embezzler also somehow comforted me.) Vera said I should move in with her and stay through my last year of high school. But she said I would have to work and pay half the expenses. I was overjoyed because there was nothing more I wanted than a real job and a normal life.

Vera ordered my birth certificate, took me to get a Social Security number and found a job for me. She called her former boss, the wealthy builder, and he agreed to take me to his bank and ask them to hire me. Within three days of my flight from home I was working full-time in the Central Files department of the second largest bank in Oklahoma City. It was an all-female department with a woman boss, the only one in the bank. She sat me down and explained that I was not really needed but she would try to keep me busy.

'About twenty percent of the employees in this bank in the summer are children of wealthy customers,' she said.

'I'm not, and I'm going to work through the school year,' I said.

'I know, but you are a friend of a wealthy customer,' she said.

Her nameplate said Elizabeth Jensen. She told me to call her Liz and smiled. She took me around to meet the ten women I'd be working with. Five of them ran small, humming machines, comptometers, which calculated the average balance of checking accounts to assess service charges for the bookkeeping department one floor below. The other women in the department created financial information files on every person and business with an account at the bank.

Steel file cabinets a head shorter than me formed a partition with the next department. The files contained narrow drawers filled with three-by-five cards. My job was to go through the entire file of tens of thousands of names to make sure no name was filed out of order, and to record checks returned for insufficient funds – 'hot checks' – and to do whatever else the supervisor told me to.

My co-workers at the bank were lifers, some on the job for only a few years but hoping to stay forever, while others were veterans afraid their health or sanity might break down before they were old enough for Social Security. The bank provided no retirement, no health insurance, only a week's vacation a year after three years' employment, and no sick leave. No work, no pay was the golden rule. They didn't use time clocks. The bank didn't need them, I found out, because the personnel director nourished a network of spies.

'You have to watch out what you all say or do in front of that Irene, else she'll take it right on to the personnel director,' Marie whispered to me on my second morning when she and I were alone, both of us early for work.

'And then what?' I asked.

'Out of the door, no explaining. Either that or if you be lucky, some hanky-panky with the personnel director might save your job,' she said and winked.

'But, like, doing or saying what?' I asked.

'Like what we're doing here right now, talking, if it was working time,' she said.

Marie was old enough to be my mother and had a daughter my age who already had a baby and no husband. Marie herself had four other young children. Her husband drove a big rig for Red Ball and was away much of the time. I could tell he'd been home the minute Marie walked into work with a black eye or split lip. Marie took me under her wing right away.

I studied Irene's face that day. She was so pleasant-looking and friendly that I didn't believe she was really a spy and told Marie so.

'Take my word for it and don't talk to her. That friendliness is put on. Number one, she'll tell everything you say and make up half of it. Number two, she'll get you talking, and then report you for talking to her on the job,' Marie said.

The bank was huge, seven floors of departments stacked on top of the lobby where the public did their business and where the vice-presidents sat behind huge, uncluttered mahogany desks, with their elite workers – who dealt with money and wealthy depositors – the executive secretaries, all women, and the tellers, all men. The public never saw us, and we were forbidden from going without permission into the public area, as if they were ashamed of us. The bank owned the whole skyscraper, but the floors above our habitat were a mystery because we were forbidden to trespass there. There was a special elevator at the side entrance of the building to whisk us thousand or so bank workers to our cages each morning and to dump us into the street in the evening.

The personnel director's office occupied most of the seventh floor, thus the watchword, 'Look out or you'll end up sevened,' meaning that a worker would be called up for a reprimand or to be fondled by the fat personnel director or fired. I had spent fifteen minutes of my first day at work filling out forms in that office and met with the personnel director for a few minutes. I prayed that there would be no occasion when I would have to be alone with him.

Once a month all the employees were gathered on the third floor to listen to a speech by one of the bank officers and the personnel director. One happened during my second week at work. They used our afternoon break on Friday for the speech. The officer told us we were part of a family, not workers, and that we should take pride in the great wealth and success of the bank, that every meal we ate, every movie we saw, every bit of furniture and clothes and cars we bought came from the generosity of the bank, allowing us to work there. Then the personnel director told us to be on the lookout for communists in our midst and to let him know if we were suspicious of anyone. He said one sure sign of a communist was a griper or someone who favored trade unions.

Besides my supervisor, all the bosses were men and most of the workers were women, except for the night shift in the Proof department, which was just over the steel file cabinets from my department. Those men, sleepy-eyed and resembling what I imagined convicts looked like, were still at work when I arrived at seven in the morning. They got off at eight when the day crew came on. The rattle and clunking and hum of the twenty IBM proof machines never ceased. I would watch the change of shifts over the file cabinets. They reminded me of trick riders in a rodeo who jump from one galloping horse to another alongside, as the day crew took the machines from the night crew.

The women who worked the proof machines interested me because they looked tough and scary and yelled at each other over the deafening noise of the machines. They kept to themselves but so did the workers in all the departments. Fraternizing with workers in other departments was discouraged. We even ate and took our breaks in the cafeteria by departments.

The bank was a mystery to me, a factory with no product, only numbers. It was impossible to figure out the whole process – where work had been before and what happened to it and where it went when it left our department.

'Don't ask questions like that, they'll think you're trying to make a union,' Marie warned me when I asked her what happened to the bookkeeping sides after she had computed the service charges on accounts. 'Anyway, I don't know and don't care. I just do my job, and you do yours,' she said.

Even Vera, who was an executive secretary at the other huge bank in the city, didn't know how the whole system worked.

'I just process loans that are approved, that's all I know. It's better not to know too much,' she said.

But it bothered me not knowing and not questioning. It seemed to me that all my life I had always known each thing I knew from beginning to end, from Daddy shooting a possum to taking it home, where he skinned it and cut it up, to Mama frying it up and all of us eating it for supper.

'Hon', just don't you worry your pretty little head over it. You do the job eight hours and leave. You have two lives. Real life stops when you get into here. You just go through the day,' Marie said.

Go through the day, the days, interminable minutes and hours and days, waiting for Friday, dreading Monday, waking up to the realization that I had to go to that place and serve my time.

After working at the bank for a month I woke up dizzy one morning. Not exactly dizzy, but everything was blurred and I was confused. I kept stumbling over my own feet. I sat down for breakfast with Vera and the egg on my plate swirled in shiny bacon grease. Nausea rippled through my whole body. I ran to the bathroom and sat on the cool tile floor with my forehead on the cool porcelain of the toilet. I couldn't throw up. The movement of the water in the toilet bowl made me dizzy. I noticed then the throb in my left eye, or behind it – not pain, but pressure, so much pressure it felt like my eye would pop out.

I managed to dress for work but with difficulty. It was taking me forever. As I was leaving to catch the bus Vera noticed that my blouse was on backwards and my slip was showing. I fixed them. I just missed a bus. I waited and waited for the next one. I had forgotten to put my watch on and had no idea what time it was. The colors of the passing cars bled into each other, creating a sort of huge sickening finger painting. I tried to look away but in all directions the morning sun reflected off shiny things – a street sign, a shop window. It was the same in the bus when it came. I'd never before noticed how so many objects glared and glittered and flashed, how ugly colors were when they weren't separated and distinct, how sickening the smell of makeup and perfume and shaving lotion. I stood on the crowded bus for the thirty-minute ride, weak in the knees, nearly crazed.

I was sure I was going to be late for work for the first time. Usually I was the first to arrive, way early, just to be safe. I tried to focus on what I would say to my supervisor as I rode the elevator up to the third floor. I couldn't think. What if she sent me to the personnel director? I nearly ran from the elevator to my department, the thundering of the proof machines almost crushing me. In the department only Marie was there, sitting by the window, looking down on the street.

'What happened, where is everyone?' I asked, terribly confused.

Marie turned and smiled. 'You know, you-all and me are the oliest ones stupid enough to get here early,' she said.

I looked at the big clock. Only 7:30, a half hour before starting time.

I sat in a chair beside Marie and stared out the window with her. She began telling me about her affairs and now she was describing a man, a saloon, dancing, a fight, but the words got all jumbled in my mind. Usually Marie's stories mesmerized me like a living soap opera.

I could see Marie's words bouncing off the Petroleum Club across the street. A wave of nausea rumbled through me. I ran to the bathroom but couldn't vomit.

I stumbled back to the office on time and sat at the work desk by the window – I didn't have my own desk because I was at the file cabinets most of the day. My first task most mornings was to rip up a pile of bookkeeping sides that appeared on the work table. I didn't know what they were or why they needed to be destroyed or even who put them there or when.

The paper kept cutting my fingers and blood spotted the bookkeeping sides, but it didn't matter since they went into the wastebasket anyway. They had to be torn in eight pieces, no more or less, why eight I didn't know. I kept losing track of the number of pieces and had to try to reassemble and recount them. I wondered if anyone checked on how many pieces they were torn into.

I was nearly finished with the pile, dreading to work at the files the rest of the day, standing, when I heard a shriek, almost in my ear.

'What are you doing? Stop, stop, oh no.'

My supervisor's voice. She was standing across the table from me grabbing at the untorn bookkeeping sides, then clawing in the wastebasket.

A pain ripped my skull. I thought I'd been shot, that my head had exploded. I automatically raised my arms and held my head. I had never experienced such pain, blinding torturous agony. It seemed palpable, a band of pain at the base of my skull, a pounding alternating with ice-pick stabs. My vision went. I could see light and motion and shadows but no forms, nothing distinct.

I woke on a cot in a small room. The pain woke me, unbearable pain. A strange smell.

'Ammonia. How often do you have migraines?' A woman in a blocked white cap and a white dress loomed over me. The whiteness gleamed and sent shock waves through my head.

'You're in First Aid. Is it any better?' she asked. The sound of her voice shot daggers into my brain.

'No, no, it hurts, go away,' I said and curled in a fetal position, my forehead against the wall.

'The medicine should kick in shortly and you'll feel better. I gave you a shot,' she said. I fell into blackness.

My first migraine headache, the first of many. Maybe it saved my job because my supervisor didn't report what I had done – torn up new bookkeeping sides, which were also placed on that same desk every morning, and that I should have recognized. Lucky for me my supervisor suffered from migraines, too. By noon the headache was gone and I felt like I was floating on air. Everything was sharp and vivid. That afternoon I joined my co-workers in taping back together all the bloodstained pieces of the sides so the comptometer operators could run the numbers. We worked until midnight.

At Vera's I found out right away that I was not a roommate and equal, but rather something between a servant and a guest. She never let me forget that it was her apartment and she could kick me out at any time. And Vera was very particular. Everything had to be spotlessly scrubbed and dusted, every dish washed and put away in its exact place immediately; the bathroom had to sparkle, closets and drawers in perfect order. She even insisted on ironed sheets, which fell to me since I wasn't very good at ironing anything else. Vera wouldn't let me cook or teach me how. I was the dishwasher and general scrub girl and errand girl. Worst of all was not having my own room. There were two bedrooms in the apartment but she insisted we share her double bed, and she made the other one into her office. She had her large desk there and an upright piano. That room was off-limits to me, so I didn't have any private space at all. I always felt like a guest, and an overworked one at that, even though I paid half the rent and for half the groceries and supplies and gasoline.

I took great pride in paying my own way, but I felt sorry for myself; I felt a sense of injustice that I paid half of all the bills and did most of the housework but my income was less than half of Vera's. She saved money and spent a great deal on stylish clothes and shoes. I never had any money left for anything and had to borrow from her, which she kept account of. I stewed about it but didn't complain. Vera could always kick me out and I would be back in the chaos of Jan and Laurence's place and sleeping in a room with three children.

Vera won the Oklahoma City Secretary of the Year award. She received some money and prizes, one of which was a huge oil portrait of herself, elaborately framed. A whole page of the Society section of the Sunday paper was devoted to Vera, with a big picture of her. I was proud of my sister, until I read the article. There was a whole paragraph about me, saying that Vera had brought me to the city to live with her to go to a better school, without naming the school or reporting that I worked; instead the article said that Vera was fully supporting me.

'How could you tell them that, it's not true,' I said to her.

'You know you couldn't make it on your own,' she said, as if that explained everything.

School was not much better than work or home. Oklahoma City Central High on North Robinson at Northwest Ninth Street looked, I imagined, like the reformatory my mother had been in at my age. The fifty-year-old marble dungeon filled a whole city block and stood three stories high. The wooden floors were scarred, the walls peeling, the corridors wide and dimly lit, the chair-desks wobbly, blackboards permanently chalky and scratched, windows broken, classrooms drafty, the library dingy with most of the books missing or defaced. A plaque on the building with a God's-eye Masonic symbol said it was originally a Masonic Hall, which the Masons had contributed to the city to establish the first high school in the state.

Central High operated the city's trade school, and only Central allowed students to work full-time and receive course credit toward graduation, with the employer assigning the grade. Working students from all school districts landed at Central High. It was only an eight-block walk to my job, where I now worked from eleven to five. The trades offered were business, homemaking, shop, auto mechanics, refrigeration, radio/telephone, printing and newspaper production. There was also a university-track program, and that was pretty much how the school was divided along class lines. There were those on the vocational track and those on the academic, or those who worked and those who did not. Those of us who worked were cheap – if not contract or slave – labor for Oklahoma City businesses.

As a working student I was in trade school. I signed up for the secretarial program and didn't have to worry about the business courses because of my prior training at Piedmont. My classes ran from seven to eleven in the morning, after which I went to my job. The school halls bristled with switchblades and hunting knives and even handguns. It was the first year of integration in Oklahoma City and racial clashes were daily fare. It was the year of James Dean's *Rebel Without a Cause*, and of his sudden death. It was the year of *Blackboard Jungle*, which could easily have been a documentary on Central High. Bill Haley's 'Rock Around the Clock,' featured in the movie, was our theme song. Classes did not always take place. Few students showed up for classes. Teachers didn't always appear, either; and when they did, they were sometimes drunk and nearly always targets for erasers and curses or worse. In the beginning I tried to stay out of the crossfire and avoid the basement locker area and the cafeteria, where most of the fights took place.

The first friend I made at Central was a girl who worked for two hours each day after school as a page in the same bank where I worked. She was not in trade school, however, but on academic track. LaNiece was an honor student and had been a champion tennis player in junior high. She didn't have to work but had bought a car and used her income for clothes and records. Her family was working class but her father worked as an airplane mechanic at the navy base and made good money, and her mother was a full-time housewife. LaNiece was athletic, a blue-eyed blonde filled with enthusiasm and laughter, as bright and active as I was dark and skinny, always vulnerable to viruses that could provoke deadly asthma attacks. LaNiece insisted that I be included in the social world of Central, such as it was, and invited me to her home.

LaNiece taught me to bop to Fats Domino's 'Mona' and 'Blueberry

Hill,' to Ruth Brown's 'So Long' and 'Teardrops from My Eyes,' and LaVern Baker's 'Soul on Fire' and 'Tweedly Dee,' and Little Willie John's 'Fever.' LaNiece dragged me to concerts and football games, and on Saturday afternoons to record shops where we listened to the top ten records in a booth, then on to department stores to try on clothes without buying anything. I felt like I was living the life of the Typical Teenager I read about in magazines. LaNiece never asked about my family and I didn't volunteer information, only that I lived with my sister. My brother Hank's celebrity as a basketball star was enough for her and the other girls I met. I shamelessly exploited the association.

LaNiece sponsored my membership in her club, the Red Skirts, who were allied with the male Red Shirts. The Red's adversaries were the Black Skirts and the Black Shirts. Red and Black were the school colors, and the cardinal was its symbol. (As a political radical later I wondered why the school had chosen these famously anarchist colors.) Until two years earlier the clubs had been secret, really little more than gangs, with conflicts between the Blacks and the Reds. After a number of suicides and mysterious deaths and beatings, secret clubs had been banned in high schools statewide. Now the clubs were legal and monitored but still not easy to get into, and entrance required a member-sponsor.

The main reason I decided to pledge the Red Skirts was that they worked as ushers at the Municipal Auditorium. I would get to see concerts for free. It was the upcoming appearance of Elvis Presley that tempted me – the show had sold out after the first hour of ticket sales.

LaNiece and I went to work Elvis's concert together. When we got there more than an hour before showtime thousands of teenagers already jammed the broad flight of steps and the whole plaza in front of the Municipal Auditorium. Hundreds of heavily armed policemen were outnumbered and stood rigidly, silhouetted against the limestone facade, blocking the five wide doorways. Dressed in our red and black uniforms we were allowed through. Along with a dozen other Red Skirts we took our places by the doors and waited. But when the doors opened thousands of teens rushed in and we were helpless to insist they take their designated seats. Fistfights broke out over seats up front, knives flashed.

I had never seen so many people, people my age in one place. Even though the schools had just been integrated, and Elvis was a hillbilly like me doing black rhythm and blues, there wasn't a black face in the crowd. I'd also never seen so many police in one place; they marched down the aisles pushing kids into seats, whacking some with their billy clubs. One boy near me was bleeding. LaNiece and I looked at each other, and ran for two seats in the second row. Usually the ushers sat down only after the show began. The noise was deafening. I started thinking of the Nathanael West novel *The Year of the Locust,* which Dr. Mariner had given me to read the year before, and I looked for exits. The MC came on stage and everyone stomped and chanted 'Elvis, Elvis, Elvis.' The MC could not be heard.

Elvis ran out from behind the curtains. 'This is the most important moment of my life' was what flashed through my mind. He wore a gold lamé jacket and tight pants, and fancy gold cowboy boots. He was gorgeous and not much older than us. The noise didn't stop, but Elvis could be heard above the roar. Everyone stood and started dancing in place. Some kids crowded into the aisles and went up near the stage. The police cleared the aisles, bashing heads, arms and shoulders. Some who fell didn't get back up. Then others would fill the aisles, meeting the same fate. LaNiece and I danced in place. Tears came to my eyes when Elvis wailed 'Heartbreak Hotel': 'I walk a lonely street, so lonely I could die.'

At first I was distracted by the violence. How could police get by with that behavior? They seemed consumed by fear. But why did they feel so threatened by kids? After a while I no longer noticed the cops but was overcome by the electricity in the air, the beat, the power of all those bodies and minds acting as one person merged with the voice and persona of Elvis. Elvis could lead us, fearless, anywhere, I thought to myself.

Still, that didn't mean that I had abandoned my hard-core fundamentalist beliefs. I had a third life in Oklahoma City, one completely distinct from school and work and social life. That was church. I joined the Trinity Baptist Church where Vera had been going. It was within walking distance of us, just at the east edge of the Oklahoma City University campus, a big, wealthy congregation. The services were far more formal than in our country church, and not a single person from my school went there. Most Central students lived in the poorer sections of the city, on the east or south sides. LaNiece lived near me, but her family was Church of Christ. So I rubbed shoulders with a few rich young Baptists at Trinity.

I realized that what I had called rich before in Piedmont was poor compared with the rich in the City. One girl, Judy, befriended me and took me home for Sunday dinner many times. She was an only child and her father owned *The Farmer Stockman* weekly, which had subscribers all over North America. That newspaper had been Daddy's bible when I was growing up. It was peculiar to me to think of a newspaper being owned by a rich man because the small-town newspapers my mother wrote for were owned by ordinary men. Judy's father had never even been a farmer or a stockman, or even planted a bean or ridden a horse in his life. He had inherited the newspaper from his father.

Judy's house was in the old-rich, north section of the city, in the Classen district. It was a mansion in my eyes, a two-story brick house with so many rooms, halls and bathrooms that a person could get lost in them. There was also a basement the size of the house, a 'recreation' room Judy called it, with a Ping-Pong table, television, hi-fi, and deep sofas and chairs – the place where Judy was supposed to entertain her friends.

But the problem with Judy was that she didn't have any friends. She really latched on to me when we met at the youth Baptist Training Union – BTU, we called it – at Trinity Baptist Church. I never figured out why Judy didn't have friends, because she was pretty, slim, blonde, smart, and nice. But she went to an expensive private girls' school across town and her parents didn't allow her to go to shows or out cruising. Judy was square.

Sunday dinners at Judy's house were uncomfortable for me. Judy and I and her parents sat stiffly and were served by a middle-aged black woman who wore all white like a nurse. Judy told me that the woman was the full-time housekeeper and lived in the house although she had five children who lived with their grandmother on the east side, where she was allowed to go visit them on Saturdays. Judy said that the black housekeeper had taken care of her from the time she was born. What was strange to me was that they never even introduced the housekeeper to me and I never caught her name. As we sat at Sunday dinner, Judy's mother would jingle a golden bell that sat beside her on the table when she wanted something.

The first time I ate there I was so relieved when the food came out and it was fried chicken. Hard as Vera tried to teach me how to eat with a knife and fork she never succeeded. I simply avoided meat, saying that I didn't like it although I did; I would order a hamburger or fried chicken, which I could eat with my hands. But at Judy's, once we all had chosen our favorite pieces – there were two fryers so I had no problem grabbing a drumstick – they all began cutting thin slices off their chicken with a knife and eating it with a fork as if it were a steak. Judy had chosen a drumstick, too, and deftly cut pieces off the bone with no problem. I succeeded in more or less stripping the chicken meat off its bone, then cut it into pieces that I forked to eat. But it didn't taste like fried chicken that way. Even Vera ate fried chicken with her fingers. But Judy and her parents didn't seem to notice my clumsiness in cutting up my chicken that first day or on other occasions; Sunday dinner there was always fried chicken.

Judy had her own brand-new red Ford, and she assumed that Vera's car was mine. I lied and told her I had grown up on a ranch northwest of the city. She and her parents seemed to assume that I was rich like them. Judy knew I went to Central High and worked nearly full-time, but she referred admiringly to it as something I was doing to build my character. She had the idea that I wanted to be a social worker, which was her own goal, and thought I was working to get real life experience, which is what she felt deprived of in her private school. It was easy to fool Judy and her family without even trying, because they seemed incapable of even imagining anyone being poor.

Judy and I were together only during and after church functions. Besides Sunday dinner, we sometimes went for sundaes after Sunday night BTU or Wednesday night prayer meeting with her parents at the nearby Carnation Creamery; green mint with hot fudge was always my choice. Judy didn't go to drive-in hamburger joints or the pizza place or the submarine sandwich shop or to shows, and she didn't cruise in her Ford or drag race like I did with my Central High friends, and I didn't tell her about my other life. I think she believed she was my only friend as I was hers. Judy was the poor little rich girl I'd read about as a child, and I did not envy her for her fancy bedroom with a canopy bed, her private bathroom, her closet full of clothes and shoes, her own recreation room, her own new car, her maid. I felt sorry for her.

Just before Judy and I graduated from high school our friendship ended. She figured out I wasn't whom she thought I was and didn't speak to me after that. It was a strange incident that happened one Sunday night during training union. We always read Bible passages aloud for a half hour starting at six on Sunday evening, then had another hour for refreshments and games. The BTU teacher was always thinking up new parlor games for us to play, and there were a half-dozen Ping- Pong tables and we would often have matches. I was a whiz at Ping-Pong. But that particular night the teacher surprised us with something new, a strip of newly painted lines and circles with numbers in them on the polished wooden floor with wooden disks of various colors lined up at the end of the strip.

'Does anyone know what this is?' the teacher asked.

We all looked dumbly down at the mysterious lines and circles and shook our heads.

'This is shuffleboard, and I'm going to teach you how to play,' she said proudly.

'Shuffleboard – I know how to play that,' I said, stupid loudmouth that I was when I thought I knew something.

'Wonderful, Roxie. Come demonstrate for us,' she said.

I had played shuffleboard in the Piedmont beer joint for ten years, and I was a champ at the game.

This setup was clearly different. It was played on the floor, and the disks were wooden instead of steel and twice as big. There was no sawdust on the strip but I figured the principle of the game was the same. Shuffleboard was shuffleboard in my mind. Enthusiastically showing off, I got down on my hands and knees and aimed a wooden disc and hit the top number circle. I looked up proudly at the teacher, but she was not smiling or approving. All the young people stood in a semicircle watching. Something was terribly wrong.

'Roxie, where did you learn to play barroom shuffleboard?' the teacher asked. I got up and stared down at the floor and noticed paddle-like sticks leaning against the wall.

'I guess this is different, more like croquet?' I said, hoping she wouldn't insist on knowing how I'd learned to play barroom shuffleboard.

But she did insist, and I tried to explain. I could see the look in the teacher's eyes and the expressions of shock and revulsion in those young people's faces as I told them about the Piedmont Cafe: I was 'white trash.'

'You know, Roxie, that good Christians don't go into taverns and they don't gamble. Now this here is a game usually found on cruise ships and it's a clean game,' the teacher said. It was several years before it occurred to me to wonder how the Baptist Training Union teacher had learned about barroom shuffleboard.

Although I was in Oklahoma City and felt safe from my mother there, I was not free of her, as I soon discovered. Hank gave me four passes to the big Oklahoma City–Seattle University basketball game. All the home games were held at the Municipal Auditorium downtown to handle the huge crowds. I invited LaNiece and two other Red Skirts, Shari and Linda, to go with me. I dressed carefully, wearing my one cashmere sweater, which I had saved for months to buy – a peach-colored pullover – and a full-circle felt skirt that matched, brown and white saddle shoes and white anklets. My short coat was exactly the same as nearly every teenaged girl in Oklahoma City wore that winter – a white, fluffy fake fur.

The night was cold with a Norther bringing arctic winds and promising sleet or snow. We entered the auditorium and headed straight for the 'Ladies' Lounge' to study ourselves in the floor-to-ceiling mirrors. The auditorium was familiar to me by then, because I had been ushering frequently. (After Elvis, I had been a Red Skirt usher in the auditorium for the appearances of Fats Domino, Ruth Brown, LaVern Baker, Little Richard, Chuck Berry, the Midnighters, Little Willie John and the Dominos, all even more violent events than the Elvis show because the artists were black, and the crowds were black and white. The shows turned into race wars, with the police looking the other way. I watched, listened and danced, mesmerized, and stayed out of the crossfire.)

The women's lounge had an entry room lined with mirrors and chairs at dressing tables. The toilets, twenty or so, were in an adjacent room. The entire place gleamed of spotless chrome, mirror and tile. We each took out our makeup, lipstick and hairbrushes, and tried each other's lipsticks.

'What color's that?' LaNiece asked, and grabbed my new Revlon lipstick.

'Persian Melon,' I said.

'Hmm, matches your sweater – nice,' Shari said.

I hated those girl sessions in front of mirrors. In the winter my white spots were barely visible with makeup on, but I always feared that someone would ask about them. The ones on my hands were noticeable, but I always claimed to have been burned as a child – somehow it was less shameful and didn't require further explanation about mysterious melanin or raise questions about whether it was 'catching.'

Suddenly the heavy chrome lounge door flew open and banged against the wall. Reflected in the mirror I saw a wild woman, an older, wilder version of myself. I gripped the chair. My friends stopped chattering and turned, then laughed.

'Drunken Indian hag, what's she doing here?' Shari said.

They turned back to their makeup and chatter. The wild woman continued, weaving, to the toilets. Banging and cursing filled the air from the other room.

'Hey kids, let's go back. My brother said he'd come out and talk to us before the warm-up,' I lied.

I was in terror that Mama would recognize me and expose me to my friends. But she did not. All during the game I could see her and Daddy on the other side of the court. I could hear her shouts, yelling my brother's name above all the roar of the crowd. Either Mama and Daddy didn't see me or they were kind enough, or ashamed enough, not to embarrass me. At halftime Hank came over to say hello. He flirted with my friends and charmed them, but his eyes telegraphed our shared embarrassment. I was not alone.

Life with Vera improved when she bought a brand-new yellow and white Oldsmobile hardtop and let me drive it any time I wanted, on agreement that I would also serve as her general chauffeur. That snazzy automobile gave me status with my friends that equaled my having a brother who was a basketball star. With a carload of teens, I cruised and hung out at drive-in hamburger joints and drag raced in the big parking lot behind the state capitol building.

Vera never asked me any questions about where I was going or who I'd been with. She was busy with her own life, going to night school at the city university to get a degree in finance, working full-time, and dating. For a while she was madly in love with a former rodeo champion who was now a famous clown because he had been gored in the leg by a steer he was wrestling. For two months or so she spent every weekend on the rodeo circuit with him. After they broke up she went out with a naval officer from Oklahoma City who was stationed in New Orleans, and she flew down to be with him most weekends. So I was home alone with the car many weekends. I guess she knew she could trust me, or maybe she didn't care. Only later I found out that she was not amused that I had drag raced her car.

Over the strong objections of the school counselor, who wanted me to stick to business courses, I had signed up for the course on producing the weekly school paper – I had after all done my own school newspaper in Piedmont for years. *The Sooner Spirit* became my life. Only thirty students qualified for journalism, and a few were reputed to be Beats. I'd never heard about Beats before but I found two in the basement of Central High in my newspaper class. Four of my fellow reporters, including the two Beats, became close friends. Billy was one of the Beats, a Black Shirt who risked his life by being openly gay; he was a good writer, and into heroin. Billy's best friend, the other Beat, was a Black Skirt who called herself Sparkie. She dyed her blonde hair black and dressed in black and wrote poetry that I liked. They had both left terrible homes and now shared a 'pad,' as they called their run-down house, with some older Beats who had dropped out of school. They worked full-time in a print shop. My two other friends, Tommy and Bobby, were both football stars, muscle men who were working on the newspaper because it was an easy grade. Top athletes never made anything less than a B in classes. They were Red Shirts, too. But in the newspaper class we left our club affiliations at the door.

My Beat friends teased me about being square – I didn't even drink or smoke, much less smoke 'reefer' or shoot 'shit' – but they took me in. Mr. Beane, our teacher, called us his 'band of outsiders.' I loved that idea. Small, dark and Irish Catholic, with a receding hairline, Mr. Beane didn't have a beard but always looked as if he hadn't shaved. His eyes were usually bloodshot. I recognized the whisper of alcohol on his breath. But he always showed up for class. I heard the others admiringly call him a 'queer' and a drunk.

Since my brother was a star athlete and I knew every batting average in both leagues and all there was to know about college basketball, I wrote many of the sports articles. Then I started writing feature stories as well – stories about racial violence against blacks in the hallways, about physical abuse by some of the shop teachers, about the drug dealers who hung around the school, about the school policy preventing girls from taking shop or printing or auto mechanics, about the snobbery of the social clubs (I received a demerit from the Red Skirts for that).

After I wrote an article headlined 'Central Steals Douglass Athletes' I found my locker painted with 'nigger lover' and signed 'KKK.' Douglass High School was the all-black high school on the east side. Soon after, a big white guy shoved me in the hallway and another tripped me. That was when I signed up for the Urban League from an ad I'd seen in the newspaper. I never attended a meeting or demonstration, or even heard of one, but I sent in my dollar monthly and flashed my membership card when anyone made racist remarks. My journalism colleagues defended me. Tommy insisted he was my bodyguard – Tommy was the football quarterback and captain and no one messed with him. He was the first guy from Oklahoma I knew to bleach his hair; it was bright yellow with a green tinge, California surfer style.

Near the end of the school year, the journalism students held a paper drive to raise money to buy a gift for Mr. Beane. I said I knew where there was a gold mine of newspapers. Billy, Sparkie and I cut our morning classes and drove out to Piedmont. I hadn't traveled that highway for nearly a year, not since I'd escaped.

Sparkie read a long poem she'd just written about high society and the stockyards. I stared out the window. I hadn't noticed the sky for a long time – it was hard to see the sky in the city. Now it was so clear and so blue. Recent rain had darkened the red shale beds that cut through the deep green alfalfa fields.

It was a weekday morning and I expected to find the house empty, but Mama was there. She sat at the dining room table, a half-filled page of writing in front of her. She drank, openly, and smoked.

'Have a drink, there's some ice cubes in the icebox.'

Billy and Sparkie poured themselves half-glasses of gin and lit up cigarettes.

'Mama, we rode out to collect paper for our journalism class. Can I take all those newspapers in the garage?'

'Go ahead and take them – belong to Moyer but he won't care, don't come out here no more,' she said.

We loaded up the trunk and back seat of the car with the newspapers. I went back into the house to tell Mama we were leaving. She stared at the page in front of her.

'Thanks, Mama. You take care of yourself.'

'You have nice friends, a nice life,' she said. She seemed to be talking to herself, not me.

The visit freed me for a while of fear, because I had returned to the scene of the crime and found the perpetrator so harmless.

I graduated from Central High School number one in a class of 335 seniors, the only student with straight As throughout high school. By being first in my class I won a scholarship to Oklahoma Women's College in Chickasha, southwest of Oklahoma City, but I decided to go to Oklahoma University to study journalism, inspired by my journalism teacher. I had no idea how I would support myself there.

After Central High School was closed some years ago, Southwestern Bell bought the landmarked Masonic building and spent millions restoring it, including a Central High museum. Back home at Christmas 1994, I visited the museum, which contains the memorabilia of Central High. (The building was badly damaged and the museum destroyed when the nearby federal office building was bombed in 1995.) I spent hours there, reading everything and staring at all the pictures of the class, my class, of 1956. Long ago I'd lost my copy of the yearbook, but I found one on display in the museum.

The 1956 *Cardinal*, the Central High yearbook, astonished me, as if every picture and every page were airbrushed, such clean-cut looking young people, so happy, and the teachers so distinguished and intelligent. The yearbook opened with a dubious claim:

Now in midst of great metropolis,
In the shade of spires of Central,
Come the student, white and Negro,
To abolish segregation
… hours of study, relaxation, fun, making friends, and becoming better citizens.

I thought about the KKK graffiti on my locker, the attacks on black students, the exploitation of black athletes, the drug dealers on the corner, the fact that all the teachers were white, how rarely anyone ever studied, and if one worked full-time like I did how little time there was for relaxation and fun; and about the lies we have to tell ourselves in order to reconcile our pasts with who we think we have become.

There are three pictures of me in that yearbook. In the mug shot for the graduating class, I smile broadly and appear to be a perfectly normal, incredibly proper and pretty enough young woman. In the group photograph with the senior members of the Red Skirts, there are twenty-four of us. I recognize only LaNiece and three others. We wear our Red Skirt uniforms. I appear uncomfortable and out of place. The picture of me with my fellow journalism students is my favorite, and the caption reminds me how that class and the teacher saved me from the white working-class girl's destiny of secretarial work:

> Cries of 'Where's the copy!' pierce the air in Room 18 twice a month, letting everyone know that the next edition of the *Sooner Spirit* is about to go to press … All students must have at least a 'B' average in English to be in journalism. After they make the class, they learn by doing the actual writing … Central students are the only ones in the city who print their own paper and take all their own pictures.

In the yearbook, my signature – Roxie Dunbar – is the first of the senior signatures, the John Hancock of the Class of 1956 at Central High. I don't remember if that was because I may have been the only student in class when the list came around or because I graduated number one. They didn't have valedictorians and salutatorians or any other award for scholarship at Central. I can't even recall if I went to my graduation. I know I didn't buy a class ring. I already had my golden ring, bought as a junior, from Piedmont, and that's where my heart was.

Lorene graduated alone from our Piedmont class. I wanted to go to the graduation but didn't want to run into Mama or Daddy, and perhaps I didn't want to be asked questions about why I had left Piedmont. But Lorene wrote me, triumphantly, that when she was asked, as the lone senior, what preacher she wanted for the Baccalaureate, she said she wanted her priest from Yukon.

'All hell broke loose but what could they do? A Catholic priest giving a sermon in the Piedmont auditorium? They had to allow it,' she wrote.

Lorene said that everyone stayed away in droves from the ceremony, including all the eighth-grade graduates and their parents, and that only two other people besides her own family came to that ceremony – my mother and father.

I cried when I read that letter. Mama and Daddy were there for me, and for my friendship with Lorene. Oh how I loved Mama and Daddy when I read that letter, and how I wished I could have been graduating with Lorene so I could have insisted on having the Catholic priest, too.

Twelve

Higher Education

> I felt it then
> I know it now
>
> little children (lost)
> were cruelly blamed
> WILMA ELIZABETH MCDANIEL,
> from 'Orphans'

Midsummer 1956. It was Saturday night and I was a high school graduate with no idea what to do next. I dressed for a party, a kind of big girls' slumber party, women only, all night, a chance for the girls to be away from their boyfriends.

'It will make us more tantalizing to them afterwards,' the hostess had said when she called to invite me. She was a Central High Red Skirt whom I knew only by sight, but my friend LaNiece put my name on the guest list when she was invited. I didn't really qualify because I had no boyfriend to tantalize. LaNiece, Shari, Linda, every girl I knew and my sister, too, had boyfriends. While at Central High I never had a regular boyfriend, although I had more than my share of male buddies, most of whom I had crushes on but who regarded me as a sister. Several Central boys asked me out but didn't call back when I refused to sleep with them. Hank's basketball roommates in the athletic dorm would call me up and take me out to a movie or to a drive-in hamburger place, but they never went further, not with Hank to answer to.

I took measure of myself in the full-length mirror and approved mostly, at least from the neck up. I'd bleached my hair with Light 'N Bright to a yellow that matched my shirt. I wore makeup that covered my white spots, and orange lipstick. But I had a body the shape of a pencil from all angles. My legs looked like brown toothpicks protruding from my khaki short-shorts. My skin was the color of a pecan shell. The white rings around my fingers, mouth, eyes and elbows were barely visible, camouflaged by the flaming red of being in the sun all day. I spent every Saturday at the Black Hawk, and some evenings too. (It was the gathering spot for working-class teenagers from all over the City, white teenagers. Way out on the eastern edge of the City, right in the heart of the black community, Black Hawk was privately owned and for whites only. Little black kids hung on to the chain-link fence and watched us swimming and laughing, bopping to the black rhythm and blues that blasted over loudspeakers.)

I was ready early as usual, a half-hour before LaNiece was to pick me up. Vera was applying her makeup in the bathroom, getting ready for a date. When she came out she stopped in her tracks.

'Look at you – too bad no boys will be at that party. They'd all fall for you.'

We both jumped at the sudden loud pounding on the back door. Nobody came to that door except Hank, and he was out of town playing semi-pro baseball for the Oklahoma Stockyards, where he also worked summers between college.

'Maybe Laurence?' I said, a question in my voice.

'Who is it?' Vera screeched.

'Daddy.'

Vera and I exchanged glances; there was alarm in her eyes and surely she saw the fear in mine. I did not want to see Daddy, and feared that Mama might be with him. More than anything I did not want LaNiece to arrive while he was there. Vera opened the door. I hadn't seen Daddy up close for over a year, only at a distance at Hank's ball games. The man looked only vaguely familiar to me, heavier with a beer belly. He appeared unkempt and dirty. He'd always been so fastidious, even in his work clothes. There were dark spots on his light blue cowboy shirt. Blood.

'Have you been in a wreck, Daddy?' Vera asked.

He stepped into the brightly lit kitchen. There were cuts on his face, his lip was swollen, his shirt torn.

'It's your mother. I was out there at the house and she had a fit and started breaking windows, furniture, throwing things at me. She cut herself pretty bad on window glass. I tried to help stop the bleeding but she took a butcher knife to me. I tried to hold her down and take the knife but I couldn't do nothing with her. She's a mess. She wants me to move out, thinks I'm seeing a woman and says she'll kill us both.'

'Well, aren't you seeing a woman?' Vera accused more than asked him. Hank had already told us that he'd run into Daddy at the Alibi Tavern with a good-looking younger woman who worked there. Vera blamed Daddy's running around for our mother's condition.

Daddy looked down and studied his hand, turning it over. It was swollen.

'Will you go out there and check on her, see if she's all right? She won't let me near her,' he said, ignoring Vera's question.

'She should be in the insane asylum. She's going to kill herself or somebody else,' I said.

'Louise would go crazy locked up. I'd never do that to her,' he said.

'Get Laurence to go – he can handle it,' Vera said.

We called Laurence and he agreed. Daddy left and two minutes later LaNiece was at the front door, dressed all in white – short shorts and a halter, her skin tanned dark gold, her long, naturally blonde hair exuding light and air, her eyes perfectly set sapphires. And I wanted to run and hide and cry.

At the party I sat by the window and stared out at the tree-lined street. I strolled out and sat in the wooden porch swing, watching the lightning bugs flash on and off. Everyone except me drank bootleg whiskey. Low-riding Chevrolet Bel Airs and Ford Fairlanes, engines revving, stuffed with catcalling, ducktailed boys cruised back and forth in front of the house. I felt like a very old person in a kindergarten class. LaNiece pulled me inside the house to bop now and then. I moved sluggishly without feeling the beat, and just listened to the words, all about love, but they had several different meanings for me. 'Ain't that a shame, tears fall like rain' pounded in my head. 'Oh yes I'm the great pretender, pretending that I'm not alone' brought hot tears to my eyes. Looking back now, I realize that I had succeeded in becoming more or less a typical teenager, alienated and terrified.

I had saved every penny I could the summer after I graduated from high school by working full-time, but it wasn't enough to pay my room and board at Oklahoma University. The student aid office said all its money was committed and the student employment office cautioned me not to expect a regular job.

I decided to ask Daddy for money. He had not contributed a penny to my last year of high school. Hank said Daddy was living with his woman, a barmaid, in the southwest part of Oklahoma City near Packing Town and gave me the telephone number. I called and Daddy tried to persuade me to go to Edmond Teachers' College and live with friends of his who needed a live-in babysitter. I thought he was just being stingy but when I insisted on OU, to my surprise, he agreed to pay my room and board.

Daddy came to the apartment and handed me a check for $160 to cover my expenses for one semester.

'You know that place isn't for people like us.' He looked as if he might break out crying.

'What do you mean?' I asked.

'Poor people, country folk don't go there. It's the rich kids' school. You won't fit in there, you'll be a stranger,' he said.

I shrugged and he left. I intended to prove him wrong. But Daddy was right.

In my first year at the university, even though OU was tuition-free and open to any state high school graduate regardless of grades, I met no one else there like me. Small-town and rural youth there were in abundance, but no one who was poor.

I had never made any grade except an A in my eleven years of rural schooling and final year of urban trade school. I thought I was smart. But I'd never had a science or math course beyond the basics, never looked into a microscope, never studied any history beyond ancient Mesopotamia and biblical lore and a list of US presidents, nor studied a foreign language. I had never taken a multiple-choice exam. So my score in the SAT-type tests at OU was so low that I was put into remedial classes in science and math. And in English. One thing I thought I did have solid grounding in was language and literature. I considered myself a writer and well-read. Yet I ended up in remedial English composition.

In my English class there were a few truly slow learners, but most of the students were simply uninterested and were at the university for other reasons, or *one* other reason – football. They were either freshmen athletes on scholarship or wealthy young women who had designs of their own on the athletes. OU was the number one football team in the country and had been and would be for a long time.

People thought that the rich girls in the class had intentionally scored low on their tests so they could be in classes with football players who themselves scored low, and maybe not intentionally. The girls were elegant, each wearing what to me was a fortune in clothes and shoes. They were eighteen like me but seemed older than my twenty-seven-year-old sister. I was rail-thin and owned three blouses, three sweaters, three skirts, one pair of shoes and a winter coat. And I worked thirty hours a week on two jobs to pay my extra expenses.

Yet I loved my English class. Even though it was remedial, the handsome, tweed-jacketed, pipe-smoking man who taught it invested his whole heart into making us fall in love with the English language, with sentences, paragraphs and his favorite writers, T.S. Eliot and Ernest Hemingway. The teacher quickly realized I did not belong in the remedial class. He told me so but said that nothing could be done about it. While the pleasant blond athletes and the beautiful blonde girls exchanged notes and giggled through class, I sat on the front row, enraptured, enthusiastically writing out assignments. For two weeks I was ecstatic.

Then the teacher asked us to write a short story. He gave us Hemingway's 'The End of Something' as an example. I tried to copy Hemingway's style and wrote a story about an adolescent girl whose mother was a violent alcoholic who beat her up nightly; after two years of such terror the girl ran away to the city and worked and finished her last year of high school in a trade school.

When the teacher returned my paper there was an A on it and a note: 'This is a brilliant story. You are a talented writer. Please see me after class.' I was overcome with joy and for the next fifty minutes could not concentrate. I read the teacher's short note over and over. After class I stayed seated until the athletes and rich girls had stomped out, arm in arm, laughing. The teacher sat down beside me.

'I want to help you,' he said. I thought he meant with my writing and I smiled, my whole insides on fire with excitement.

'I'm going to major in journalism,' I said.

'That's a good idea, but I mean I want to take you to the university psychiatrist. There is a fee, but I will take care of that,' he said.

I was confused and suddenly embarrassed, then afraid. Only a few miles from the university was the state insane asylum.

But most of all, I was crushed.

'You didn't mean it was a good story,' I said, choking back tears.

'Yes, it is a good story, but you need help,' he said.

'Isn't it enough that it's a good story?'

I bolted from the chair, grabbed my books and ran out. I could never look the teacher in the eye again. And after that I didn't write about myself, but rather about philosophy and history.

I had a part-time job on weekends babysitting for Darla. I babysat for her a few times my last year of high school when she was still managing the beauty salon and lived nearby with Oliver. Then they built a house in Nichols Hills, the wealthy new suburb north of the old wealthy section of Oklahoma City. Soon after, Darla divorced Oliver and kept the house. She quit the beauty shop, and I assumed that Oliver was paying her alimony because she didn't have a job.

The house was huge with two bathrooms and four bedrooms. The children, who were both in school, had their own rooms. Darla's room, the master bedroom she called it, had a sliding glass door to a patio, and its own elegant, marble bathroom with gold-plated fixtures. She had a canopy bed draped on top with wine-colored satin. The thick carpet was the same color. Even Darla's towels and bathrobe were wine-colored. When I stayed there I had the den to myself. There was a comfortable leather sofa I slept on and a desk where I could do my homework.

Darla treated me like a house guest, not a servant. She had a maid come in three times a week to clean and buy groceries and wouldn't even let me wash a dish. 'Just put them in the dishwasher and Sally'll do them. There's plenty more clean dishes,' she said.

The freezer was always stuffed with TV dinners and frozen meat and vegetables, frozen pies and ice cream.

It was nice to have a home away from the dormitory to go to on weekends. I wasn't welcome at Vera's since her fiancé spent weekends there. The credit investigation company Laurence worked for had transferred him to Ada in southeastern Oklahoma, so on Friday evenings I would take the bus the twenty miles from OU to downtown Oklahoma City and Darla and the kids would pick me up. We all went together to a drive-in for hamburgers and malts, then to a movie, Darla paying for everything. On Saturdays I spent most of the day studying and playing with the kids, or watching TV with them. Saturday was Darla's day for beauty treatments. She gave herself a facial, did her hair – she had her own hood hairdryer – and painted her fingernails and toenails. Then she went out to buy a new dress and shoes. She always wore white and red on her Saturday night dates, low-cut, tight, slinky dresses, red strap-sandal spike heels, and sheer hose. She explained her color scheme of bright red and white by saying it was Oklahoma University's colors but I didn't yet understand the connection.

Darla's Saturday night dates were always different men, but men very much alike, men younger than her. By then Darla was in her early thirties and the men were closer to my age. They were usually blond, husky with thick necks, most of them good-looking. I would stay up watching television until she and her date came home and went to her bedroom. They stayed there until noon on Sunday when the man slipped out. I never saw the dates leave because they exited through the patio from her bedroom. Darla called the men 'dates' but I figured that they were paying and I was used to that by now with Darla. My job was to babysit while Darla was on a date and keep the children occupied and away from her bedroom on Sunday morning. I took them to a nearby Baptist church and then to the park.

After three or four times of that weekend routine Darla asked me if I recognized the hunk she'd brought home the night before.

'No, but he's cute,' I said.

'You don't like football, do you?' she asked.

I shrugged. 'Not much.'

'Well, that guy who was here last night is the captain of the OU football team, number one in the country,' she said.

'You had a date with him? How'd you meet him?' I asked. I was amazed because the star players were celebrities whom we rarely saw on campus.

'Hey, the whole damned OU football team has been here by now. They are my customers – I have a contract,' she said. I felt the blush that must have filled my face. I would never know for certain if she had a formalized relationship with the team.

'Hey Roxie, I have my own business now. I don't need Oliver any more. I'm on my own and make good money and have fun besides. Does it bother you?'

'No,' I said and meant it. The news impressed me more than it bothered me, but I wondered what I would do if Darla brought home one of the freshman football players from my English class. After that I hid out in the den when Darla came home so I wouldn't find out.

Eventually I stopped babysitting for Darla and took a job on campus. After a while Darla no longer called me and disappeared from my life as I entered a new world, to reappear only briefly two years later.

I read for a blind student, George, every afternoon. He not only paid me with the welfare funds he received to hire a reader, but also tipped me. 'Take it. I bootleg and make a lot of money. Who would suspect a blind man?' he said. Oklahoma remained prohibitionist but enforcement was lax.

George was an intellectual, a graduate student in philosophy. Most of the books he had to master were not translated into Braille and he tape-recorded as I read and took notes with his Braille gadget. We spent most of the time on Hegel because he was doing a paper on Hegel's concept of freedom. I would read a phrase like 'Freedom lies in not having to choose' or 'The cradle of the child is the tomb of the parents,' and he would stop me and ask what I thought of it. Hegel made no sense to me at first, but George managed to make me understand the concept of thesis, antithesis and synthesis, and I was taken by the whole notion of dialectical reasoning and the great unconscious. I learned about *zeitgeist* – spirit of the times, and *weltanshauung* – worldview.

George talked about current world events that I had no knowledge of and no way of comprehending – the Hungarian uprising, the US taking over the Middle East to control its oil. He detested President Eisenhower and the Dulles brothers, and believed that the military ran everything. He said our government was overthrowing other governments and installing and financing murderous dictators in Iran and Guatemala. George talked a great deal about socialism and he gave me articles by I.F. Stone. Thelma, my dormitory housemother, a middle-aged single woman reputed to be a lesbian, was also a socialist and a friend of George's – that's how I got the job.

They encouraged me to be an intellectual and to laugh at the social scene I wasn't likely to be accepted in anyway.

There were some 'beatniks' at the university, mainly in the School of Art and the School of Architecture, but none lived in the dorms – they cheated and lived communally and illegally off campus. I wanted to meet these Beats but didn't know how. I took a job modeling as an adolescent nude girl (I wore a one-piece swimsuit) in art classes but no one befriended me. The architecture school was famous and famously scandalous. Outside Oklahoma it had been considered one of the best, and aspiring architects applied from all over the world because it was headed by Bruce Goff, Frank Lloyd Wright's most famous student. Goff was loudly homosexual, outspoken and flamboyant, and thumbed his nose at his Baptist attackers, holding orgies at the bizarre house he had designed and lived in outside Norman. At the end of the spring semester before I arrived he had been fired on 'morals' charges.

Thelma and George and the ephemeral Beats were among a tiny minority at Oklahoma University. During the first year all students were required to live in strictly curfewed male/female segregated dormitories, but nearly all were pledging sororities and fraternities. The few of us who were not pledging and were stuck in the dorms were considered either 'eggheads' if male, or 'dogs' if we were women.

Then by accident or fate I met one of the Beats from Architecture. A few weeks after classes began, a fellow named Jack who dated a girl in my dorm asked me if I wanted to take a spin in his MG. We drove around and clashed immediately and intensely when he said, 'Your housemother's a dyke, did you know that?' Then we argued about sororities and fraternities – he was a Sigma Chi although he didn't live in their house.

'I've got just the right guy for you, Roxie: my roommate,' he said as he dropped me off. He called later and said he had arranged a blind date.

In the lobby of my dormitory were several guys waiting for their dates. I knew instantly which one was mine, the one with the deep-set, brooding blue eyes, high cheekbones, and no smile, the one whose light brown hair strayed below the neckline, the one who looked like Paul Newman as the boxer in *Somebody Up There Likes*

Me. Jimmy was a second-year architecture student, chosen for the program by Bruce Goff himself. Jimmy's mother had died in May that year, on his birthday, of a quick-killing cancer, two months between diagnosis and death.

'I lost my mother and the man I admired most in the world the same month,' he said.

Half our romance seemed to be about our shared distress over lost mothers and we invested all our desires and dreams in each other. I could talk to Jimmy about my mother and why I left home without feeling ashamed or afraid he would reject me. We became each other's mothers and teachers. He was a math whiz and got me through algebra. He had trouble in classes where he had to write papers so I helped him. He lived off campus with Jack and two other old friends from high school who liked to drink and party, which Jimmy had done his first year. Now he drank, but mournfully. Neither of us had any money. Jimmy had already spent his summer's savings from working as a carpenter for his father, who was superintendent of a construction company. He borrowed from Jack, and I borrowed from George, who would never let me repay him. But what most attracted me to Jimmy was that he was an authentic rebel. After we'd been inseparable for a month a woman in my dorm took me aside and warned me about Jimmy.

'He was one year ahead of me at Northeast High School. He had a terrible reputation as a juvenile delinquent. You know his best friend is in the federal reformatory at El Reno for an armed robbery that Jimmy was involved in, too. His dad got him off by bribing the judge.'

I told Jimmy what I'd heard and who had told me. He went into a tirade against her. He said he hated what he called 'girl-girls,' all proper and social, but did not deny the story. Of course that rebellious aura made him even more attractive to me.

Jimmy loved the Beats and knew their poetry by heart. We hung out in a smoky basement coffee house that played jazz records and held poetry readings. The coffee was plain Okie java, not espresso. We dreamed of visiting San Francisco's North Beach to rub shoulders with Beat poets in the famous coffee houses. By that time *Life* and *Time* had made Ginsberg, Ferlinghetti and Kerouac into celebrity anti-heroes. Our one coffee house, in a basement across from the campus, was called the Green Door after a current rock and roll song. It was always under threat of being closed by Oklahoma politicians, who called Oklahoma University 'a hotbed of communism' and the Green Door 'a den of iniquity.'

Jimmy wasn't certain what he thought of socialism but strongly favored trade unions – he was a journeyman union carpenter and his father hired only union labor. He dressed in worn cords and heavy sweaters and he hated everything associated with cowboy styles or any other style. He scorned the campus Greeks and the rich, spoiled kids. He liked football but was no athlete because he was afflicted with painful rheumatoid arthritis in his hip. With my asthma and migraines and his limp we regarded ourselves as semi-invalids and kindred souls thereby more cerebral and pure than all the cheerful, healthy, rich young people around us.

Jimmy's only close student friend on campus besides his room-mates was a Palestinian engineering student, a senior who had been a boyfriend of his sister Helen when she was an OU art student. From Saîd Abu Lughod, I learned in a short time more about the Middle East, especially the Palestinians, than I knew about the United States, and, in the process, learned much about US foreign policy. Saîd introduced us to all the Palestinians, Jordanians, Syrians and other Arab students on campus – there were around a hundred Middle Eastern students at OU studying petroleum engineering.

Jimmy found a new mentor that fall when he changed his major to civil engineering: his calculus professor, an astronomer who also managed the university observatory. Old Dr. Whitney took the two of us in like lost children. We spent evenings drinking gunpowder tea with him, studying the heavens through the telescope, watching me-teor showers. Jimmy said that Whitney was reputed to know all the logarithms by heart. He was something of a mystic with a knowledge of Hinduism and ancient languages, including Sanskrit. He did not believe in God, and Jimmy did not believe in God. I did not remain a Baptist for long.

'Okay, so your mother is an alcoholic, but that doesn't mean drink-ing alcohol is a sin. Alcoholism is a disease, and not everyone who drinks is an alcoholic,' Jimmy said when I objected to his drinking.

'It's a sin, the Bible says so,' I said.

'Now where does the Bible say that?' he asked. He had me there.

'I just know Jesus said it,' I said.

'What about the wedding party when Jesus turned water into wine?' he asked.

I smiled. I knew the answer to that one. 'He turned the water into unfermented grape juice,' I said.

Jimmy laughed. He couldn't stop laughing. My words rang in my head, the words I had heard a thousand times from Baptist preachers and Sunday school teachers. The absurdity of the words set my face afire. If the Baptists had lied to me about that, what else? Would Africans go to hell because they weren't saved, because they were deprived of Christian missionaries? Was there a heaven with streets paved of gold? Was there a hell where sinners burned for all eternity? Were the scriptures absolute truth? They had lied and lied. My grandfather and my father and Laurence had been right. I became a willing disciple to anyone who would teach me anything new, and a quick study.

George was quite pleased with my transformation and introduced me to his philosophy advisor. I enrolled in Dr. Feaver's Ethics course the second semester. It was a popular class with over two hundred students. Professor Feaver practiced yoga and often taught while standing on his head or sitting on the desk cross-legged, yoga-style. He introduced me to Tagore, Plato and Aristotle, Hume and Locke, Kant and Goethe.

Dr. Feaver's brother was a popular minister of the university Presbyterian church and I began going there. I wasn't ready to give up religion entirely just because I had turned against the Baptists. Even Jimmy liked to go with me because Reverend Feaver, like his philosopher brother, were descendants of Scots and had doctorates in physics from Princeton. I persuaded Jimmy to join the church with me so we became Presbyterians in a very special congregation. Probably except for Reverend Feaver I would have rejected belief in God and organized religion then rather than four years later in California.

One day I had a message from the university president's secretary that the president wanted to meet with me. I had visions of scholarships, of official recognition of my writing, of skipping remedial classes and advancing immediately to the Journalism School. But instead the president began talking about the newly elected head of the student council, apologizing that he was black. I was totally confused and assumed there was a mistake of identity. I didn't even know a black man was student president. I told the dour president that I was happy to hear a black student had been elected, that he was mistaken about me.

'I understand that you can talk about your fear of blacks only with your mother,' he said.

Mama! Shame and anger flooded over me. My knees weakened.

'Look, my mother is a drunk, she's crazy,' I said.

'Oh no, she made sense. She called, and I talked to her myself on the telephone. We understand and just want you to know it.'

'But I believe in integration, I'm a member of the Urban League. My mother is crazy. Please just forget about the whole thing.'

I rushed out of the president's office straight to the nearest phone and reached Mama. I had not seen nor spoken with her since I was last in Piedmont in the spring. After listening to her tell me that she had been fired at the newspaper and about her new job as a cook at Deaconess Hospital in Oklahoma City, I asked why she had called the president of the university.

'It's a big place. I thought it would help for you to meet the president.' That's how Mama was, never daunted by social barriers.

I swore I would never see her again, under any circumstances. But I did two months later.

I came down with tonsillitis at the beginning of finals week but trudged on to my exams anyway. Jimmy's exams were all the first day, and he left to help his father move back from Kansas after he had finished a construction project. By the middle of the week I could not swallow food and my throat throbbed in agonizing pain that nearly made me black out. On Thursday I finally went to the infirmary and the doctor said the infection could cause rheumatic fever and kill me, that he would check me into the campus hospital where I would be put on IV feeding and antibiotics. I refused because I had one more exam.

When I got back from the infirmary, I fell into a deep dark sleep. When I came to, my room was black and I heard music – 'Joy to the world, the lord has come.' I was certain I had died. I raised myself to the window and saw carolers holding candles and a soft snow falling. My entire body burned with fever and the pain was unbearable. I couldn't even swallow the antibiotics or water. I would die. Everyone

I knew had left for Christmas break, even my housemother and George. I had no one to call to come get me. Jimmy was in Kansas, Hank on the road with the basketball team, Vera and her fiancé off to Galveston for Christmas, and Jan and Laurence lived a hundred miles away. I called my mother.

Mama came for me and drove me to the hospital where she worked. I was nearly delirious. After a week in a near-coma I was well enough to have my tonsils removed. During that time, my first hospital stay, Mama was either working in the hospital kitchen and would drop by to see me, or, when off-duty, sit beside my bed, talking and telling me stories. She never slept. I had become the sickly child dependent on my mother again. She wasn't cold sober – I still caught whiffs of gin – but almost her old self. When Jimmy came to take me away, he met my mother for the first time. I was embarrassed by her, he afraid for me because of the horror stories I'd told him about my last year at home. He insisted that I not maintain contact with her, and I promised him I would never see my mother again.

Thirteen

Diamond in the Rough

... another class of people put us somewhere just below – One more reason for my mama's hungry eyes.

Merle Haggard,
from 'Mama's Hungry Eyes,' 1969

Despite fantasies of becoming a movie or sports star and get-rich-quick schemes, the two most successful means of class-climbing for poor whites, like other poor groups, is marrying up and out and/or education. Marrying up and out is probably more possible for women than men, and is certainly something my mother preached to my sister and me. Indeed, marriage was my way out of my class and into the middle class. It was during those six years of marriage and that transformation that I slowly comprehended the class question.

I was eighteen and Jimmy was nineteen when we married. Jimmy had grown up on the family estate outside Oklahoma City. The house, which his father had built himself, was to me a fantasy world, the kind of place I could only imagine from reading Jane Austen novels – a rambling five-bedroom, two-bath, native-stone mansion with a stone fireplace, thick carpets, fine antiques, chandeliers, and cut-glass crystal and bone china displayed in mahogany 'breakfronts,' as they called the glass-front display cabinets. The place was surrounded by a stream and woods and gardens. At the end of a long stone path was a huge stone patio and barbecue pit. Unlike in a

Victorian novel, there were even two working oil wells on the property.

As Jimmy showed me around the first time he took me to meet his
family, he was suddenly a stranger to me. I could not even comprehend growing up like he had, and, of course, he could not even
imagine how I'd grown up. The land had been homesteaded by his
mother's Scots-Irish family who farmed it. When his mother married
his father, who was descended from Dutch Protestants, they lived
there, then inherited the land. They were simple farming people,
potentially poor whites, but during the Depression and World War II
the construction company Jimmy's father worked for grew huge and
rich off government contracts, and he climbed from journeyman
carpenter to chief superintendent. After the war he sold some of the
land to the state to build the Tulsa Turnpike, invested in real estate,
then built the new house. Jimmy grew up rich. The only blight on his
and the family's perfect world was that his mother – he called her 'an
angel' – had died. I suppressed a tiny warning signal that I now
interpret as the fear that I was repeating what my mother had done –
marrying up and never being able to be as 'good' as the mother/ma-
triarch; because she was dead, Jimmy's mother shone all the brighter,
her angelic and righteous presence never absent. She was the model
I was supposed to imitate.

Jimmy's father fit my image of a patriarch or an English country
gentleman out of one of my favorite novels at the time, Galsworthy's
The Forsyth Saga – a man of property. He wore a fine cashmere
overcoat and a fur cap. I had never seen anyone with a fur cap. He
greeted me by shaking my hand, a gesture I had never before experienced – shaking hands was not something we did in Piedmont.

A strange thought passed through my mind as I walked down the
aisle holding my father's arm. It occurred to me that my father may
have had my new father-in-law for a boss when he worked for the
WPA during the thirties. The thought made me feel like a traitor and
haunted me during the marriage.

At my wedding, if Daddy had asked me, 'Do you really want to go
through with this?' maybe I would have said, 'No, Daddy, oh no,
please save me from this fate.' I knew I was not getting married for
anything but protection and class-climbing. But Daddy did not ask
and instead of taking me away, he gave me away. Years later he would

tell me that indeed he came close to objecting.

One reason I married Jimmy was so I could continue at the university. His father offered to pay our tuition and provide a free place for us to live and a car. Yet within a week after the wedding Jimmy announced that he wanted us to be self-supporting and persuaded me to work.

'You support me until I graduate, then I'll support you to go back to school. It's only three years,' he argued, adding the clincher: 'My sisters think you might be a gold-digger just looking for a free ride off the family, but if you work they would know that's not true.'

What Jimmy's older sisters thought of me mattered a great deal, to him and to me. I agreed to work. So began the pattern that would doom our marriage. With a huge sense of humiliation, after having left to make something better of myself, I returned to the bank to beg for a job.

'This time we hope you are sure you want to stay with the bank. Leaving our family is something we don't expect of our employees; loyalty is foremost,' the same old sleazy personnel director said.

'Yes sir, I am sure; if I go back to college it'll just be night school. I'm married now,' I said.

'You know if you get in the family way you can't work here, and there's no guarantee a job will be waiting.' he said.

'I understand. We don't plan to have babies for a long time,' I said.

'That college business may not be as easy as it sounds. I'm putting you in the Proof department and the girls there have to stay until they balance out, sometimes up around midnight when the night crew comes on. Anyway we don't want you getting too smart on us, getting ideas,' he said, looking at me hard, his broad pink face glistening with sweat.

'I thought I'd be back in Central Files. I know the work there and wouldn't need training,' I said, shocked at the news.

'I talked to Liz Jensen about that when you applied, but she doesn't need any help. You know she was pretty sore about training you and all and you up and leaving,' he said.

And so two weeks after my wedding I was back working at the bank, training to be an IBM proof machine operator, a tough cowgirl riding the big machine. I left the bank that hot summer day I was rehired, lonely and depressed, trapped. Before I had quit to go to

Oklahoma University, my supervisor in Central Files had entrusted me with new tasks, including typing, and she allowed Marie to begin training me on the comptometer during the hour before work. Liz had always made it clear she expected me to stay forever. I had not told her about my plans to quit and go to OU because I knew she would fire me if I did and I needed the money to live on, and to save for college. I believed I would never have to work at that kind of job again. I was climbing to higher ground.

But there I was, crawling back, eighteen and a married woman, feeling old and trapped. How had it come to that? I asked myself.

I lasted for nearly a year as a proof machine operator at the bank. During that time I lived two distinct lives, work and home, just as Marie had advised. But work nearly swallowed me.

The initial blow came the first day of work when I went in early to talk to Marie like I always had before. We had stayed in touch during the time I was at OU with notes and cards. She had even called me a few times to catch me up on her latest affairs. Now she looked scared.

'We can't talk any more, honey. Liz told all of us not to talk to you or we'd be fired,' she said.

'But that's ridiculous. We're friends, let's talk to Liz,' I said.

'You remember what I told you, no talking between departments? I can't afford it. I'm sorry.' I went to the restroom and cried. Maybe Marie did, too.

Within the bank, as in all corporations, a class system existed among the workers. Below management, the tellers were at the top of the pyramid in status, although their pay was very little more than those at the bottom. Now back at the bank I realized that Central Files had been second in status after the tellers; next came Bookkeeping, and at the very bottom was the Proof department. I had fallen into a hole from which there was no escape.

Many evenings I worked until seven or eight and even up to midnight a few times. We stayed until we balanced the deposits and withdrawals of over a hundred small banks around the state that used our bank as a clearinghouse. There were no buses to the family place where we lived, so Jimmy drove the ten miles to downtown Oklahoma City to pick me up after work. By the time I cooked dinner and we ate, it was bedtime. The morning started at five so I could be at work by seven, an hour early. Jimmy dropped me off and drove on to Norman for his eight o'clock class. On Fridays when the bank was open until six we rarely balanced before midnight. Instead of paying us overtime when we worked late, the supervisor gave us the afternoon off.

'Go shopping, girls, go to a movie. Be back at seven,' he'd say around one in the afternoon. I wandered around the department stores with no money to spend. There were no bookstores downtown, so I read in the Main Library until it closed at four. I would walk up Robinson the eight blocks to Central High and feel nostalgic for my life before.

Already thin, I lost weight and fell below a hundred pounds. Migraines plagued me. I suffered agonizing menstrual cramps. Asthma struck rarely, but colds and flu wracked my body. Boils erupted all over my body and bladder infections flared, yet I never missed a day of work. One day an operator about my age next to me screamed, jumped up and began pounding her machine. She threw checks in the air laughing hysterically. Two male supervisors took her away, kicking and screaming. The next day at lunch the other operators said that she had been committed, that she'd had a nervous breakdown and would receive shock treatments

Reading Marx some years later, I had a pretty visceral reaction to his term 'alienated labor.'

Very early I had signed up with an employment agency to find another job, but there were no jobs in the midst of the economic 'recession,' as Eisenhower called it. After nearly a year of that work routine I was fired one Friday in June after lunch.

As usual, a half-dozen of us women operators sat together in the cafeteria, eating and griping about having to work late without overtime, griping about speed-ups and our low pay, some of them complaining about the bosses making passes.

'We need a union,' I said.

My co-workers abruptly left the table. I walked back into the huge noisy workroom and my supervisor beckoned me to his desk. He pantomimed cutting his head off and pointed to me. I felt dizzy.

'What?' I yelled.

He wrote on a notepad and held it up: 'Do not pass Go. Collect your final paycheck in Personnel.'

During the following two scorching summer months I pounded

the sidewalks looking for a job. The recession was lifting and more
jobs were advertised, but I didn't get any of them. On several occasions, I was practically hired and given a starting date only to receive
a call telling me someone more qualified had been hired or that
they'd decided they didn't need anyone.

One day I received that kind of call from the Oklahoma Natural
Gas Company where I had applied. Then the secretary said, 'By the
way, are you related to Hank Dunbar?'

'My brother.'

'Yes, well, in that case Mr. Sands, the personnel director, would
like to see you,' she said.

The downtown office of the gas company's personnel manager was
chock-full of gold and silver baseball trophies on mahogany pedestals
– the gas company had one of the best semi-pro baseball teams in the
region.

'Hi, I'm Sam Sands. Besides being in charge of personnel I'm the
coach of our ball club.'

'I've watched your team play. My brother used to pitch for the
Stockyards team last summer,' I said.

'Yeah, missy, I know all about Hank Dunbar. What an athlete. I
said to myself, no sister of Hank Dunbar could be a bad egg, least of
all a communist.'

'A communist?' I giggled nervously.

Mr. Sands slid a sheet of paper across his desk toward me, watching my face closely. I picked it up and saw my name at the top.

Troublemaker; union organizer; agitator; Urban League member;
subscribes to *The New Republic*; father-in-law long-term union and
integration advocate.

'What is this, where did this come from?' I thought he was joking
for some unfathomable reason.

'Sister, that there's a blacklist and you be on it,' he said.

'But how, why?' I thought I must be in the middle of a nightmare.

'Don't worry. I plan on hiring you-all. Like I said, no sister of Hank
Dunbar could be like that there. But listen up, if you even breathe
union, or make any trouble, you walk that day. Got the message?'

'Yes sir,' I said. As I started to fold the paper to take with me, he
grabbed it, winking.

Mr. Sands placed me in the Oklahoma Natural Gas Company's

service center, which was in an industrial park on the northeast edge of Oklahoma City, only three miles from where we lived. No over-time, nice working conditions – even free coffee and lunch – but still at minimum wage and no medical benefits.

In the orientation I was told: 'In addition to natural gas for homes and offices regionally, Oklahoma Natural Gas produces a third of the total natural gasoline used for jet fuel in the United States as well as most of the country's propane and butane.'

There were only eight of us white-collar employees in the huge plant and only one other woman in my department, an older woman who was the personal secretary of the plant manager. But some three hundred men worked in the meter repair shop, and the meter readers and gas line repairmen, the troubleshooters and installers, all men, worked out of there. The plant had its own radio tower and a dis-patcher to choreograph service.

My job was to assist the meter records clerk. I noted on familiar three-by-five index cards the placement and removal of gas meters and the model and capacity of the meters. (To this day, I notice every gas meter wherever I am, registering whether it is an ironclad or aluminum and what capacity; despite high-tech transformation dur-ing the past four decades, gas meters have remained the same, a fact that always gives me some comfort.)

The job was so easy that it crossed my mind that Mr. Sands had made up the job to bail me out of being blacklisted because he admired my brother.

The best part about working at the gas plant was that two of our Arab acquaintances from Oklahoma University were interning there as petroleum engineers. Every day I had lunch with Rafic, a Jorda-nian, and Nouri from Syria, and they told me the latest news from the Middle East. It was the time of the Suez crisis and they admired Nasser. Before I came to work, they said, their only friends at the plant had been Howard, Lorenzo and Red, the three black employ-ees, an elderly man and his two nephews who cleaned and made coffee and lunch. So they became my friends as well. At Christmas when the company gave each employee a ten-pound cured ham for a bonus, Rafic and Nouri, who couldn't eat pork because they were Muslims, gave theirs to our black friends, so I did, too. And Saîd, our Palestinian friend, visited every weekend.

The meter records clerk, my supervisor, was a fanatic Nazarene who'd grown up in Bethany, west of Oklahoma City, an evangelical-founded town with a Bible college. Next to my Church of Christ grandmother, Neal was the most self-righteous person I'd met in my life. He 'suggested' that I not wear tights under my skirt because 'the men will wonder how far up they go.'

I ignored his 'suggestion.' He preached to me all day and cautioned me not to fraternize with the black and Arab employees: 'Some people might get the wrong idea.'

Each day Neal greeted me with a new racist joke. I told him I liked Senator John Kennedy and hoped he would run for president. Neal was outraged and railed about the 'Papists' and communists taking over America.

I always brought a novel with me to read on my breaks. Neal said that reading fiction was sinful and was horrified when I brought *Lolita* and *Lady Chatterley's Lover* on purpose to rile him.

But I never mentioned the word 'union.'

The one thing Neal did that I appreciated was to give me a crystal radio with a tiny earpiece. His idea was to save me from backsliding. He set the tiny radio to the Nazarene station. But I jiggled the crystal and received CBS radio news, and there I found blow-by-blow reports on the Cuban revolution in progress. I smiled blissfully as I listened to Fidel's victories for four months, right up to New Year's Day 1959 when they marched into Havana and took power. All along, Neal smiled happily, assured that I was getting religion.

Life was much easier with my new job and growing confidence that I successfully had escaped my class fate and was fully accepted into my new family.

Jimmy and I lived in the three-room garage apartment – near the 'big house' – which had once been the servants' quarters; now they hired day laborers and housekeepers to maintain the house and the grounds. I idolized Jimmy's family and adopted them as my own, especially his sister Helen, who lived with her husband in a cottage they had built nearby. She called me 'a diamond in the rough.' I accepted the role and submitted to being polished. Helen said I was from good peasant stock like Tolstoy's characters and embodied the nobility of the peasantry, enriched by being part Indian. I shivered with pleasure when she told me those things.

The whole family opposed racism and segregation. Despite his wealth and being a boss, Jimmy's father was a trade union advocate, and thought, as ridiculous as it sounds to me now, that the ignorance of poor white people, my kind of people, was responsible for racism. Even before the Supreme Court decision on school segregation, he'd fought for integration, not very successfully, in the Carpenters' Union, and as a superintendent on projects he had hired black laborers and hod carriers. He invited his construction workers and their families, including the blacks, to his famous barbecues. I imagined that my new father-in-law was like my Wobbly grandfather, although when I asked him once what he thought of the Wobblies he said they had been anarchists and crazy and un-American.

Everyone in the family read *Time* and *The New Republic,* and knew all about what was happening in the world. I soaked up everything they said, and I read and read.

I did not read to escape, not even novels. I read for knowledge. Ayn Rand's *Atlas Shrugged* comforted and excited me. The idea of a hidden utopia seemed like the solution to the world's problems as I perceived them. I admired what seemed to me Ayn Rand's burning passion and total commitment. Her women characters were central and independent, equal in all respects to men; they were whole, autonomous beings – sure, confident, intelligent, strong but not aggressive.

I kept rereading *The Fountainhead* and *Atlas Shrugged,* but each time I was more confused by Ayn Rand's 'philosophy of wealth,' as she called it. Finally, at the library I found her first book, *Anthem*, a thin autobiographical novel, and I understood her views better. By then I had read a great deal about the Russian Revolution and realized that Rand was a White Russian whose rich family had been exiled and that she hated communism, which she thought was taking over the United States. I abandoned Ayn Rand.

I read other books on utopias – Edward Bellamy's *Looking Backward*, Milovan Djilas's *The New Class*, which explained why communism had failed and how it should be implemented. That got me interested in the Russian Revolution and I read about it. For the first time, I read Marx's *Communist Manifesto* and thought it sounded exactly like the IWW Constitution, but I couldn't find a copy of the IWW document to compare it with.

Then I discovered Robert Lindner's *Rebel Without a Cause: Hypnoanalysis of a Criminal Psychopath*. I recognized myself in the portrait he drew of the 'psychopath.' Jimmy and his family believed in inherited traits, either through genes or socialization. They never let me forget, by carefully helping me, how much I had to overcome with my poor upbringing and crazy mother, or the possibility that I was a 'bad seed.' But Lindner explained my malaise in a different way. Lindner defined the psychopath as a rebel without a cause, an individual in a chronic state of mutiny. He believed that my whole generation to one degree or other had become psychopathic, that the youth of the Western world was touched with madness, sick with a condition of mind once limited to a few, now an epidemic over the entire earth. Not only us young people as individuals but national governments, all of western civilization were psychopathic. Lindner said that for at least thirty years civilization had demonstrated behavior – Buchenwald, Warsaw, Hiroshima, Nagasaki, Los Alamos – that if diagnosed in an individual would cause that person to be permanently institutionalized as mentally deranged. He attributed the gas chambers, genocide and the atomic bomb to the mass insanity he had identified in society. It was an epidemic, like polio, but caused not by a virus but by society. I could not cure my illness without the society changing. What was I to do?

After I read Lindner's *Rebel Without a Cause*, I looked for other books by him. The librarian told me he had committed suicide in 1956 and there were no more books. She said I might be interested in Jean-Paul Sartre. I checked out *Being and Nothingness*. The words exploded in my head. I read that huge, turgid book, retaining words that defined my feelings – ennui, alienation, nausea. Then I read Sartre's fiction and plays – *The Flies, No Exit* – and his theories made more sense. Simone de Beauvoir's novel *The Mandarins* made even more sense. I longed to be in Paris with people who would understand me and teach me. Within the covers of that book I understood for the first time the significance of the horrors of Hiroshima and the Holocaust, and, unrelated, of the grand precolonial Indian civilization of Mexico.

I read everything I could find about being alienated – Ralph Ellison's *Invisible Man*, Camus' *The Stranger* and *The Plague*, Kafka's *The Metamorphosis, The Castle* and *The Trial*, Kerouac's *The Subterraneans*.

I identified with J.D. Salinger's alienated characters in 'A Perfect Day for Bananafish,' *The Catcher in the Rye* and especially *Franny and Zooey*. I read Dostoevsky's *Crime and Punishment* and *The Idiot* for the first time. I realized that I had been the *idiot* in my family, that the Family itself, not just *my* family, was at the root of the problem.

I began to observe Jimmy's family more critically.

Some symptoms I suffered ever since my family fell apart grew far worse after I got married. For no apparent reason I would be overcome by a blinding white rage. I could see and hear and control my movements, and it seemed to me that I chose to scream or to run and hide or to kick a chair or slam a door. Yet I couldn't prevent or stop it. The fits would last from a few minutes to hours. Inside the fit I felt terror and sometimes a strange euphoria, a feeling of safety. The first time it happened with Jimmy, before we married, I thought he would leave me but he wrote me a page-long note saying I was too good for the evil world around me, that I had a pure mind and soul, that I was perfect except for that tiny flaw in my personality that came from my inferior background, and that it was his destiny and mission in life to protect and care for me.

On other occasions, Jimmy would shake me awake, saying I was grinding my teeth. Once he recorded it for me to hear. The sound was loud and eerie. Insomnia plagued me. I was afraid to go to sleep, not knowing what I would do. During those times I had blinding, disabling migraine headaches and nausea.

The more I read the more my fits and migraines diminished in number and intensity. It was then that I realized that self-knowledge and education are curatives, and it was then I believe that I determined to become a teacher one day. I tried to talk to Jimmy about what I was learning, but he was lost in differential equations and strength of materials. Our mental worlds diverged. He was relieved that I was better but he thought all my problems were caused by a bad family life and could be cured with a good family, his family. Helen gave me books to read that made me understand the madness of the world around me. A book called *The Nature of the Non-Western World* explained colonialism. *The Great Fear in Latin America* by John Gerassi, a former *Time* reporter who had been fired for writing it, was a tract against US imperialism. Helen's favorite books, which became mine, too, were Rachael Carson's *The Sea Around Us,* and Vance

Packard's *The Hidden Persuaders*, which showed how unbridled capitalist development was poisoning our food and water, and how advertising manipulated people. I read in *Time* that Packard had testified before a US Senate committee against rhythm and blues music being broadcast on the radio because he said it was designed to 'stir the animal instinct in modern teenagers.' I stopped listening to rock and all pop music.

And then I met Uncle Bob. After a car wreck, Jimmy and I took out a loan – the driver of the other car had no insurance nor did we – and bought a new, black Volvo coupe, one of the first sold in Oklahoma. We took a trip to Grand Junction, Colorado, to stay with his mother's sister, Thelma, and her husband, Bob.

Aunt Thelma was a tiny, soft-spoken, intellectual woman and Uncle Bob a talker and very intelligent. He'd been forced to retire a few years before from working for the United Nations. Before that he'd been a professor of agriculture at Iowa State University. Their three-story frame house was filled with exotic objects and rugs and works of art from China and Afghanistan, the two countries where Uncle Bob had served as a UN agricultural advisor. He loved China; they had been there three years when Mao kicked the UN and all foreign advisers out, he said. Then he was posted to Afghanistan, which he also loved.

Jimmy cautioned me that Uncle Bob was bitter and extremist in his views, that he was a socialist, but Uncle Bob found a real listener in me. 'China is the future of the world not only because of its size and population but its knowledge and wisdom. They were right to kick out us Westerners,' he said.

Uncle Bob told me a dark, complex story – which had made headlines a few years before, but I'd never heard about it – of another UN economic advisor named Owen Lattimore with whom he had worked in China. After Mao kicked them out of China, Lattimore wrote that Chiang Kai-shek's government had not fallen because of a communist conspiracy but because of Chiang's corruption. Lattimore recommended that the US recognize communist China. The UN reassigned Lattimore to Afghanistan but he didn't last long, because Truman pressured the UN to fire him. Then, Uncle Bob said, Lattimore was hounded and publicly denounced in the witch hunts of the early fifties. The UN sent Uncle Bob to Afghanistan to replace Lattimore, but he was also forced out by Truman, forced to retire early from the UN, also suspected of communist sympathies.

'My crimes? I was trying to convince the Afghan peasants to grow wheat and corn to feed their families, and for the market, instead of poppies for the CIA heroin trade. The American advisors insisted on 'cash crops' and encouraged poppy growing. The CIA was involved in drug trafficking, I saw it with my own eyes. And I protested about the Americans putting their own seal on food aid they sent to Afghanistan through the UN. No other country did that.'

Uncle Bob said that after he was fired he was blacklisted as a security risk and no university would hire him to teach.

'I'm a socialist and proud of it, nothing wrong with that. Capitalism is evil and it's going to get us all blown up if it isn't destroyed,' he said. Uncle Bob dug through newspaper clippings and magazines on his cluttered desk and pulled out a printed page and handed it to me. 'Here, read what I.F. Stone says.' The piece was dated November 1956. I read:

> What the Russians are doing in Budapest is so dreadful that even the Indian, Icelandic and American Communist parties protest. Moscow is ready to do anything in order to keep in its 'zone of security' governments politically satisfactory to it. But haven't we just finished a campaign in which the Republicans boasted of the quick way we toppled the Arbenz government in Guatemala ... We in the Caracas agreement tried to ensure that no anti-American and anti-capitalist governments could be formed in our hemisphere. How we honor brave fighters for freedom ... until they shoot down our tyrant friends, as recently in Nicaragua.

A flush of embarrassment came over me as I read, realizing I had no idea what the words meant. But I did know a lot about the Middle East from my Arab friends and it all seemed to add up to the same problem – US imperialism.

Saying he wanted to show me something, Uncle Bob took me on a drive around Grand Junction, a kind of Western boom town up until the recession had hit the year before.

'Okay, now look around at all the new buildings and the ones going up. What are they?' he challenged me.

I looked carefully and spotted a new brick Methodist church building and nearby another Christian church under construction. In

the center of town were several new banks and a savings and loan
building almost completed. I reported my observations.

'You see, churches and banks, and casinos out in Nevada, they're
the ones that benefit from hard times. The rich get richer and the
poor suckers get saved and trust in Christ for a better life in the
hereafter.'

I was back home, a child listening to my father tell his stories
about workers' rights and I told Uncle Bob about my grandfather in
the IWW, and he said I had a blessed heritage. He pulled out a book
and read to me the words of Eugene Debs, from when he was the
Socialist Party presidential candidate in 1916 and my grandfather
voted for him: 'I have no country to fight for; my country is the earth;
I am a citizen of the world ... I am opposed to every war but one; I
am for that war with heart and soul, and that is the world-wide war
of the social revolution.'

I regretted leaving. I wanted to stay and sit at Uncle Bob's feet and
learn from him everything he knew. When we were in the car ready
to pull out Uncle Bob said, 'Wait a minute, I have something for
Roxie.' He returned with a book and handed it to me: *The Political
Economy of Growth* by Paul Baran.

'Study this book. Some of my UN reports are cited in there.'

That night in a motel in Raton I read but didn't understand much.
Uncle Bob had said to study, not read. That book would take a lot of
studying. It said that Russia wasn't really communist or socialist, that
no country was, that socialism was yet to be realized but necessary
for the future. The book was about western imperialism, especially
the US, and revolutions in Africa, Asia and Latin America. I dreamed
that night that Uncle Bob was invited to a very important UN meeting in Geneva and he asked me to accompany him as an advisor. I
was thrilled and afraid but certain I could do the job.

Back home, I followed the news of the United Nations closely, as
reported on television by Pauline Fredericks, who became my new
role model. That fall, day after day, heads of newly independent states
of Africa arrived at UN headquarters to take their seats as equals
among nations. The sight was more thrilling than seeing Elvis Presley
four years before. I had new heroes and dreams.

I began to wonder about the price I had to pay for my new status when one really hot summer Saturday afternoon Jimmy and I with his sister and her husband went to drink beer in a joint we hadn't been to before, attracted by the air-conditioning sign. The barmaid turned out to be Darla. I hadn't seen or talked to her for nearly two years.

'Darla, what are you doing here? How are you and the kids?' I asked. I was surprised by my own joy in seeing her.

Darla wore a tight-fitting red sundress. Her bosom, which I knew to be false, protruded seductively. She looked different, not so much older but somehow hard, her skin rough. Yet she remained strikingly beautiful with her mane of thick black hair and her smoky skin. Darla hesitated and I thought she didn't remember me. I followed her eyes – she was studying my companions.

'Fancy seeing you here. How are you, stranger?' she said, a teasing tone in her voice. Then I realized she was shocked because she had known me as a devout teetotaling Baptist. She looked amused and approving.

'I got married. Darla, this is Jimmy, and his sister and brother-in-law,' I said.

Jimmy looked up at her sideways and said, 'Howdy do.' Suddenly I was aware that Jimmy did not approve of Darla. He glared at me as if I were a stranger, or a traitor.

When Darla returned to serve us, she handed me a slip of paper with her phone number on it. 'Give me a call. I'm off now.' She left with a man who had been sitting at the bar.

'You got some outstanding old friends, Roxie,' Jimmy said, not with a smile.

'She's from my hometown. I used to babysit for her, you remember me telling you about her.' There was apology in my voice, and shame.

Later, when we were alone, Jimmy said, 'You're not going to call that woman, are you?'

'I thought I might. Why not?'

'She's a prostitute.'

'She's my friend.'

'Not any more. You associate with lowlife like that and you will become like them,' he said.

I said nothing and never called Darla and never saw her again.

Other warning signals alerted me to the class chasm between
Jimmy and his family and me – for instance, on that trip to Colorado
to meet Uncle Bob. All along the highways were broken-down cars
and pickups with women and children and old people sitting in the
shade while a man worked under the hood. They beckoned for us to
stop and help. Jimmy passed them by.

'Why don't we stop?' I asked. No one in my family would ever
have passed up a stranded motorist, but then we never strayed far
from home.

'They're hustlers, rob you blind, highway bandits,' Jimmy said.

'How do you know?'

'I just know. They use the kids and old people for bait to get you
to stop, then rob you. They're transients, fruit pickers, white trash.'

I stared at the sad faces as we passed by and tried to see the con
artists and criminals behind the masks. But they merely looked familiar, like my own relatives. Yet we got plenty of help on the highway.
Practically everything that could go wrong with a car plagued ours –
the radiator burst, the voltage regulator busted, the carburetor
spewed gas, even the ignition wire broke, and we had flat tires on
several occasions. Each time we broke down, always in the middle of
nowhere, someone stopped to help us or gave Jimmy a ride to the
next station.

'How come they don't think we're highway robbers?' I asked. The
people who stopped to help us were invariably driving old cars or
pickups and looked a lot like the people who tried to get us to stop.
New cars whizzed on by.

'They can tell,' Jimmy said. As Ken Kesey, himself an Okie, notes:
'It isn't a new car that pulls over to help you when you are broke
down with the senile carburetor; it is somebody who knows what it
is to be broke down with a hurt machine.'

Then one autumn day in the third year of my marriage I was home
sick with the flu and found myself the only person on the grounds. I
had never been alone there before. The place was so serene and
lovely, the oak leaves bright yellow, a maple tree flaming red, the
blackjacks burnished copper. The huge lawn that sloped down to the
creek was still a carpet of green thanks to the sprinkler system. I sat
down on the stone bench in the patio that was halfway between the
creek and the big house. Even though I was only thirty-five miles

from where I grew up it was so different, rolling hills with trees rather than flat and barren, no cannibalized old cars and junk around.

'How lucky I am,' I said aloud and felt like yelling it since no one would hear. I could never have dreamed of being a part of that kind of life three years before. Jimmy's family had taken me in as one of their own. Forever and ever I would be safe and secure and loved. I loved my sisters-in-law and father-in-law as if they were my own flesh. I would never be poor or want for anything again. I tingled with happiness, tears of joy streaming down my face.

The sound of a car startled me out of my reverie. The mail carrier: he always brought everyone's mail to the big house and put it on the back porch where we could each fish out our own. I strolled up the hill to check. I pulled out a manila envelope, exactly like many others I had received, from the White Citizens' Council. Inside was a pamphlet dated 1958, which began:

> We are proud of our white blood and our white heritage of 6 centuries. If we are bigoted, prejudiced, un-American, etc., so were George Washington, Thomas Jefferson, Abraham Lincoln, and other illustrious forebears who believed in segregation. We choose the old paths of our founding fathers and refuse to appease anyone, even the internationalists.

I tore the pamphlet in half and rifled through the rest of the mail. There was a letter to Helen from the sister who had moved to California. The envelope was barely sealed, just at the tip. I stuck my little finger under the flap and it popped open. I slipped the letter out of the envelope and unfolded the two pages. My eyes fell on the middle of the first page and the words hit me like a blast of icy wind:

> I think you are right that it remains to be seen if Roxie will drag Jimmy down to her level or if he can pull her up to his. Coming from her background she may be beyond rescue. I wish Jimmy would leave her.

I had to sit down to keep from falling. I could not believe what I was reading, and that there had been other letters and conversations, letters about me ruining Jimmy. The letter was almost entirely about me, mostly a discussion of the condition of 'white trash,' whether it was genetic or social, and the 'complication' that I was part Indian. I read the letter a second time, telling myself they were concerned about me because they loved me and wanted to help me. But it wasn't there, only concern for Jimmy and the wish that I would disappear or had never appeared. The letter ended by saying that Jimmy had met me at a vulnerable time in his life just after their mother's death, and I, being a gold-digger and devious, had entrapped him and pressured him for a quick marriage.

I felt like running, packing a suitcase and leaving without a word. I would not be able to tell Jimmy because he would know I'd opened the letter. I vowed to remain quiet, to finish what I'd started, sending Jimmy to school. He would graduate in three months, then I would insist that we leave. I would carry out my part of the bargain and I would not lose Jimmy. But I found myself the only one left around who might rescue Mama.

Hank had married, not Mary Jane but a Yukon cheerleader. I had gone to the wedding a few months before, serving as the punch pourer at the reception. Mama had been there, so spaced out she didn't even notice my presence. Hank and his bride were getting ready to move to Quantico, Virginia. Hank's draft notice had come the minute he graduated and he enlisted in the Marines, pretty much ending his bid for the big leagues. Many years later he would confide in me his disillusionment, which surprised me.

How proud I had been of Hank's success as an athlete, in college basketball as a guard and super-shooter, and as a semipro baseball pitcher who could enter the big leagues if he chose. His picture was in an October 1954 issue of *Look* magazine.

Later he would tell me about how badly he had been treated, as if he were an Indian, being hazed as such at OCU, and in the Marine Corps. Hank was dark and had black eyes and straight hair, high cheekbones. But his most striking memory is about that summer when he pitched for a semipro team all over North America. In Calgary, Canada, he was greeted by jeering crowds who'd read in the morning's newspaper the news that Hank was a 'savage,' a 'Sioux Indian.' While he pitched the voices from the bleachers cried out racial insults like 'dog eater,' 'dirty Indian,' and 'go home, savage.' When he told me about this many years later he said he was confused because he had never really thought of himself as an Indian, but also, from that day forward, he was very sensitive to racism in all its forms. And he won that game for his team in Calgary.

'I just can't take it anymore. Mama won't let Daddy near the house and I'm the only one watching out for her. Charlotte doesn't want me to go, and we have a trailer packed ready to leave early tomorrow. Please go out there and check on her,' Hank said on the telephone. He explained to me that Mama's next-door neighbor had called him and said that Mama had gone berserk and was wrecking everything in the house. I agreed to go out and check.

Jimmy and I went to Piedmont, his first visit there. The house was dimly lit. I found Mama crumpled on the bed, fully dressed, passed out. Her hands and arms were bloody, her face swollen almost beyond recognition. Every piece of furniture was broken, the windows and the dishes – that china so precious to her that Vera had given her. And the silver coffee pot Vera had bought Mama for her twenty-fifth wedding anniversary in 1953 at one of her last sober moments, an item Mama so treasured, was dented beyond recognition from being slammed against the concrete floor of the porch.

I got a dishpan of water and a washrag and wiped the blood off as best I could. There were no deep cuts and the bleeding stopped. I asked myself: With Hank gone will this be my task?

'We're not going to do this again. There's no way you can help, it'll just make you sick again. Let's get out of here,' Jimmy said. I knew he was right.

I was the only child left near our mother. Vera had remarried and moved to Louisiana and Laurence had been transferred by his credit investigation company again, this time to Topeka the year before. I decided never to see or communicate with my mother again. And I developed a nearly pathological fear that Mama would call or come find me. I had nightmares of her attacking me while I slept, of killing Jimmy and his family. As far as I knew Mama didn't know where I lived: my brothers and sister were sworn to secrecy. Yet I knew she had her ways of finding out anything she put her mind to. On my birthday a month earlier I had received a gift through the mail from her, a child's music box.

After that encounter in Piedmont, on a crisp clear autumn day in mid-November, Mama appeared. It was a Saturday afternoon and I was reading. Jimmy was working at the gas station on the highway and had taken the car. Everyone else was away shopping.

I looked out the window and saw her with Aunt Ruth walking up the grassy hill toward the house. Mama and Aunt Ruth stood in the open doorway of my garage apartment. Aunt Ruth hugged me, obviously believing I'd invited them to visit. They came in and sat down on the divan. I could not speak. I stood at the door. Jimmy was suddenly beside me. I grabbed him and hung on. He enveloped me in his arms.

'Make her leave, make her leave, please,' I heard the echo of my voice. I ran out the door and down the hill to the creek. Some time passed but I had no sense of time. I was numb and afraid. Jimmy found me there.

'She's gone. Come back home, I'll take care of you,' he said.

'We have to leave, go far away, please,' I said.

'We will, I promise, as soon as I graduate, just two months, we'll go to California.'

I never saw my mother again.

I was shaken for days, more afraid than ever. And until we left Oklahoma I was terrified, riveted with migraines and fits. I felt I was no longer a member of Jimmy's family and did not want to assume the responsibility for my mother. I knew the only choices I had were to leave Jimmy, or for he and I to get away from there. I wanted to leave alone, but I did not have the courage.

As we entered the Painted Desert of Arizona I was at the wheel while Jimmy slept. We were driving straight through to San Francisco, so he had to relent and let me drive. I felt the sweetness of solitude and began really studying the landscape. The colors that give that desert its name were not visible, because the midday sun cast a sheen of white. The desert appeared endless, the sky a colossal blue dome. I could sense the curve of the earth.

'It's a ball,' I said out loud.

Jimmy did not wake. Suddenly my existence shrank and I felt tiny and irrelevant. The vision of the roundness of the planet made the universe real and my place in it no more than a speck of life. The realization of my own insignificance did not depress or frighten me; rather, a calm such as I'd never felt before came over me, a sort of coming to terms with who I was and just where I might fit into the universe, myself a singular atom with no past. My mind opened like a flower in spring. I looked directly into infinity and felt myself as an irrelevant dot. God disappeared and I felt one with the universe.

And, at that moment, I acknowledged that my destiny would not be with Jimmy. I would have to find my way alone somehow, some-day, without family or protection.

I found myself headed for the Promised Land, without God, with-out a history, born again in a sense, in search of freedom. Yet when we stopped by the Colorado River after crossing the bridge into California I felt an emptiness and loneliness. A song played in my mind. Tears filled my eyes. I heard Mama singing and playing on the old piano.

> Shall we gather at the river
> the beautiful, beautiful river;
> Gather with the saints at the river
> Close to the throne of God?
> Yes we'll gather at the river,
> The beautiful, the beautiful river,
> Gather with the saints at the river
> That flows by the throne of God.

When the peasants are deprived of fields to work, so goes the chorus of an old Irish ballad, 'All that's left is a love of the land.'

That's my father's life story, too, and the story of the Okies who moved to towns and cities and to California and Oregon when they were pushed off the land.

While I was growing up, like my mother, I thought nostalgia for the land was stupid. Who wanted to do the backbreaking work involved in caring for the land? As far as loving the land, I didn't think I did. I didn't want to. But I do. I finally acknowledged that in myself on the twenty-fifth anniversary of my mother's death, when I sat most of a day by her grave looking out over the endless red earth.

Just below the skin that I show the world resides a peasant girl who absorbed ancient memories of the land. Love of the land is not located so much in the mind, or in the heart, as in the skin; how the skin feels when you go back. I know it by how my skin feels when I'm there, in that ten-mile-square area where I grew up, and when my eyes sweep over the expanse of red dirt.

Epilogue

California Litany

> I pull out the bottom
> drawer
> of my mind
> marked Oklahoma
> which holds a list
> of small raw towns ...
> Bowlegs
> Depew
> Pretty Water
> Idabel
> Gypsy Corner
>
> WILMA ELIZABETH MCDANIEL,
> from 'Oklahoma Litany'

I have made my home in California nearly all the past thirty-six years, most of that time in San Francisco, with four years in Los Angeles. Until recently, California had felt to me like a foreign country, a place of exile, which was exactly what I wanted of it.

When my husband and I moved to San Francisco in 1960, our Oklahoma license tags provoked angry honking and obscene gestures from other drivers, hisses of 'Go home, Okies' and 'Dumb Okies.' Although we had a grace period of one year to maintain our Oklahoma registration, we had it changed within weeks. And I began to work on getting rid of my Okie accent and usages – my speech gave me away. Not only was it hard for others to understand me, but I couldn't fathom half of what I heard. People spoke so rapidly in San Francisco and pronounced words differently from me. I called the elm tree 'ellum,' an aerial 'errol,' an inch and a fish 'eench' and 'feesh.' While I said 'prolly' they said 'probably,' and I 'renched' rather than rinsed. I knew how to spell almost faultlessly and though I thought I spelled phonetically my ear heard differently than San Franciscans. I stumbled through what I thought was my own language, trying to find my bearings, saying 'shadder' meaning shadow, 'small' meaning smile and 'chimley,' which they called chimney, and called a female sheep a 'yo.'

I was aware that out there just over the Coastal Range lay a vast valley, stretching from Redding in the north to Bakersfield in the south, populated by people like me, or like I didn't want to be – 'Dust Bowl Okies.' And I was aware that in the Santa Clara Valley in northern California and in the San Bernardino Valley and in Orange County in southern California were dense pockets of people like me, or like I did not want to be – 'defense Okies' – those who came during World War II to work in the war industry. And although I supported the United Farm Workers movement I did so from a distance and did not venture into that valley where Mexican farm workers and descendants of Okie farm workers lived at odds. I must have traveled Highway 99, and later I-5 when it was built parallel to 99, up and down California's Central Valley a thousand times, passing through, headed for L.A. or Portland, Mexico or Canada, New Mexico or Oklahoma. But I stopped in the Central Valley only if necessary. I did not want to talk to the people I knew were there, people I didn't want to be like.

When I was at UCLA in the mid-sixties, I was well aware that most of the cops in the Los Angeles Police Department were people like me, or like I did not want to be. And I was embarrassed and secretive about that knowledge, particularly during the Watts uprising in the summer of 1965, after white LAPD cops shot a black man in cold blood.

In 1967, during the height of the anti-Vietnam war and counterculture youth movements, a friend and I were walking away from a movie theater in West Los Angeles around midnight when an LAPD patrol car skidded to a stop beside us, red lights flashing. There was a 9 p.m. curfew for anyone under twenty-one since the Sunset Boulevard police riot against celebrating street youth the year before. We were over twenty-one but never got a chance to prove it. My friend, a foreign student, was clearly terrified; he had a student visa but was from a country where being stopped by the police or army meant pain and suffering if not death, especially if a bribe wasn't offered, and he had little money on him. He reached inside his jacket, he told me later, to calm his pounding heart. In a flash, the two cops drew their Smith and Wesson .38s, just like in the cowboy and Indian movies, and crouched into firing positions. My friend had the good sense to raise his arms, palms open, way above his head, and I followed suit. However, the cops remained in firing position, apparently unimpressed by our disarmed helplessness. They finally stood up, rammed their revolvers into their holsters, stomped around us, kicked at the trunk of a palm tree, all the while calling us 'hippies,' 'communists,' 'peaceniks,' and they tried to scare us with threats while discussing between themselves what to do with us.

But they gave themselves away: I recognized the way they moved, the way they talked, not just their Okie accents but as if they moved and talked in slow motion, compared with most Californians I knew, managing to appear humble and arrogant, graceful as cats and that dangerous all at the same time. I was no longer scared. I said, 'Where y'll from? I'm from near El Reno.' The effect was immediate. Suddenly the two cops, probably a decade older than me, my oldest brother's age, became friendly Okies. We chatted, mostly letting them talk because my Oklahoma accent did not come back easily to me, about our origins and family ties – their parents had been Dust Bowl Okies from Choctaw and from Prague in southeastern Oklahoma – then about the weather, and they apologized for the trouble, and asked if they could give us a ride – 'No thanks!' I said – and then they drove away. They never even checked our identification.

It was hard to explain to my foreign friend what magic I had performed. I can't say that I really understood it myself at the time. But that was a moment of necessity, of survival; it wasn't often that I revealed my roots, and other rootless Californians like myself rarely asked, 'Where are you from?' or if they did, they really meant, Where do you live?, not Where do you come from originally? or Who are you really?

Even when I began working on this book I still had no desire for any relationship or interchange with those people like me out there beyond California's cities. I was interested in Oklahoma history, in the radicalism my grandfather was part of, that legacy. I identified myself as working class, part poor white, part Indian, anything but 'Okie.'

Then I met Wilma Elizabeth McDaniel, the poet known throughout the Central Valley as the 'Okie bard' and 'Okie poet laureate,' and found myself at home among California Okies for the first time. Wilma's poems and stories made me realize that I could not write a memoir about growing up in Oklahoma without acknowledging my ties to those who had left and who have, through their struggles, their music and their stories, preserved and reinvented our history as a people: I ached with joy and sadness when she read to me her most famous poem, the one that won her the nickname 'The Gravy Poet':

> You can
>> put your trust
>>> in gravy
>> the way it stretches
>>> out the sausage
>> the way it stretches out
>> the dreams from payday
>> till tomorrow.

That first time I met Wilma, I drove down Highway 99, noticing and stopping at those Okie towns – Turlock, Hilmar, Herndon, Fowler – and found Wilma in her small apartment in a dusty cotton town, Tulare, about which Merle Haggard wrote a ballad, 'Tulare Dust.'

At Christmastime last year, Wilma and I decided to visit Weed Patch, the migrant labor camp set up by Roosevelt for the Okie migrants, where Steinbeck's Joad family lived, and where Dorothea Lange took so many of her classic photographs. I thought it remarkable that Wilma had never in her nearly sixty years living in the Central Valley visited the famous site. I knew why I myself had never driven the six miles off Highway 99 to see the place: I was ashamed of being associated with Okies. Wilma said she had always wished to visit that shrine, Weed Patch, but that no one ever took her there – she never learned to drive – and no one else in the family seemed interested since they had suffered elsewhere. She rarely ventured more than twenty or thirty miles from home, typically Okie, except for the ones of us who caught, in Merle Haggard's words, 'white line fever' – the truckers, like my stepsister and my cousin, and long-distance drivers, like me and my brothers.

The hundred-mile trip down Highway 99 from Tulare to Weed Patch, which is south of Bakersfield, took about two hours. As we drove that stretch, Wilma told me stories about the people, the hardships, the courage, the tragedies, about her own family and the many stories she had heard from others. Every place had a story – Tipton, Pixley, Earlimart, Delano and McFarland (whose history I had known only through the UFW movement), Rosedale, Oildale, Lamont. Then we arrived at Weed Patch.

To our surprise, we found that it's still a functioning farm worker camp, nearly deserted in the middle of a weekday with the workers in the fields. Signs were in Spanish and English. The weather-stripped wooden buildings at the camp entrance must have been the original ones, no longer in use, but there were no markers or museum to explain anything. Most of the small cabins had been built since the thirties, but were fairly shabby. The camp was bounded by a tall chain-link fence and I could almost imagine a guard tower with armed security officers, like a low-security California prison.

As Wilma and I poked around, the camp manager approached us, alert with suspicion. The sign at the entrance clearly stated: *This center is for residents and visitors of residents only. Others are trespassers and will be prosecuted.* Another sign read *No Credit.* I tried to explain why we were there; the manager was Mexican so I tried in Spanish, too, but the suspicion in his face only melded into bewilderment. He told us to go ahead and look around and went back inside the building.

There was not much to see, just a barren, run-down labor camp in the middle of plowed-up cotton fields on a chilly and windy December day. Yet Wilma and I stood there in awe, as if at a sacred site. Later we confided in each other that we each thought we had heard voices, Okie voices, and we were each overwhelmed by a sense that that place was profoundly connected to who we've been and who we've become.

Wilma was hungry when we left Weed Patch. Later she wrote this poem, 'First Visit to Weedpatch,' explaining her hunger:

> I went there
>   and walked on the years
> ever so carefully
> as if on broken glass
> yet my feet bled

through my shoes
seeping from my heart

And my hands blistered
from imaginary hoes
thrust into them
from the rawness of the past

And there was no mistake
   I felt hunger
    it started from a sign
    that read *No Credit*
and increased the length
of Weedpatch Highway.

And so we stopped in Lamont, the nearest town, at a restaurant called Molly's Home Kitchen. Wilma said, 'This has to be an Okie establishment,' as we walked toward the place and saw the plastic Christmas decorations in the windows. I agreed that the place felt familiar.

Once inside, indeed the place felt like home, that feeling in the skin when I go back home to Oklahoma. It was a simple coffee shop; the hour was late, around 4 p.m., and we were the only patrons. Wilma studied a black-and-white blown-up photograph above us which we guessed to be the owner and his son. Wilma said, 'I'll bet you his name's Leon.' How Wilma could guess this, which turned out to be true – Leon was there and talked with us – I do not know. We ate bowls of Campbell's chicken noodle soup and cornbread, drank our java, and left sustained.

Back in San Francisco, I called Daddy and told him about the Weed Patch camp – he's read *The Grapes of Wrath* several times. He said, 'Yeah, them poor folks sure did suffer, couldn't even grow their own food. Least you kids never went hungry like them.'

For the first time in my life I felt unashamed, and even proud, that the bottom line of my life is that I never had to go hungry.

Afterword to the Oklahoma Edition

Red Dirt first appeared in 1997. At that time, the "red state–blue state" description distinguishing Republican and Democratic political parties had not yet been created. Red is now supposed to indicate Republican and blue, Democratic. Of course, nothing is that simple. Some states have razor-thin majorities of one or the other, while other states have regions or cities whose colors are different from the states as a whole. Yet, one thing is certain: Oklahoma fits comfortably into the red-state category, and has for some time, long before the signifiers were coined.

But that was not always the case. "Red" in the title of *Red Dirt* predated the label "red" for right wing, although the new connotation can be added to the litany of reasons I chose the word. I was thinking, first, of the red soil in rural Canadian County where I grew up and where my father tried to scratch out a living as a tenant farmer. Second, Oklahoma originally was territory that the federal government established as a homeland for the American Indians whom it forcibly removed from the Southeast during the 1830s. My mother was in part descended from those "red" people. Third, my paternal grandfather was a socialist and a Wobbly, active in the Socialist Party and in the Industrial Workers of the World (IWW). He and other Reds were victims of the Wilson administration's "red scare." Not only my grandfather, but also at least 20 percent of Oklahomans during that time were "reds," and many more were sympathetic. The Socialist Party won local elections all over the state, and a significant percentage of voters supported their own presidential candidate in five elections. Their activity and general pro-unionism in Oklahoma created the most pro-worker state constitution in the country. The "dirt" in Red Dirt echoes childhood memories of poor farmers being called "dirt farmers," and Native people being called "dirty Indians," and socialists being called "dirty reds."

By the time I was coming of age in the 1950s, Oklahoma had been for over two decades a tightly run proto-fascist state, with oil and wheat keeping a small ruling class super-wealthy. And the rest of the population, strongly influenced by fundamentalist preachers, was poor and ignorant. The wealthy ruling class controlled every institution, including the media. Those of us who disagreed were expected to go somewhere else, and those of us who were able to did so, leaving a hard heart of corporate control and a fearful population. Oklahoma's transition from traditional Dixiecrat Democrat to right-wing Republican, in step with the South as a whole, resulted from the Republican Party's "southern strategy," carried out during the Nixon era.

How I came to disagree with Oklahoma's new ideology can be attributed to two family secrets that were whispered in oblique stories. One was about my mother's mother being part Indian. The other was about my father's father being a Red – a radical socialist and member of the IWW. My grandmother's part-Indian heritage was kept secret because it was both dangerous and shameful to be an Indian in Oklahoma before the 1960s. My father told me stories about his Wobbly father but warned me to keep them a secret, because it was dangerous and shameful to be a Red at the time during the anti-communist McCarthy period.

My family experiences have informed my assessment of the present red state–blue state configuration, with Protestant fundamentalism, laissez-faire capitalism, and super-patriotism now linked with war, the ruling political ideology. Having grown up Southern Baptist and super-patriotic, I know what it is like to view the world that way. At the time, I felt powerless to affect change. As knowledge of my family's past deepened, it became my source for alternative, and empowering, views of the world around me.

Perhaps more important than the symbolism of the color red is the question of why it has changed meaning. Thomas Frank, in his 2004 bestseller, *What's the Matter with Kansas?: How Conservatives won the*

Heart of America, asks the same question about Kansas and, implicitly, the rest of the "red" states, but his answers do not satisfy me. Frank appears to idealize the Roosevelt New Deal era of the Democratic Party, as do most elected officials and activists in that party. Furthermore, he takes for granted that the New Deal really was about the poor and working people. My father used to tell me that Roosevelt had saved the bankers and the rich in general but did not change the condition of the un-rich, nor was he interested in doing so. Roosevelt's interest was in rescuing the capitalist system and preventing a workers' revolution in the United States, as well as in industrializing agriculture.

What happens to a society that literally loses its roots in the earth? Why do we as a society choose to replace ten thousand farmers with an absentee corporation? This system is not more productive, but even if it were, is it practical to destroy the lives of so many who want only to farm?

My father was a born farmer, and he never owned his own farm; instead, he rented and sharecropped. When he could no longer do that – because the medium-sized farmers who employed him also went under and were replaced by corporations – something in him died. The second half of his life was painful. It was only in the process of writing *Red Dirt* that I realized his tragedy, and ours as a society, although I doubt that he could have enunciated it.

My father died in June 2001, two months before what would have been his ninety-fourth birthday. I had spent two hot, humid days with him a year before he died, when we actually said our farewells, or I felt we had. He didn't have a life-threatening illness, but his will to live had been waning since his companion of more than forty years – my stepmother – suddenly died of a heart attack in 1998. My brother Fred, the only one of us siblings still living in Oklahoma, had cared for our father's needs for years and could no longer do it, so he moved him into a hospice a couple of months before he died. My other brother, my sister, and I, all living in California, went back for the burial. There was no formal ceremony, as my father never attended church, but there was a small ceremony officiated by my brother Fred at the burial site in Matthewson Cemetery, just outside of Piedmont, where most of our relatives are buried. Besides us siblings, a few of our first cousins were there, ones who had idolized my father. We each said a few words. In the casket, Daddy looked peaceful, but determined as ever. As I had predicted would happen when I reconciled with him a decade earlier, I miss him terribly and both salute and mourn his life. He didn't like this book much because, he said, it made him appear unable to support his family, something I did not intend and don't believe I wrote or implied. On the contrary, I marvel at how the poor survive in this rich country. They are my heroes. Had I been in charge of his tombstone, I would have written:

Here lies a farmer, whose dreams were killed by the greed of the wealthy.

ROXANNE DUNBAR-ORTIZ
August 2005